Sept '19
Nick,
Read abs
To a truly athlete
+ elite athlete

Sincerely,
"Jake"

LOVE YOUR ENEMIES IN CASE YOUR FRIENDS TURN OUT TO BE BASTARDS

ORGANIZATIONAL CASE STUDIES EXAMINING WORKSITE POLITICS

LOVE YOUR ENEMIES
in Case Your Friends Turn Out To Be Bastards

Organizational Case Studies Examining Worksite Politics

By
Jake Hagerman

PORTLAND • OREGON
INKWATERPRESS.COM

Scan this QR Code to learn more about this title.

Copyright © 2014 by Jake Hagerman

Cover and interior design by Jayme Vincent

Man Pushing a Boulder on a Mountain © Sasin Tipchai. BigStockPhoto.com

All rights reserved. No part of this book may be reproduced or transmitted in any form or by any means whatsoever, including photocopying, recording or by any information storage and retrieval system, without written permission from the publisher and/or author. Contact Inkwater Press at 6750 SW Franklin Street, Suite A, Portland, OR 97223-2542. 503.968.6777

Publisher: Inkwater Press | www.inkwaterpress.com

Hardcover
ISBN-13 978-1-62901-143-1 | ISBN-10 1-62901-143-6

Kindle
ISBN-13 978-1-62901-144-8 | ISBN-10 1-62901-144-4

Printed in the U.S.A.
All paper is acid free and meets all ANSI standards for archival quality paper.

1 3 5 7 9 10 8 6 4 2

CONTENTS

Acknowledgments ix

SECTION ONE
Organizational Case Studies 1
Preface 3
Chapter One 6
   Vignette 1 6
   Vignette 2 9
   Vignette 3 10
   Vignette 4 11
   Vignette 5 13
   Vignette 6 15
   Vignette 7 17
   Vignette 8 19
   Vignette 9 22
   Vignette 10 24
   Vignette 11 26
   Vignette 12 28

  Chapter Two 31
   Vignette 13 31
   Vignette 14 36
   Vignette 15 39
   Vignette 16 43
   Vignette 17 46
   Vignette 18 51

Vignette 19 54
Vignette 20 57

Chapter Three... 61
Vignette 21 61
Vignette 22 67
Vignette 23 69
Vignette 24 72
Vignette 25 74
Vignette 26 77

Chapter Four.. 82
Vignette 27 82

Chapter Five... 94
Vignette 28 94

Chapter Six... 105
Vignette 29 105

Chapter Seven 119
Vignette 30 119
Vignette 31 131
Vignette 32 136
Vignette 33 140

Chapter Eight... 149
Vignette 34 149
Vignette 35 155
Vignette 36 158
Vignette 37 160

SECTION TWO
Sharks, Slimeballs, and Malcontents:
An Organizational Survival Guide................................ 167

Preamble 169

Chapter Nine.. 173
Organization Delinquents: Miscreants Who Create
    Systemic Tyranny 173
Preamble 173
Competence and Loyalty 176

How to Maintain Emotional Buoyancy and Survive
in a Political Ecosystem..179
How to Accomplish Goals in Spite of an
Organization Manipulator's Presence.......................181

Chapter Ten 184
Adult Children of Alcoholics (ACOAs) in the
Organization: How to Identify and What to Do 184
Preamble 184
ACOA Behavior 184
What Factors Contribute to a Normal Worksite
Atmosphere..188
ACOAs' Disruptive Behavior at the Worksite 190
Interventions with ACOAs in the Work Environment...191

Chapter Eleven 195
Evaluating the Workplace Political Ecosystem:............. 195
Preamble 195
Determining Change Threshold Within the
Organization 195
Location 197
Safety 201
Navigation 204

Chapter Twelve 207
Organizational Dynamics: Positioning; Meta-
Communication; Guile (Ganef) 207
Preamble 207
Morale..208
Changing the Organizational Structure 209
Changing Organization Administration.........................209
Strategic Planning and Evaluation 210
Positioning 211
Meta-Communication 213
Guile (ganef) 215

Chapter Thirteen 217
The Matrix System of Management: Strengths and
Needs 217
Preamble 217
Historical Context 224
The Problem in a "Nutshell"..225
How to Survive in the Matrix System of Management .226

Summary 228

Chapter Fourteen 229
   Set-ups, Cons, and Other Nefarious Activities 229
   Preamble 229
   Set-ups 230
   Cons and Other Nefarious Activities 232
   Identifiers – Problematic Behaviors That Indicate
      Trouble Lies Ahead 234
   How to Effectively Challenge Nefarious Behavior
      by the Organization Manipulator 236

References 241

ACKNOWLEDGMENTS

To my wife and sons whom I love and treasure very much, my late friends Drs. Pazaratz and Markow, my late brother and sister, and of course colleagues who have survived misadventures with an organization manipulator – carry on with your careers and I hope this book provides some enjoyment and solace. I wish you success in all future endeavors.

SINCERELY WITH REGARD,
JAKE HAGERMAN
Fall, 2014

SECTION ONE

ORGANIZATIONAL CASE STUDIES

PREFACE

My name is Jake Hagerman, a pseudonym actually, a long time, non-secular professional in the field of Mental Health Services who lives in North America and enjoys Jewish literature. The following chapters are written for a professional audience qualified in a clinical capacity, thereby reducing the need for explanations, definitions, and clarifications of esoteric terminology. Call it laziness, but from my perspective it makes for easier, fluid, audio transcription as I dictate the book. The Vignettes in Section One are generally humorous, but occasionally not so humorous. Nevertheless they are a series of anecdotes experienced by colleagues, acquaintances, and last but not least me. Some are intentionally exaggerated, some combine stories, some are fictitious, and others even understated. In essence, they represent personal experiences that never end and have provided innumerable laughs over the years. If you're having a difficult day and want to disengage, please read the book! I'm sure you can match the many accounts I provide with your own experiences in this complex but stimulating profession we share.

The book is divided into two sections; the first section, entitled Organizational Case Studies, comprises eight chapters describing thirty-seven vignettes that occurred during my career over the past four decades. The second section, entitled Sharks, Slimeballs, and Malcontents – An Organizational Survival Guide, includes six chapters and is actually more serious academically, title aside, providing the reader with practical information, coping strategies and techniques to effectively survive in the political ecosystem of a troubled organization.

It has not been my intent to write a book that could be perceived as ridiculing or belittling the Mental Health/Social Service Industry! But the fact remains that during the past thirty years in both North America and Great Britain, Mental Health Services have been reduced in many cases to a redundant operation, thereby substantiating, in the Government's mind, reduction in financial support. The consequent impact in quality of life to the recipients of such services has been of catastrophic proportion. But I digress, who wants to listen to a "downer"?

So, what to do? Are you a secular humanist, or a post-structuralist of whom Foucault would be proud? One who investigates ad nauseam the "guts and trappings" of Mental Health Services and makes a better world! Perhaps, however, for me personally and if truth were to be told, I wrote Section One of the book to mollify my need to share many humorous and often unbelievable anecdotes. An act of catharsis, pure and simple! In doing so I have set forth a series of events that describes my career experiences commencing in the early 1970s until 2000. I've recently begun my last job in a professional career that has been hard and not come easily, which, in part, influenced my decision to put to paper these many interesting stories and coping strategies before old age dims their memory.

In any event, I hope you brought your best sense of humor and imagination to recognize and laugh at the many foibles and ridiculous mishaps encountered by our colleagues described in the first portion of the book. Thank you for listening and please keep an open mind. Many of the scenarios have happened in some degree to all of us, if we were to be completely honest.

Lastly, I purposely stopped the Vignettes at the year 2000, just prior to commencing my previous job from the one that I have now. It would be too close for comfort if I included some of the hilarious anecdotes from that job!? Regardless – my gut tells me to wait a few more years and gain increased courage before dignity of risk forces me to "take the plunge" and write more Vignettes. Please, while reading the book, keep in mind the following suggestions:

Each Organization should:
1. Investigate and identify critical dimensions of team and leadership performance;
2. Employ "Behavior Observation Scales" which identify specific behaviors and means to report the frequency with which these behaviors occur amongst the Team; the Leadership; and Instructor performance;
3. Assess frequencies of specific (i.e., critical) behaviors that reflect dimensions of team performance (e.g., adaptability; situational awareness; closed and open communication; single and double-loop feedback) and;
4. Train Observers who will code Team and Leader behavior. This training will increase the accuracy and inter-rater reliability of Observer ratings.

One more request. I enlist your support to improve organizational outcomes at your respective job sites by incorporating the aforementioned strategies.

The book's Section Two is meant as a Training Tool to identify and improve your "skill-set" for survival in the workplace. It is also written to augment a knowledge base for aspiring Managers; Leaders; Industrial-Organizational Psychologists; Clinical Consultants; Business/Commerce and MBA students; Counseling, Nursing and Social Work students – you name it.

Finally, the book was written to advance your knowledge on mostly what *not* to do in your careers! Specifically, your analysis of the Vignettes in Section One and the Coping Strategies/Survival Techniques with organization manipulators in Section Two identifies issues that can become problematic. It also provides cogent information on how to improve job performance at those worksites where you provide consultation and a mentoring role. That's it.

GOOD LUCK IN ALL FUTURE ENDEAVORS AND NOW ON WITH THE BOOK!

CHAPTER ONE

VIGNETTE 1

A "FLASHBACK" TO THE EARLY 1970S IN A HOSPITAL LOCATED IN A LARGE North American city. The team I worked with consisted of a various assortment of personalities, two or three of whom had a propensity to achieve at all cost, in utter disregard for their fellow colleagues, who found surviving in this political ecosystem hard enough, let alone having to contend with "backstabbing S.O.B.'s"! Let me spend some time describing the personality quirks of a number of individuals:

Jerry H. was in his early twenties, a slightly overweight ex-athlete overachiever with professional parents, whom he dearly wished to surpass in all work accomplishments, at all costs. This guy was particularly dangerous as he "cozied up" to mid-management in the most obsequious, servile manner!

Jerry H.'s opposite number on the other clinical team was Rolf G., a "henpecked," albeit intelligent individual who had a serious eating disorder. His weight would fluctuate 40 (18 kg.) to 70 pounds (30 kg.) up and down the scale, necessitating two and sometimes three sizes of clothing in his wardrobe. Rolf G. continually complained about his weight, "hit the gym once in a blue moon," and was a procrastinator extraordinaire.

Betty H., the team leader, was a "wild child" and a product of the 1960s, misparenting, unresolved anger, and a propensity to seek out and "bed" unassuming Social Work males. She felt she could control and dominate them through various sexual proclivities, which I observed on numerous occasions during staff parties. At one point Betty H. was found screwing a colleague underneath a king-size bed telling her partner to "rev it up Billy, rev it up"! During one such party Betty H. became so intoxicated that she decided she needed a chaperone while walking in the neighborhood after one of her sexual dalliances – unfortunately this time there was a snowstorm outside! I got the chaperone job and she was "shadowed" by yours truly down a lonely street in the suburbs, then, from out of nowhere, fell to the ground and lay in a prone position for what seemed an eternity, but was really just a few pregnant seconds. So what you say, just pick up the drunken woman, drag her to the side of the road, throw some snow on her face and "Bob's your uncle." Yeah right, Betty H. weighed in at 280 pounds (130 kg.) and was 5'10" (1 m. 78 cm.) in flats. Oh dear, what to do? *Nothing can top this, Jake!?* Dun da dun dun…and remember it's approximately 3 a.m.! I needed thoroughbred energy to haul this very large incapacitated, "blind drunk" woman out of harm's way.

Somehow I was able to drag Betty H. away from the center of the road and several slipping, sliding, swerving cars. But inevitably she would crawl back into harm's way, swearing and cursing that I was an "A-hole" – it was a nightmare and then some, but who says life is fair! Over the next half hour I threw snow on her face, slapped her cheeks, pinched her wrists, shouted at her, cajoled her, you name it – trying to move this drunken creature to the safety of the sidewalk was no easy feat. Twenty feet (6 m.) seemed like twenty miles (32 km.). There must be a God or at least Jesus Christ because she started to moan and come around, then talk in halting, slurred tones about whom she was going to shlofen[1] later. The next Herculean task was getting Betty H. to her feet, moving, as in motion, was the operative intention, and by this time I was "bagged," really exhausted! At two different points she fell on top of me, full dead weight "squishing" me when we tumbled onto the occasionally fluffy, but generally ice-packed road. Needless to say I was frightened of being smothered, or at least being made incapacitated. As an aside, when my friend at the party heard I'd volunteered to chaperone "topsy-turvy" Betty

---

1   sleep with

H., he stated, "Are you nuts – she's pretty heavy, Jake!" Back to the story – after a further twenty minutes she was beginning to sober up and got to her feet; then, and I say this in all sincerity, she began playing "nickey, nickey nine door." Going up and down the street, at three in the morning mind you, walking up to a stranger's house, hammering on their door knocker and making a racket, then running away when the lights came on and an irate inhabitant, awakened from his or her sleep, came to the door! Most often I was able to hide behind a tree or a bush and hoped the police would arrive or at least be called. Without stating the obvious, but I'll state it anyway, by this time I was getting tired of being "Mr. Nice Guy"!! *Jake – get on with the story!* Okay, okay.

Nice guys finish last, you say, and you're probably right, but I had to get this drunken "femme fatale" back to safety at the party, which incidentally was being held at my third-floor apartment! The cold, inclement weather was almost unbearable! Hypothermia and dehydration was a big factor causing me to stay by her side, not loyalty! Don't ask me how, but I was able to maneuver, cajole, and beg Betty H. to follow me back to my apartment, which by this time was approximately 1 mile (1.6 km.) away. Once we got inside the front door of the 100-year-old Victorian mansion, converted into six apartments on three floors, I gathered myself behind and underneath this very large, and by now, moderately drunken woman. I placed both hands on her broad derrière and with my shoulder on her lower back pushed her up, one stair at a time, mind you, three flights of stairs at a very steep incline in this stark, Victorian home! The bannister was "rickety," the last batch of stairs leading directly to my apartment were at a forty-degree angle and the climb, which just about killed me, was perilously dangerous!! If Betty H. had slipped and fallen, I would've been driven backward, down the stairs with her on top of me and wouldn't be dictating this story! Once we entered my apartment I was able to push her into the bedroom (get those filthy thoughts out of your mind), get her winter clothes off – only the external winter clothes mind you, and push her onto my bed. She fell in a heap, lay on her back, and in less than fifteen seconds was off in "dreamland." Muttering profanities,

I congratulated myself on a job well done! Who says your best years are in your twenties?! The following day, halfway through my shift at work, I received a telephone call from Betty H. apologizing profusely and stating when she'd woken up, she checked herself "all over" to make sure everything was okay. Whatever the hell that means? To a twenty-two-year-old, overly salacious male, this statement was enough to put me off sex for the next decade at least, or so I thought at the time. But I digress; on to the next Vignette.

VIGNETTE 2

BETTY H.'S FRIEND NICKY WAS GENERALLY A NICE PERSON AND VERY EXPErienced at doing her job. The only problem was her propensity to overindulge in eating candy, which was on a daily basis the appetizer, lunch, and evening meal!? Day in and day out SHE ATE CANDY – this was a serious problem as Nicky's energy level over the six months I worked with her was "spiked" by the candy's sugar and consequent malnutrition, which led to some pretty hairy experiences! Her labile mood, influenced by elevated blood sugar levels, precipitated erratic behavior, more specifically, impulsivity, anger dyscontrol, and thought disturbance. No amount of encouragement, discussions at coffee break, at which time she used copious amounts of sugar in her coffee, could dissuade Nicky from changing her sugar habit. She was, and had been, a sugar addict for approximately ten years! From my vantage point, one thing kept her alive – her husband's love and the demands he placed on her regarding eating the occasional meal that he cooked, which followed a food guide recipe containing carbohydrates, protein, and fats. Otherwise this "electrified fence" of a personality, as described by a colleague, imposed herself on colleagues on a daily basis, however, never on clientele surprisingly.

The problem was that her best friend, Betty H. the team leader – remember her? – defended Nicky and was in current vernacular an "enabler" of this self-destructive and flamboyant personality. What to do? After the birth of a child, the conception of which was a miracle in itself, within three months Nicky was hospitalized due to the effects of malnutrition and general exhaustion, let alone what was being done to the infant she breastfed!? The hospital admission ostensibly ended Nicky's career in this field and saved our collective sanity at work and probably her newborn baby's life. The good thing was that Nicky received therapy from a very competent hospital multidisciplinary team, which included much-needed nutritional training from the Dietitian on the team: the bottom line being the risks of maintaining a "candy diet" and its effects on her newborn child while she was breastfeeding!?

And you thought you had it bad! Yes, you can say she had ownership of the problem and received professional guidance. Yeah right, where the hell was Human Resources when all this was going on?! During this fiasco the staff, her colleagues working "in the trenches," were "double timing" it for a very long period of time! Unfortunately as you will read, this behavior increased and exacerbated the "gamesmanship" of the professionals on my team. Please, read on.

VIGNETTE 3

DICK F. HAD WATCHED A 1950s WEEKLY TELEVISION SERIES, *77 SUNSET Strip,* was much enamored with the jive talk of one of the actors, Ed "Kooky" Burns, and used to rhyme off Kooky's expressions throughout his shifts at work. You were a square if you didn't dig jive talk!? He would use the following expressions day in and day out, which became pretty lame after a while and from a 2014 perspective, pretty sexist and very "corny" (1950s expression). Anyway, let's see if you can decipher some of them: "Cool it Chick this Cat has eyes for another"; "Get lost I'm looking for kicks"; "Hi doll face do ya wanna groove"; "Why don't we trip the light fantastic – can you dig it"; "Baby you're the ginchiest"; "I'm gonna zonk downtown and buy some threads"; "Hey man don't flip your lid"; "Be there or be square"; "Come on get with it – let's kick out the jams"; "Susan Smith's on the pill she won't get pregnant"; "Keep your shirt on"; etc., etc. Working with this guy was humorous at times, but eventually wore everyone down including yours truly. What to do? One of the Psychiatrists assigned to the Unit cautioned Dick F. on the need to use jive talk while performing his duties! You would think a simple, yet direct challenge from a senior clinician concerning your deportment would result in a simple, yet direct change in behavior (i.e., cause-effect paradigm). No way, Dick F.'s retort generally summed up his attitude, "Cool it Cat don't be a drag." As you can imagine, his career on our team ended shortly thereafter. But you'll read about it in a later Vignette, stay cool!

The staff debrief after Dick F.'s departure included the usual "barbed" comments from Jerry H. – Mr. ambitious, backstabbing, upwardly mobile, the end justifies the mean, professional miscreant! Jerry H. stated his analysis as follows, "It's obvious – the stress on the job affected Dick's mental health and the neologisms comforted him, allowing a sense of empowerment, albeit at the expense of the team's increased stress and frustration." Here's the laugh, Dick F. became a very successful medical specialist in a Midwestern locale. I wonder who had the last laugh? And Jerry H.? After many years of walking over, through, and around his colleagues, he "ground" his way up the ladder of success, attaining a very senior management position with a budget over two billion dollars and thousands of subordinates. *Jake, there appears to be a theme going on here, didn't you know that justice is fleeting, get with the program!* Okay, okay.

VIGNETTE 4

RON B. WAS ANOTHER STAFF MEMBER WHO WAS "JOE FRIGGIN' COOL," excellent at his job but the worst form of "fence sitter" who eventually shat over yours truly, many, many years later. We'll talk about it another time, another book, another life! Ron B., a man who "read" the politics, stayed out of trouble at all costs, and pursued his career with the least amount of conflict. He eventually ended up at a post-secondary Institution of Higher Learning!? Beyond that promotional "blip" early in his career, he never advanced in station, due to a problem with having the guts (i.e., dignity of risk) it takes to climb the ladder of success. *Jake, you're so judgmental.* Yeah, so what? However, his one claim to fame was going to a seedy, other side of the tracks restaurant/grill with yours truly after a shift one night and ordering a meal. A big difficulty arose when we forgot to check the patrons of the establishment, because lo and behold, a few of them were members of the Hells Angels Motorcycle Club. When Ron B.'s meal arrived and he started using ketchup, one of the Angels asked if HE could have the ketchup, in a polite tone I might add. But more to the point were his exact words, "Can I borrow some of the red stuff" to which Ron B. retorted, "For sure and you can have some of the white stuff too," pointing to a bottle of vinegar. A pretty gutsy statement from a 21-year-old, one hundred-forty pound (65 kg.), 6 foot tall (1 m. 82 cm.) geek, to a 35-year-old seasoned, outlaw biker well over 6 foot tall and approximately 230 pounds (110 kg.). Unfortunately for Ron B. two weeks later, one of his "quips" blew up in his face, metaphorically speaking. One night after picking up a girl at a local bar they walked out to his British sports car and after putting her in the passenger's seat and walking to the driver's side, he was physically assaulted by her ex-boyfriend, who then proceeded to threaten Ron B., steal his wallet, take his car keys, and drive away in the beloved British sports car, with the ex-girlfriend! Ron B. was so shaken up he was unable to give the police a full description of the assailant, or remember the name of the "Clubbie" he'd just picked up and because he was intoxicated with no identification (i.e., I.D.) the police thought he was making up the story! Ron B. was thrown in the "drunk tank" overnight and guess who he met in the drunk tank? One thousand and one, one thousand and two…the outlaw biker he'd met in the restaurant/grill two weeks earlier!

This impressed Mr. Biker, who recognized Ron B. the geek immediately and asked, "What are your charges"? Ron B. stated in a clear, resounding tone, "I was mugged, had my car and wallet stolen and the police think I'm making it up and arrested me for public drunkenness," to which the outlaw biker retorted, "that beats pass the red stuff, white stuff B.S. you gave me two weeks ago – want to ride with us sometime"? To which Ron B. responded, "I need to pee" and passed out (after peeing).

VIGNETTE 5

As I cast my memory back to the early days of my career and think of this particular Unit other personalities come to mind, some nice, some not so nice! One particular individual, from a Scandinavian country, thought he was the strongest man in the city. He'd been a highly successful weightlifter in his earlier years (bronze medalist of Scandinavia); he was a Martial Arts expert in two different disciplines and was a dedicated "ladies man" while still unhappily married. Sven had many, many funny things happen to him! When asked by yours truly – Sven at this time was in his early 30s – what he was aspiring to be in his career, he stated in a matter-of-fact voice, "I want to be willage wise man." Yes "Willage," Sven had difficulty pronouncing his Vs. By this time in his life he'd worked as a tradesman with automobiles in the daytime, was completing a Bachelor's Degree in Philosophy in the evening, and was a Bouncer at the Graduate Bar at the local University. Earlier in his career he had relocated to the Northeast and completed a commercial airline pilot training program. He had also completed his Armed Forces training in Scandinavia and spent time soldiering in Africa during the early 1960s and was an accomplished scuba diver. Enough background, his most famous line when he became enamored with a female was (vulgarity aside) "if you don't want to fox me you can sax me off" which often meant nothing to his object of desire and potential conquest. But in Sven's own words, "Jake, you try 10 times you score one." *Jake, continue with the story, we get the picture.* Okay, Okay.

One incident stands out in my mind very clearly, even 40 years later. Here I was in my early 20s being mentored by this older Scandinavian man in his early 30s, bored with life and supporting three children and a nagging, unforgiving spouse. To liven things up he would "hustle" young coeds at the University after doing a handstand on a bar table!? Yes, on the bar table, you got it right!! Well he's a "Bouncer," what d'ya think they do after hours? One night, while sitting at a table at the bar where Sven "bounced," a beautiful young blonde, approximately 22 years of age, "spray paint" jeans, the halter top "no bra Friday" look, ran up and gave him a big hug.

She then told Sven how much she enjoyed his discussion at the philosophy tutorial group earlier that day and was so impressed that he was a committed Buddhist, yeah right!

Ms. Enamored invited Sven back to her apartment "to discuss philosophy," more specifically, Buddhism. As Sven was leaving the bar, he looked over his shoulder and lifted his eyebrows quickly a couple of times with a sly smile. I couldn't believe it; I'm lying through my teeth, I could believe it! Sven was very adept at using his physique, accent, and European charm to seduce many, many, women. Later on in the week when we met up again, Sven as usual debriefed, in very graphic and technical detail, his liaison with this most recent conquest, which included his usual malapropisms, "I had two orgasmas and she readily enjoyed oral general intercourse when I was spend!" Apparently when they got to her apartment she stated she had to go to the bathroom for a few moments and would return "eager to discuss Buddhism." Sven used this opportunity to strip naked in her living room and present her with a lovely big erection when she returned from the bathroom. I won't go into the gory details but you can imagine the rest of the story, which was a revolving tale throughout the six years I hung with the guy. There are many, many more Sven stories, but they all end up the same (lucky bastard)! When Sven decided to leave the city, he phoned me and said, "I have decided to become a Willage Wiseman and will bicycle from Marseille to India, I do not correspond, I'm sorry to say goodbye but hope you won't forget me." He left the city that week in April, 1978, and I've never seen nor heard from him since. I don't think I'll ever meet another Sven as long as I live! Talk about "alter ego," living vicariously – listening to his pedantic (or pathetic – you choose), mono-dimensional stories with always the same plot – "conquering" young women and wondering whether his charm would ever rub off on me? I did conquer occasionally, but could not replicate his style and joie de vivre. No way – Sven was one of a kind!

VIGNETTE 6

Working at this particular jobsite with the myriad of personalities, challenging clientele, clinical demands, and political activism caused many a rift between staff members. One of the longest, ongoing "range wars" entailed a male and female dyad that worked on the same team and quickly learned to hate each other's guts, regardless of the setting they were thrust into.

Derek G. was in his late 20s, an outspoken, experienced "line worker" who knew his job well, but was abrasive, confrontational, and loved to provoke his female counterpart, whom he despised, and he made his contempt very obvious! One situation entailed his nemesis Jill B. bragging, as it appeared to the staff members anyway, of being molested when she was growing up. She stated this very, very frequently, which thinking back was rightly or wrongly challenged on many occasions as being needy, unprofessional, and at the very least inflammatory, to those women who were legitimate victims of sexual abuse (i.e., which she might well have been). People encouraged Jill B. to seek professional help to resolve this issue but to no avail. It appeared Jill B. needed the attention/empathy from her co-workers and used the disclosure to meet unfulfilled needs – on work time!? The problem was and it was a big one – we weren't her therapists and stated this innumerable times!

During the late evening shift after the clientele had gone to bed, Derek G. and Jill B. found themselves in the staff room writing up process notation, debriefing the patients' shift behavior. Jill B., for what appeared to be the "umpteenth" time, began discussing in rather lewd detail the molestation story, at which point Derek G. had had enough! When he suggested that the frequency of discussing this topic indicated she might benefit from "third party" intervention, Jill B. responded sarcastically, "What did you have in mind?" Derek G. exploded with six months' worth of pent-up frustration and rage, expletives spewing from his mouth a mile a minute! Unfortunately at that time Jill B.'s husband Nathan walked into the room and quickly took to his wife's defense, chiding Derek G. and suggesting they "step outside." This honorable act would have seemed appropriate, but for the immense size difference, making it appear comic opera, Derek G. being approximately 6 feet (1 m. 82 cm.) and 180 pounds (82 kg.) and Nathan being approximately 5'5" tall (1 m. 65 cm.) and 130 pounds (60 kg.). In conjunction, Nathan was wearing a "loud" Hawaiian shirt, tie-dyed cut-off jeans, and a long, ostentatious gold chain with a crucifix hanging from his neck. Derek G. paused for a micro second during his tirade and burst into hysterical laughter, "wetting" himself in the process! Derek G. continued to laugh holding his wet pants while he limped to the bathroom, with Jill B.'s husband shouting "Come back you friggin' coward where the hell do ya think you're going?!"

From inside the bathroom as Derek G. removed his wet pants/underwear and washed them with a wet cloth, he pondered the situation, speculating how he was going to "save face." Unfortunately, at that point the evening staff came "rolling in" to replace Derek G. and Jill B. and wondered what the hell had transpired. A valid explanation was not forthcoming. After a few moments, which according to Derek G. felt like a few decades, he swallowed his pride and walked out of the bathroom holding a towel around his waist to cover his "private parts" AND his folded pants and underwear over his other arm. You can only imagine the response from the staff members!!

This scenario for obvious reasons got around with various versions, the one just described was the tamest and most realistic from the writer's point of view. And before I forget, the jive talk from Dick F. describing/embellishing the version he'd heard went something like, "this scene's from nowheresville, it's not cool, the party pack's gone bananas, can you dig. Cool it, I mean let's get with the program!" People on the various teams felt Dick F., this time at least, was "right on" or at least "hep" with his evaluation of the scandal. Human Resources had one hell of a time getting to the truth with this one. They had been previously apprised by various members of the team regarding Jill B.'s tendency to embellish an unresolved situation in her past, which had a deleterious effect on the Unit's morale. At the same time, Human Resources could not let Derek G. get away with such an outlandish, irresponsible outburst. What to do? Quite frankly everything was pushed under the rug – does that sound familiar, it will, please read on!? Anybody who's worked in an Institutional setting can match and probably surpass this scenario with a dozen stories. However, at the time, from my point of view and from my colleagues' vantage point, "heads should've rolled" but they didn't, and life went on! Derek G. continued to harass and repudiate everything coming from Jill B.'s mouth and eventually sent her husband a congratulations card! Specifically, when Nathan had had enough of Jill B.'s negative attention seeking and decided to leave the marriage and get on with his life! Where have we heard that one before? Oh 'bout a 1000 times, at least if you've been in this "minefield" of an Industry during the past three or four decades!

VIGNETTE 7

AROUND THAT PERIOD, ANOTHER TEAM MEMBER, MURRAY J. A RECREATIONAL drug user and a burly, 220 pounds (100 kg.) was having serious problems with his identity as a male. No, it's not what you think, he wasn't having gender orientation issues – contemplating "vacating the closet," etc. Remember this is the early 1970s, just four years after the 1969 raid on a New York gay bar, which brought homosexuality to the forefront of North American rights and freedom of expression. No, Murray J.'s problem was his desire to be a more "naturally endowed" male, as a number of his previous conquests had complained about the size of his penis. This was bad news for a male during that era and perhaps any period of time, I really don't keep up with the "dating chatter." What I do know is about this period, or it could have been a few years later, possibly the late '70s, Murray J. heard about an operation that could extend his penis, but he'd have to travel overseas to have it done. He was led to believe that after an incision was made an additional 1.5 inches (6 cm.) of the shaft could be pulled down from within his body, thereby extending the penis in length. Very avant garde stuff in the 1970s.

"Cutting to the chase" – how's that for a pun, Murray J. was confident and courageous and wanted a bigger "dink," so he had the operation, came back to work, and after a couple of months was ready to try out his new member, or "friendly weapon" as he called it. Low and behold he met a young lady in a downtown bar, after he'd dropped some window pane acid (i.e., LSD) which he bragged was " far out, you're talking from behind your head, let's trip the light fantastic," which he borrowed from Dick F.'s phraseology, indicating he was ready for action. The young, nubile female, stimulated by this drug-induced social foreplay, wanted "some action" as well and agreed to return home with Murray J. The long and short of it, oh dear another pun – was the "workout" Murray J.'s newly developed member was put through that particular evening and into the early morning hours! Next day at work, he made the mistake or maybe purposely, no one really knows, of discussing the previous night's "sexcapade," which got around the Hospital Units and various staff disciplines like a house afire. Without exaggeration, Murray J. was subsequently contacted by a number of women who were interested in dating and "good times" from this new and improved lothario! *Come on, pull the other one, Jake, the guy gets his "dink" enlarged and a bunch of women phone him up for a date?!* C'mon!! "Yeah, they did" is my answer. Remember Germaine Greer's ground breaker, *The Female Eunuch*, had just been published in March, 1971, heralding the feminist movement. Equality for both sexes, denouncing masculine domination and extolling sexual liberation! Who the hell knows the reason why Murray J. was all of a sudden a big hit with the women! As opposed to being an overweight, stagnant, boring "screw"! His new instrument of pleasure was an instant success, which had life-altering ramifications. Murray J. "hit the gym," cut down partaking in mood-altering drugs, and lost 30 pounds (14 kg.). So instead of being plump, with a mushy roll around his middle, his stomach was less rotund and unless he sat down and leaned over, had the semblance of a physique! His attitude at work was buoyant, less serious, generally more fun loving, and he was an easier person to be around socially! *Once again, Jake, who are you trying to kid? A larger dink changes this guy's life that much?!* All I can say is, after his surgery he didn't have too many complaints from the women he dated! A few of the snide colleagues who in the past would deride Murray J. were now purchasing various magazines and reviewing the "adverts" by "medical specialists" who were promoting the best deal regarding penis enlargement. Eventually, Murray J. met and married a nice, genuine person and if my memory serves me correctly, raised a family and had a very happy life until his untimely death in 2007. *Jake, what's the moral of the story?* Grow a big dink? – who the hell knows, but it's a good story.

VIGNETTE 8

THROUGHOUT MY EARLY APPRENTICESHIP AT THIS FIRST JOB, THERE WAS one particular individual, Malcolm B., whose personality did not "mesh" well with the clientele, with whom he'd been working for many years and from whom he was burned out. Neither Management nor Human Resources had taken the time to seriously or even effectively intervene with this individual. The chronic mental fatigue from working in a demanding and unrelenting institutional milieu, with an emotionally disturbed and ruthless clientele, had taken its toll! In the early 1970s there was no such thing as the "Psychologically Healthy Workplace" philosophy/infrastructure, providing staff support. How many good and competent people were lost in that era? It's anybody's guess, but from my perspective far, far too many! Malcolm B. was not just forthright but in lay language, friggin' aggressive! He loved a good fight during staff meetings and used staff fledglings like yours truly for "cannon fodder." He also ruled the clientele with an "iron hand," in plain English, his aggressive, confrontational verbiage was over-the-top. The fear that was precipitated when the clientele heard Malcolm B. was scheduled for the afternoon shift caused at the very least, severe distress and I'm sure for some people, apoplexy, metaphorically speaking, there's that word again! Of note and in all fairness while thinking back, Malcolm B. did not betray confidences and was in common parlance a "standup guy."

His primary problem was being in the field too long with this particular clientele! Management – both mid and senior levels – and

Human Resources had ostensibly "washed their hands" of this guy's behavior, which was disastrous for staff morale on Malcolm B.'s particular Unit! My one recollection that stands out to this day was Malcolm B. taking six clients swimming and brushing off any staff suggestion that he required, or would benefit from additional staff support. It was simply beneath his dignity to feel he needed any type of support and his macho persona – the baritone voice, 200-pound (91 kg.) frame on a 5'.10" (1 m. 78 cm.) body – belied any sense of fear or insecurity. Cutting to the chase, a problem ensued in the changing room at the swimming pool, when one of the clients decided to go for a swim in his "birthday suit." Malcolm B. was preoccupied with another client, who had attempted to vandalize a locker. A problem of equal significance involved an elderly woman who was having her 80th birthday, basically a pool party, hosting about 10 of her female friends, who were approximately her age and some even older. Are you starting to get the picture? One more important point that I forgot to mention: the "contagion effect" with Malcolm B.'s clientele was at its height! If one client "acted out" you can bet the others would follow suit. Quelling the riot that ensued was difficult, near impossible, without external support from security guards, city police, or any other civil servant/hospital employee – if it was on the grounds of the Institutional facility. Try complete bedlam/pandemonium off-site in the community at a local swimming pool!! A scary, scary situation to be faced with if you're the only staff member! Remember back in the day, there were no cell phones or e-mails – they hadn't been invented! In these situations staff were frequently taken advantage of by the clients and unable to get to a pay phone, or use other means of communication. Specifically, the acute behavioral "acting out" by the clientele could become quite menacing! You had to "keep your cool" and talk your way out of it, "sweat bullets," and hope for the best. But I digress.

Getting back to Malcolm B.'s particular situation with Mr. Exhibitionist! Two of the lifeguards intervened, jumped into the pool with a flotation device, pushed it near this person's head and dragged him to the side of the pool. As the action occurred, standing nearby at the side of the pool, waiting to help if the need arose, were two attractive female lifeguards. Their Speedo bathing suits showed off every inch/millimeter of their slender, curvaceous figures. As our young, recalcitrant client was at the age when Mother Nature and hormones collide, you can imagine what happened next when he spied the pretty, young, teenage lifeguards! An elderly woman, "maiden aunt" at the party swooned and fell into the pool! Of course the young females, for a short period of time, were too busy staring at...to engage in life-saving the elderly woman. The splashing water and yelling brought them back to reality. Suddenly in the back of the changing room, Malcolm B.'s loud, abrasive language towards the client he'd caught attempting to vandalize a locker was drifting, or better stated, echoing throughout the building at about 80 dB! Needless to say when the police arrived, the elderly woman who'd fallen into the pool had been rescued and was receiving artificial respiration. The birthday party was a shambles, the client who'd crashed the party in his "birthday suit" who'd previously been in a state of excitement was now shivering cold and in so many words, limping along. Mr. Clydesdale a few short moments ago was now Mr. Shetland Pony, "teeny weeny" – who said Mother Nature is kind!

The police hearing the tirade from inside the changing room had no idea what was going on. They came "inching" along the wall in single file with their hands on their guns, the lead officer motioning his men, of whom three had followed, to be quiet, as they opened the door of the changing room to locate and subdue the noisy perpetrator. You guessed it, as they walked in, there was Malcolm B. half clothed, sitting on the back of the client in a distinctly oblique position, leaning over and talking softly into the ear of this individual. Unfortunately as well, the client was wearing a Speedo bathing suit, pushed down during the raucousness to mid buttocks!? You can imagine what went through the officers' collective minds and what happened next! I won't bore you with the details, but there was a mountain of paperwork filled out by everybody when the debacle ended!! Jumping forward about an hour and a half, the Police report didn't look good for Malcolm B.! There was a very speedy return to the Institution in a "paddy wagon" with the six patients and Malcolm B., who had some SERIOUS "splainin' to do." The incident resulted in Mid/Senior Management and Human Resources requesting a formal investigation, which included structured interviews with staff who worked with Malcolm B. and five days of testimony that had to be transcribed. The guy was put through the wringer, but there is a positive ending! I heard through the "grapevine" a number of years later that sometime in the early 1980s, Malcolm B. had won the lottery – his "take" was in the millions. Also that he'd decided to retire and write a novella of his experiences and NO, it wasn't me!

This scenario I'm sure has been "played out," less a few embarrassing details, many, many times before, where "loose cannon" burned-out staff have been given too much rope to hang themselves. Mental health professionals are not paid enough money, in my professional experience, to go through what happened to Malcolm B. and not burn out! Currently, as I look at the myriad of infra-structure support systems available for distressed or debilitated employees, I wonder, no, to be perfectly honest I'm amazed at how we survived in those early years of my career! For many – recreational sex, soft drugs, and alcohol saved the day and for a few and I hope a very few, strained and broken marriages were the inevitable outcome.

VIGNETTE 9

I'M STARTING TO WIND DOWN WITH THIS INITIAL PHASE OF MY FIRST JOB experience in the Mental Health Services Industry. After six months on the job, a staff member who eventually became my closest friend and remained so until his untimely death early in 2013 decided to pack it in and leave this particular job. I worried that his move to work in another city would end our professional relationship; it didn't, so I wasted time catastrophizing. A big party was held to honor this person whom most people liked. Sven arrived, got drunk, began doing handstands in the living room and when I intervened, punched me in the face. A "nice" collegial response wouldn't you say, but let's be honest, Mental Health practitioners are no more civilized when they're under the influence of alcohol than anyone else! Sven ultimately found two or three youngish health care workers and proceeded to lecture them on the pundits of Buddhism. One of the workers thought Sven was a genius and would've gone to bed with him except her husband, who happened to be my best friend, was the staff member for which the party was being thrown.

Halfway through the party the famous Terry K. a lithe, six-foot (1 m. 82 cm.) tall narcissist arrived and boy did SHE arrive! She enjoyed causing controversy, to put it mildly, which occasionally included exhibitionism. How so you ask? Her attire this particular evening included the shortest, most revealing cutoff jeans imaginable, both "cheeks" hanging out, but more intriguing was the narrow ring of dark, black pubic hair around the sides of the "cutoff" jeans, in the midst of which was a three inch indentation!? Obviously she'd made her point, or indentation! After that we nicknamed her "The ring of fire," no bikini cut for this young lady! The visual impact of her "you know whats" generated quite a stir, so much so that the young men ogled their eyeballs out of their sockets while bouncing off the walls, in about, umm let's see, 10 seconds or less!! Conversely, the women at the party had many choice comments to make about Terry K.'s evening attire. Hell, by this time I didn't mind her faux pas, which broke some arbitrary dress code social convention, causing the party to ratchet up in volume and sexual "acting out"; I must say it was fun while it lasted! Remember Betty H.? How could you forget her!

She arrived with her boyfriend, soon-to-be fiancé, "in tow" and when she saw Terry K. in those skimpy, cutoff jeans and not to be outdone, the war of extremes had begun! After three or four drinks and some heavy petting, Betty H. and her boyfriend, nearly fiancé, went into an adjoining room to talk to a staff member and her husband. A quiet tête-à-tête so to speak, or so we thought! By that time, roughly two in the morning, everybody was "hammered," including me. As always I was trying to be the good host, wandering around asking people if they needed their drinks refilled. I happened to stumble into the adjoining room where, in the middle of the floor,

Betty H. was unzipping her boyfriend's pants in an attempt – I believe anyway – to fondle his "private parts." *No kiddin' Jake.* Okay, okay. The couple – the staff member and her husband – sat quietly trying to look nonchalant, staring up in the air, around the room, down at their drinks, at each other. Anything but making direct eye contact or making their interest in Betty H. and her boyfriend's "process" appear obvious. I sat down, looked over at the couple, and started roaring with laughter! Obviously this was a mood breaker and what transpired afterwards I can't remember because I "passed out." I was told the party ended about 6 a.m., nobody got hurt, everybody had a good time, and Terry K.'s skimpy, cutoff jeans and her accessories were the "hit" of the night! Unfortunately, I can't say whether the cutoff jeans became a trend setter, but this tall, dark-haired beauty, with those 35-inch legs and casual sitting posture will not be forgotten, by me anyway!

VIGNETTE 10

DESMOND P. WAS A SHORT, CHARISMATIC INDIVIDUAL WHO WAS VERY clever, how so, you say; by rarely causing nor allowing a "power struggle" to occur with the clients is the answer! Very, very difficult to sustain this behavior, especially when the clientele exhibit reduced impulse control, aggression, negative attention seeking, physical violence, and paranoid tendencies! They could spot a phony a mile away, but Desmond P. had honed the "cool dude" persona to near perfection. However, there comes a time and Desmond P.'s cool dude persona had run its course! Specifically, one particular instance during the hot summer months when he came to work wearing his cutoff jeans, which were much too small, allowing the boxer shorts he was wearing to protrude from the bottom of the cutoff jeans. Throughout the shift, the clients continued to tease Desmond P. about his "boxer" shorts hangin' down too far. He didn't take the hint, and at one point one of the female clients was able to grab his underwear from inside the cutoff jeans and yank them up aggressively, causing Desmond P. to let out a loud, mortifying howl!

No more Mr. Cool Dude during this shift!! Everyone burst into laughter, which eventually ended up (an hour later) in a food fight during lunch time. Unfortunately the staff forgot to monitor the kitchen adjacent to the lunch room and the rest is history!

What happened, Jake? It seems two pieces of bread that were being toasted began to burn and then smoke. Unfortunately, the toaster lay beneath a set of curtains, the curtains lit on fire, and because the lacquer on the cupboards underneath the curtains was highly flammable, the cupboards were ignited and burst into flame! In under 15 seconds a fire started on the kitchen cupboards that surrounded the kitchen! A "domino effect" occurred, causing each cupboard to go up in flames around the kitchen – POP POP POP! The children started screaming, FIRE, FIRE, running around throwing food, and when they were "hurried" outside the lunch room by the staff members, quickly ran back inside! *Jake, that's bad news!* No kidding, Ace! Pretty soon the kitchen, which was adjacent to the lunch room, was filled with smoke and fire, and the oxygen was being sucked out of the lunch room big time, which required everyone to cover their nose and mouth while crawling out to safety. One of the staff set off the fire alarm, sending the fire trucks "on the double" to the Institution. Everyone was saved and the staff were rightly blamed for this silly error, which could have cost lives.

The Fire Chief arrived and gave his two cents' worth to the Administrator of the Unit, who gave her two cents worth to the Supervisor, who gave his two cents worth to the line staff (one of which was me), and the situation seemed to resolve itself. Desmond P., who could do no wrong, Mr. Cool Dude and Pal to the clientele, subsequently changed careers with some gentle encouragement from yours truly. He eventually completed two Bachelor's degrees, a postgraduate degree, and became a very successful Administrator in his new chosen profession. I like to think the cutoff jeans/boxer shorts/fire exposé helped to clean up Desmond P.'s tendency to play Joe friggin' Cool. Specifically, his propensity to be cruel, sardonic, and belittling at his colleagues' expense was not funny and reflected an immensely aggressive personality with a narcissistic overlay. You know what I'm talking about, the Mr. Duplicity's of the worksite, who appear to have the world by the tail, the Joe Friggin' Cool veneer, but underneath are immensely insecure and "mean-spirited"! It lifts their devalued self-worth, denigrating colleagues, but maybe Desmond P. just needed a pal, who knows?! *Yeah right, Jake, "pull the other one" too much "blah, blah," enough already!* Okay, okay, I do know I'll never forget that day in the lunchroom with Desmond P. howling in pain "dancing" around, holding his crotch, trying to act "cool" and less than one hour later, the building nearly burning to the ground. And they say it keeps you young! Yeah right, on to the next vignette.

VIGNETTE 11

ARLEN M. WAS A BRILLIANT, SELF-ABSORBED, ACERBIC INDIVIDUAL WHO reminded everyone of a movie caricature, sidekick from the 1930s light comedies. He didn't mind insulting any individuals he felt couldn't defend themselves or were beneath his intellectual quotient. His soon to be ex–spouse was no better and would repeatedly remind Arlen M.'s colleagues, during the staff parties, about his unusually high aptitude for this type of work. "What a load!" As mentioned earlier in the chapter, one of the regular duties of the staff members was taking the clientele on "out-trips" to the community for recreation activities. During one of these out-trips, Arlen M., who was somewhat oversized in a particularly small pair of bathing trunks, attempted to take a dive off a particularly high diving board and lost his raiment. Easy to do under those circumstances! The bathing trunks sank in about 10 feet (3 m.) of water and there he was, in the midst of approximately 100 bathers enjoying a warm, hot summer afternoon at the beach watching their friends dive off the three-meter board. Here's the problem – Arlen M. was supervising six clients with a particularly "weak kneed" junior staff member who could be easily "contaged" and then domineered by the clients' aggressive behavior. Incidentally, a staff member, regardless of experience, who attempted to appease this particular client population could be "eaten alive" and was on many occasions, when the clients were out of control. The staff member's learning curve had to be steep in order to survive and entailed the individual who was unaccustomed to this outlandish, often dangerous conduct having to "sink or swim"! In many circumstances the "newbie" staff professionally drowned – crushed, domineered, and severely maligned by the clientele, to put it bluntly!

Jumping forward in my story – Arlen M. was not in a great situation, especially when he'd lost his bathing trunks, which had sunk to the bottom of the bay. No one was around to help him dive for the bathing trunks and he'd left his diving mask back at the Institution! What to do?

Arlen M. motioned to Ms. Weak Kneed staff member, who happened to have a petite, curvaceous body squished into a particularly revealing Speedo bathing suit – to swim out to talk to him. No mean feat to get her attention with all the yelling and noise going on, but he eventually succeeded and she swim out. The next part of the story, of which I've heard three or four different versions, ostensibly required Ms. Weak Kneed to dive for Arlen M.'s bathing trunks! As the water was particularly clear and there happened to be an inordinate number of younger children with diving masks close by, Arlen M.'s flaccid secret quickly became a hysterical crowd pleaser! The kids started to scream and laugh and point at Arlen M., who began to shake his head rigorously and motion to someone else – denial and projection the most primitive forms of defense mechanisms. *Jake, we hear ya, get on with the story.* Okay, okay.

About this time Ms. Weak Kneed re-surfaced adjacent to Arlen M. with his bathing trunks and handed them over. This resulted in paroxysms of laughter by her and everyone else, except Arlen M., who had one helluva of a time coordinating his head to submerge while simultaneously bending his legs upwards, in order to put on his bathing trunks, one leg at a time! The laughter increased the more he unsuccessfully attempted to put on his bathing trunks, sink, return to the surface spluttering, spitting out water and choking, only to repeat this routine again and fail repeatedly! Ms. Weak Kneed valiantly tread water by his side and between bouts of laughter, offered her shoulder as a support, the problem being,

Arlen M. was dragging her under the water, making it appear she was attempting unsavory sexual activity in a public location! Yes, the old "lewd and lascivious conduct" law from the early 1970s reared its ugly head! Keep your filthy thoughts to yourself! To make a long story short, Arlen M., with the help of Ms. Weak Kneed, got his bathing trunks on, after which they both managed to swim to shore, where they were met by the police department's finest! Ms. Weak Knees gave her version of the story, during which time the police ogled her body – and what about the six clients? They were completely out of control by this time, running around the beach chasing teenage girls screaming in terror, pulling a Harpo Marx rendition from the 1930s comedies. Needless to say, Arlen M. had some serious "splainin to do." *Jake, it appears a lot of that's going on in your chosen profession, what gives!?* I know, I know!

VIGNETTE 12

My last story before commencing Chapter Two entails a "comeuppance" with a particularly arrogant senior staff member, regarding one of the most seriously disturbed clients on the Unit.

There is a moral to the story: "whatever goes 'round comes round." Believe me, what I'm about to describe and the actions taken were required, necessary, and began the incorporation of a revised quality control program that was much, much in need! This professional gave everyone the creeps including his peers! His brilliant, no-nonsense behavior had a major flaw – a general inability to grasp some practical, day-to-day clinical interventions with a seriously disturbed clientele – it was occasionally unbelievable! But I digress.

A particular client had impulse control problems, (i.e., ADD) and a myriad of other psychological afflictions, too many to describe at this time. You guessed it, Dr. Genius found it necessary for some crazy reason to discharge, against the multidisciplinary team's opinion I might add, this person to the community! I couldn't, nor could my colleagues, comprehend this judgment call! In the past we'd been particularly harsh with Dr. Genius and his rigid, authoritarian approach to resolve what seemed to be very mundane "clinical dilemmas," to use his vernacular. So one day it became readily apparent to all involved that he was getting even by putting his foot down with this recent judgment call, which had disastrous results. *Get on with the story, Jake.* Okay, okay.

It was only a matter of time before the client "acted out" in the community. No more than three weeks later, in fact, which made the papers of course, the client commandeered a bus and began to "joy ride" around the community – with the police in hot pursuit! One of the occupants of the bus, an 86-year-old lady, later commented that the joy ride had livened up her day and she hoped the police wouldn't be too harsh with that "nice young man"! Indeed, needless to say the client was eventually arrested, that is, after approximately 30 minutes of "joy riding" around the suburbs of this moderately large eastern city! People cheered him on as he drove by waving, honking the horn, occasionally driving over lawns and through schoolyards to avoid police roadblocks, with a parade of police cars trailing behind him. Remember this was the mid 1970s – I shudder to think of today's actions/consequences taken by the police!

Later on I learned through the grapevine, whether true or not true, that Dr. Genius was subsequently contacted by the Chief of Police and severely reprimanded. This was followed up with the Mayor of the City, by way of a complaint sent to the Hospital Administration, challenging the competence of Dr. Genius! More specifically, recommending he receive supervision in the future by one of his peers who knew EXACTLY what the hell they were doing! Oh dear, what a blow to someone's ego and yet what a severely needed "kick in the ass" for this self-righteous, pompous professional! He thought he was superior in judgment to a ten-member multidisciplinary professional team, with over 100 years of combined, clinical experience! The last "laugh" was communicated by Dick F. of course, remember the staff member who'd been cautioned, then reprimanded by Dr. Genius, regarding his use of jive talk. "Dr. G. – Jive kings use condoms – I guess this one broke, to be safe is to be cool, can you dig." The King of Cool had done it again! Now, on to the next chapter, are you getting the feel for my

Chapter One | 29

eccentric style of Case Study? Hope so – there is lots more to come. *Jake, just get on with it.* Okay, okay.

Of Note: you will find throughout the book many examples of people who have de facto, rather than de jure authority. That is, they exercise power even if they're NOT formally authorized to do so. These are the "informal leaders" of the organization. Some good advice – observe these people in the organizational structure and record, either making mental note or in written form, their opinions. Before you read on, here are some "tidbits" to think about. Outstanding leaders usually possess four attributes; they:

1. pay attention through Vision (of the organization)
2. achieve meaning through Communication;
3. achieve Trust; and
4. organize for Innovative Learning.

According to the experts, anyway, regardless, KEEP THESE ISSUES IN MIND.

CHAPTER TWO

VIGNETTE 13

FOLLOWING A BRIEF THREE-YEAR DEPARTURE FROM MENTAL HEALTH Services, I returned after completing another credential to augment my qualifications. Also, I needed time to work in an entirely different field to ponder my future while upgrading my clinical skills, figure that one out?! Festinger's Theory of Cognitive Dissonance, the approach-avoidance paradigm, that was me, "in spades" – I was becoming more determined to be a success in one of the most difficult and perplexing Industries in North America. But I had reservations about throwing myself whole heartedly into a career, ending up "under the bus" with a bunch of professional outliers.

Remember those shibboleths I'd encountered in my first real job and discussed in Chapter One? If you hadn't guessed, the problems with the clientele are often overshadowed by the politics played out between the staff members! Some of these range wars carry on for years and years, creating unbelievable pain and suffering between the antagonists and in many circumstances, complex trauma at the end of a career. Am I telling you something new? I think not! So, here we go with Chapter Two.

My second job in the field of Mental Health Services entailed carrying a 150-caseload of Social Assistance applicants and recipients. The catchment area I was assigned was relatively large in a middle-class area of the city, but with corridors of working-class side-street "islands." You're familiar with what I'm describing, I'm sure. You have those beautiful, well-manicured boulevards, but every six or eight blocks there are side streets that proceed into minor alleys, almost too small for a vehicle to drive through, let alone park. This area was the usual domain of my clientele. One specific referral causes sharp, painful memories still to this day, even though it occurred in the late 1970s. Back then, I thought, through this new job, I could "make my bones" as the expression goes and with success, help to re-affirm that maybe, just maybe, this was the profession that I was suited to spend my entire working life. But on with the story!

I was requested to complete a Social Assistance application for a young, unwed mother, who as it turned out was blonde, petite, and good looking but with sinister motives and manipulative tendencies! I phoned prior to traveling to her downtown address, pre-arranging a time to meet that was conducive for both of us. I was familiar with the case profile by this time. After six months on the job I'd encountered a great number of single, unwed mothers with children under five years of age. The naïveté of the client's adolescent voice on the phone supported my preconception of whom I thought I would encounter. How wrong was my presumption!! When I got to the client's street and looked for the address number, I saw a young woman peer through a window from an apartment complex and then quickly move back from sight. I looked down at my day calendar, reaffirming that I had the right address, before getting out of my vehicle. I made a mental note to ask the applicant if she was currently seeking employment and was developing a Job Search list that I could review. Standard questions asked in these circumstances.

Let's cut to the chase: I knocked on the client's door, which was opened briskly and there stood a 20-year-old, blonde, blue-eyed beauty dressed in "spray paint," tighter than tight jeans, highlighting a lovely, svelte figure. I couldn't believe how this woman got into those jeans, let alone was able to sit down without passing out, they were that TIGHT! What was even more provocative was her T-shirt with the following statement printed in dark, bold letters: I'LL GIVE HEAD TILL I'M DEAD. *Um'mm, sounds like a set-up, Jake!?* It was! She invited me inside and the walk, or should I say wiggle, from the doorway to the kitchen table was meant to impress, and it did! I sat down adjacent to her, opened my valise and began taking out the Application material, while she sat staring at me intently, with those large blue eyes, going blink, blink, blink. I began the interview in the most professional voice I could muster. When I finished, she requested clarification on several points. Her voice, its cadence and relaxed manner, reflected someone who'd gone through this routine many, many times before! She was, I felt, very practiced at discerning the strengths and weaknesses of the respective Caseworkers who'd taken her Application in the past and then navigating them along to meet her agenda. Twenty minutes later this gut feeling was confirmed as I wondered who was interviewing whom. The picture on the sideboard in her living room showed her preschool son, approximately three years of age, being held by a good-looking long-haired gentleman and my client beside him in a stagnant, artificial pose. She noticed my eyes wandering around her apartment and when asked about the current nature of her relationship, stated rather calmly, nodding at the picture, "He's doing time in Federal prison." When asked when he was due for parole she answered, "I'm not exactly sure, he's in for first-degree murder." Yeah right, that about set the tempo for the rest of our interview!

Okay, on with the meeting. My client acknowledged she was currently unemployed and showed me a Job Search List and then stated she had not received any monies from an external source, indicating she was indigent, thereby making her technically eligible for Social Assistance. Next, I looked at her bank book and requested her taxation statement from the previous two years. This is when things went 180 and began to get hairy! My question and request, innocuous by any standard and required by my job, had caused a disconnect with the logical flow or more precisely, her anticipated and premeditated, rehearsed diatribe with yours truly. Remember what I stated earlier that my gut told me I was dealing with a very experienced pro and here I was about to be bitten in the proverbial ass – big time! In the late 1970s there were no cell phones, you had to use a land-line. What next occurred was a vitriolic harangue from what I perceived was an AGGRESSIVE personality-disordered, single, unemployed woman who was prepared to "pull out all the stops" to get her needs met, at my expense! Anger is putting it mildly; this woman's rage caused by a "narcissistic injury" from some flunky Welfare Worker trying to run the show – not on your life scenario! Not a nice position to be put into and I'm talking about me! Her behavior went "beyond the pale," not just some client losing her temper and giving me a blast, far beyond that level of anger, far, far beyond AND with the potential to get ugly!

You've been in these situations, you know what I'm talking about, your mouth becomes dry and you start to lose confidence, composure, and articulation. The client's big blue eyes by this point were steady-state automatons, I'm talking HATRED, no more seductive blink, blink, blink! They were riveted at me with an intense, focused stare – that antisocial, cold-blooded scary stare! I imagined she had used this ploy, whether from an unconscious or preconscious level, to intimidate, manipulate, and crush any opposition many times in her past! Instinctively I recoiled at her behavior and began to feel like mush. Intimidated!? Me! Jake Hagerman, approximately 10 years older and 50 pounds (23 kg.) heavier!? Quite frankly, size means nothing in these situations and I was fully aware the client's behavior could "ratchet up" another 20–30% in intensity and potential violence! I can look back and laugh from the "side of my mouth" mind you, but at the time I was scared, even cowed by this woman's conduct! I started looking for avenues of escape. But I digress. She intuitively felt my nerve was breaking, the will to survive compromised – my face gave it away. Jake, Jake, cool it. Okay, okay.

IT GOT WORSE. There was a knock at the door and in walked her "brother," holding her beautiful three-year-old son in his arms, asking how things were going? This guy was a dead ringer for the late character actor Jack Palance, who in his day was one of the most intimidating Hollywood "heavies" from the early 1950s to late 1980s. The client's brother looked a "nasty piece of work"! His appearance out of nowhere, in hindsight, was, I'm sure, orchestrated to maximize the threat imperative and it worked! But Jake had one last trick up his sleeve. I asked if I could use the client's phone to contact my Supervisor regarding the Application. "No problem," both stated simultaneously; once again an eerie feeling crept over me that they'd done this "schtik" many, many times before! What d'ya think? I'm sure those of you who work with potentially dangerous clientele have experienced my plight and share my feelings about that "gut feeling from hell" warning you to be VERY, VERY careful!

Old Joe, my supervisor, who was one year away from retirement, answered the phone. He was the most calm, reassuring individual you'd ever want to meet. He was and had been for 30 years a perfect foil for this type of client behavior and asked me "my problem." Here comes the next shocker, the Jack Palance look-alike brother picked up another phone in the living room to overhear our conversation! I looked over at him, shrugged my shoulders, and asked, "Can I help you?" His response came as no surprise, as he with absolutely no tact and amazing gall stated, "I pay the friggin' rent here, so I think I have the right to know what the hell's comin' down." That did it, my client WAS receiving financial support from an external source and she had lied. This probably negated her eligibility for Social Assistance under the provisions of the Welfare Act, or at least would require a further inquiry about her financial circumstances. At this point, who gave a damn! The Jack Palance look-alike brother and his sister had successfully accomplished their agenda to break my confidence and force, I can't think of another word, an abrogation of my responsibility to the taxpayer, or so they thought! Thank God for the Old Joes of the world; he had quickly surmised what was comin' down and requested my immediate return to the office, so as to provide "better service and one-to-one supervision regarding this very unique and complicated case." Yeah, right, "pull the other one," Joe! The Jack Palance look-alike brother started to blather about his rights being sullied, actually the preamble used began with an F and ended with a K. The client sister became "unhinged" and for a microsecond I thought she was going to come across the table at me! I also believe if she'd had a weapon, or a "shank" in close vicinity, she would've used it on me. No doubt in my mind!!

My phone response being overheard was of course contrived and well acted: "Joe, are you saying you want me to leave; I'm sure we can sort things out here." His retort, "Get your ass back to the office NOW," reaffirmed his boss man authority and helped to mollify the tension. I shrugged my shoulders, hung up the phone, put my Application material back into my valise, and walked slowly out the door, feeling their eyes riveted on the back of my head. I fully expected the Jack Palance look-alike brother to step in front of me as I left, or in some way impede my forward progress, which could have been interpreted as an assault under the criminal code. But he didn't! I walked down the driveway, towards my car, and took time to quickly look over my shoulder. There stood the Jack Palance look-alike brother and my client holding her three-year-old son staring, staring, glaring, and then moving away from the door and out of sight. Three words came to mind – MENACING, DANGEROUS and then SAFETY a microsecond later! When I got to my car I had a sudden urge to urinate, vomit, scream in that order! But you've been there, you've been in my skin, it ain't fun but it's a living and a very challenging one to boot!

When I got back to the office a crowd had formed by the front door, led by Old Joe! Everyone shook my hand – that was the extent of the "Psychologically Healthy Work Place" support in those days. Nonetheless, it felt good to be received in this fashion. Unknown to me, two of my colleagues had had encounters with this pair over the past several years, enduring the same intimidation ploy that I did. One of them required two weeks' stress leave from work, so in my mind I'd risen to the challenge and survived! I was proud of myself, but enough back slapping and taking bows. By the way – Jack Palance's look-alike brother was in fact the brother of her partner doing time in the Federal penitentiary for first-degree murder. This stuff, it keeps you young, doesn't it? *Yeah right, Jake.*

VIGNETTE 14

OLD JOE WAS MY BOSS FOR ALMOST TWO YEARS, TRULY A GREAT GUY, "transparent" as they say in 2014. But back in the day Old Joe was simply an old pro, sixty-four-year-old vastly experienced, mid-management boss. Someone you could go to, "shoot the breeze," and come away wondering how did he know so much and still be at a junior, mid-management position. Politics, Jake, POLITICS with a capital P. His nemesis was his thirty-something boss, who around management circles was known as a gigantic pain in the ass. An exacting, "know-it-all jerk," in plain English! No project was too big for Old Joe's boss and woe-betide anybody interfering with this guy's plans for future promotion! Stated again, no project was too large, nor too daunting, for this upwardly mobile mamzer[2]!

About a year after I was employed, I had lunchtime rotation, meaning I was responsible for evaluating emergency 15-day Social Assistance applicants who were "in crisis." More often than not their crisis was a miscue of over-spending their budgeted monies, then they would come in to claim, "fifteen days emergency assistance" to tide them over. Some of their stories were true; I know because I checked them out carefully with collateral sources before issuing a check. Others were part "whopper," part fantasy, and you couldn't help but laugh when you confronted the Applicant with your suspicions. When this occurred you were met with a well-rehearsed exaggerated pause, explanation, and pause again, as if to indicate does stupidity run in your family!? Over time I got pretty respectable at evaluating "the good, the bad, and the untrustworthy." Some pretty nasty "pieces of work" came through the door, including the lazy one I'm going to tell you about.

One of the more notorious Applicants was a former Commercial Diver, a tough dude whom I'd rejected from Social Assistance several months previously, while taking his Application at his home in my catchment area. His gaze this time around said it all, "Oh no here we go again with this jerk Social Worker." Yeah right, my gut said, I hope his story is genuine, not like last time, when his collateral sources told me he was a con and working on the side – which was proven to be correct by the way!

His story this time 'round was also flimsy, filled with conjecture, and he couldn't produce a Job Search list, nor had he the slightest intention of doing so. Is this the type of person who is in an emergent situation and in need of Social Assistance? I quickly pondered his request.

---

2   bastard

He was able bodied, with *no* medical history contravening his ability to seek employment. We were geographically located in a "fruit belt," with ample work available from the local farmers who were recruiting pickers every morning at 6 a.m. When I told Mr. Commercial Diver, out of work, in-need-of-emergency-funds-for-fifteen-days person, that there was ample work opportunity and available every morning at 6 a.m., he went ballistic! Shouting, threatening, pacing, and then shouting, threatening, and pacing again! I was firm and no amount of debate would change the situation. And then on the scene came Old Joe's boss, who'd been having a nice, quiet lunch in his office and was concerned about the serious goings on. He "shushed" me and took over the case, which exacerbated the situation ten-fold! Mr. Commercial Diver began ranting and raving at Old Joe's boss and even threatened to call the police, for what reason I don't know and then it happened, Mr. Commercial Diver lost his pants! They slid down his legs during one of his rants while he was inhaling. Not batting an eye, he started yanking up his pants with one hand while "waggling" his finger and then his fist with the other. Next and almost at the end of this fiasco, he left in a huff but not before I received a call from his wife! She stated that unless her husband got emergency Social Assistance, "I'd better watch out when I was driving, 'cause he knows your vehicle!" He'd barely left the office a minute before and I get this call, what gives? Remember, in those days no cell phones!?

But don't worry, Old Joe leapt into action and entered the fray, coming to the rescue. He debriefed with his mamzer boss, talked to me about the wife's phone call, asked me if I wanted police protection for the next forty-eight hours, warned the Commercial Diver that under no circumstances would "we" allow this behavior to happen again and would use it against him in a Court of Law if he didn't comply! All this Old Joe did while sitting, having a cup of tea, his blood sugar barely registered above 5 I'm sure! This was a typical workday for Old Joe and through it all he never lost his composure and leadership aura! Being sheltered under this competent air and unflappable nature caused an enormous weight to be lifted off our backs while we toiled in the trenches. He was a Godsend for the Social Assistance Unit; we were never under the false assumption that our competence won the day in the field. Rather, if the truth were to be told, our competence and knowledge that we had BACKUP from a great man made the Unit's reputation what it was over the years!!

During the next six months Old Joe managed to get his mamzer boss promoted out of the office and Upstairs with the "Big Boys." They ate him for breakfast as the saying goes, but miraculously he was still working at the Government agency ten years later, when I returned to say goodbye to a friend who was retiring. Old Joe's mamzer boss had AGED and then some; the years had not been kind and yet I felt deep down justice had been served, but that's not kind. *Jake, Jake, go join the Boy Scouts; he was a first class Jerk!* Okay, okay. *Old Joe – what happened to him, Jake?* If you really want to know, he met and was later re-married to a former girlfriend. A long lost love and spent his retirement in a "perfect" job, volunteering as a Review Board Complaints Evaluator! He monitored clients who felt they'd been hard done by, from people like Old Joe's mamzer boss and the Organization's "Big Shots." What goes around comes around, I left the retirement party laughing so hard I had to pull over and stop the car to relieve myself.

VIGNETTE 15

DOWN THE HALL AND ACROSS THE CORRIDOR WAS MY COUNTERPART FROM the other team, Myra J. This individual had an hourglass figure and then some and was very, very meticulous. Accuracy, effectiveness, and efficiency, the world of work is run by rules, regulations, and you better tread softly, "anal retentive" type of personality and VERY mistrustful of men! This late 20s/early 30s pedantic, reactionary tsedreyter[3] would fold her arms across her chest whenever a male approached to discuss a case, or have an innocent gossip session by the water cooler. Further clues follow; Myra J. was always physically cold, even during the midst of the summer heat, when temperatures rose to the mid-80s and low 90s Fahrenheit (35°C). She also wore sweaters or some type of loose fitting apparel to cover

---

3   eccentric

her torso FROM THOSE PRYING EYES. Lastly, and certainly not least, Myra J. had a fixed delusion about a boyfriend/fiancé Henry whom she'd been involved with for a period of seven years. Yeah right, the problem was no one had ever seen her boyfriend/fiancé Henry! Myra J. would tell long, detailed stories about their weekends together and if you were a new staff, it was very easy to get sucked into this emotional vortex. Staff attempting to challenge the veracity of Myra J's "Henry" statements would be aggressively, yes aggressively, shut down as in told to take a "flying leap," "hit the bricks," "don't be dumb," etc. In those days "clean" conversation between the sexes was still in vogue. The "F bombs" we hear today would've spelled social Siberia, total ostracism in the early 1970s, but you get the picture, Woodstock aside, swearing between the sexes was a big no-no, at least at work anyway.

Old Joe came out with one of his malapropisms when describing Myra J. "I think she's kind of psychotic-neurotic if you know what I mean" and left it at that, because Myra J. was damn good at her job! Here's the problem, remember old Joe's mamzer boss. He was so impressed with Myra J.'s casework ability that he loaded more and more work on her desk and because Myra J. sought approval and couldn't say no, she kept working and working AND working! After a month of doing Trojan work with little to no respite, Myra J. began talking to herself while walking down the hall; she didn't respond to social cues from her colleagues regarding her eccentric behavior; her hair was usually unwashed and her work clothes were often rumpled, messy, and unkempt. In essence, she was entering a clinical depression, having a "breakdown" in lay English. At our weekly staff meeting, Old Joe's mamzer boss marched into the room one day and proceeded to address the staff about some minor policy and procedure change and then complimented Myra J. "She's such a hard worker, everybody's go-to person and one of the best staff members the Organization has employed in the past 30 years," etc., etc. You can imagine how the barrage of compliments impacted this very socially inhibited, almost schizoidal personality. Old Joe's mamzer boss strutted away shortly thereafter, people shuffled their papers, and made small talk and no one (except yours truly) saw

Myra J. slowly stand up from her desk, bend over, pick up roughly a dozen files and throw them eight feet in the air! Papers floated all over the room in total disarray!

Everyone roared with laughter and started to clap, until Myra J. walked slowly towards the large panoramic picture window, placed both hands above her head, palms down, on this monster window and stared outside with those unblinking, vacant brown eyes. The clapping and laughing slowly subsided and someone went over and gave Myra J. a slap on the back (we did that in those days) and said it was one of the funniest things he'd ever seen! Myra J. didn't move, not a fraction! She stood straight as a statue, unblinking, staring that vacant stare out the window, with her arms outstretched, the palms of her hands pressed against the window!

By now, people were starting to get worried and one of the staff members who'd been in the nursing profession many years earlier told everyone to shut up and walked over to Myra J. An attempt was made at conversation, but to no avail, Myra J. was in a dissociative state and could not be reached. Several of the support staff started to cry and then someone remembered to phone 911! When the ambulance arrived – they weren't called paramedics in those days – two attendants entered the room and attempted to move Myra J., trying to get her to walk. Dream on, McDuff, it's called dead weight! Myra J. was "frozen," staring out the window, lost in her own world! Someone phoned her mother, whom Myra J. adored, debriefed the woman about her daughter's mental state, and offered to drive over and bring her back to the office to provide assistance. Impressively, Myra J.'s mother under the circumstances kept phenomenal poise! We, collectively as Social Assistance Caseworkers, talked about the mother's behavior and total dedication to her daughter's plight for years afterwards. I was at a staff reunion eight or ten years later and after a few drinks, we got around to talking about that fateful day and the courage shown by Myra J.'s mother!

But on with the story – Myra J's mother entered the room, walked slowly to her daughter's side, and started talking to her in a low, controlled, whisper voice, at the same time massaging Myra J.'s right shoulder and arm. People were thankfully respectful that a soft

Chapter Two | 41

approach was being used to soothe a very disturbed and detached mental state.

With time it became obvious that Myra J.'s mother was connecting with her daughter at a very deep and therapeutic level. All the advanced, "modern" therapeutic training took a back seat in my mind that day! The mother was attempting to retrieve her daughter's mental faculties and the staff – with all our combined and collective clinical training – just stood there transfixed!? No one said a word, no one intervened – we did nothing!! Approximately fifteen minutes later, which seemed at the time like five, Myra J. began to verbalize in soft, hesitating, infantile language, which her mother responded to in kind. Another ten minutes followed, at which time Myra J.'s mother asked Myra J. to take her hand, which she did, and follow her outside to the ambulance – which she did! They got into the back seat of the ambulance and were driven to the local acute-care hospital, where Myra J. was assessed and found in contravention of the Mental Health Act and "sectioned" as it was called in those days. She spent the next 30 days in the psychiatric ward of this facility and was subsequently transferred to a nearby Psychiatric Hospital, where she spent the next eight months in therapy.

Eventually Myra J. did recover, came back and was given an easier and much reduced caseload! This time thanks to the Union putting its foot down, she wasn't "fed to the lions"! Here comes the $64,000 question. Was there an internal investigation regarding the nature of the events that led to the emotional breakdown of this fragile, young Caseworker? Absolutely not – remember those were the bad old days!? "Suck it up, if you don't watch out, it could happen to you!" "He who survives wins!" "If you stay on your feet you've got a chance to win!" Remember all that macho B.S. crap. *Yeah, but what happens to the Myra J.'s of the world, Jake?* They can still contribute and shouldn't be put through this kind of ordeal is the obvious answer! Yes, she can learn to be more assertive and give appropriate boundaries, but she wasn't comfortable with authority roles. *Then why was she placed in this kind of confrontational, demanding position in the first place, Jake!?* Obviously, somebody in H.R. had overlooked this problem for years before, and bosses should be more sensitive by providing a safe and secure work environment is the answer! The moral of the story, according to my late father, goes something like this, "When you learn that life IS NOT fair, that's when you're an adult, Jake" – according to Dad anyway. Seriously, thank God for allowing the "Psychologically Healthy Workplace Model" to be invented, designed, and implemented! It currently exists in most North American work environments and is here to stay and it's damn unfortunate the timing was thirty years too late for Myra J.

VIGNETTE 16

DURING MY TWO-YEAR EXPERIENCE AS A SOCIAL ASSISTANCE CASEWORKER, I was on-duty during lunch hour on a four-week rotation basis. One particular day a gentleman entered the building, approached the Intake Room where I was stationed, and then waited patiently to be seen and an Application taken for emergency Social Assistance. Two Admin. Assistants appraised the man's appearance and made an unfortunate snap judgment, by his looks and not his action, that he was unsavory and was probably out to bilk the system. Unfortunately, they made their prejudice and extreme bias noticed to both the client and myself! I took them aside and stated in no uncertain words my disappointment in their professional deportment; actually I told them to, "straighten out their acts" or I'd get Old Joe's mamzer boss involved! Good old-fashioned confrontation sometimes wins the day and it did – that day anyway. The two Admin. Assistants stopped their behavior and walked away in a huff. The gentleman sat there quietly watching and a very subtle smile crossed his mouth, as I'm sure they misinterpreted my comment as "stick out your racks" instead of "straighten out your acts." They often did the former, to get the attention of the younger men (me included) in the office. These ladies would sit, gossip, "buff" their nails, and make cruel, incessant jokes about the various staff, the boring job, and how they'd "fix" the office if they were in power, now d'ya get the picture? *We get it, Jake!* Okay, okay.

It came the client's turn and one of the Admin. Assistants ushered him into the Intake room and chair opposite my desk. As I recall he was wearing an old-fashioned weather-beaten leather jacket with a hockey insignia. The jacket was so old the leather had cracked and the fading color was not red but ochre. Almost disguising the team name sown below the decal was a crest just visible, with Montréal Canadiens emblazoned inside. I was mildly curious but held back questions regarding the nature of the jacket until after the Application had been completed. I assessed his "financial needs" and found the gentleman eligible to receive 15 days' emergency Social Assistance, which would carry him through to his first paycheck. No big deal you say, until I asked him about the jacket and how he acquired it.

The gentleman, by now in his mid-70s, told me an unbelievable story and I have no reason to disbelieve him, as a number of years later I made discreet inquiries, which confirmed to a "T" everything he'd said to me was believable – believable is slightly different than true. Listen some more.

He was telling me the truth, or so I thought, kind of that is. This person had played professional hockey in Canada and the United States for approximately 12 years during the 1920s and 30s and on three different teams. He stated he'd been one of the hockey players who carried the great Howie Morenz off the ice (1937) after Morenz was "checked" and sustained a broken leg, from which he never recovered, dying of blood poisoning three weeks later. The older gentleman's stories about professional sports in the 1920s and '30s from the perspective of a journeyman player – the way he described himself – were the exact words my sources used to describe his skill and talent on the ice. Whether this was the same individual from that era, or simply a man impersonating this person with the same name and in the same general age bracket, is anyone's guess. But I loved his candor and gift as a raconteur and found him simply a good guy! But what had happened over the years I wondered? He had the usual stock answers which we've heard many, many times from people who are down and out. Nevertheless, he had an aura of immense dignity about playing professional hockey back in the day, when there were no million dollar contracts and you played simply for the love of the game. I asked him where he was living and he stated in a Northern city most of the time, but during the summer months would return to this area to pick fruit, catch up with his friends, and make, in his words, "a mint", which was in those days approximately $50–$70 per day. He also stated his philosophy of life, "Yeah, I've had my ups and downs but compared to other guys I've had it pretty good, no complaints, a loving wife who recently passed away, two children and three grandchildren."

He went on to discuss two friends who lived down the hall from him in a "seedy" center town hotel, of which he currently resided during the "picking season." The friends were veterans of the WW II Battle of Dieppe, a precursor to D Day. Both had been teenagers lying about their age when they signed up, wanting to see some "action" as recently trained Rangers. One had been in the second wave of landing crafts, loaded with troops heading towards the beach, witnessing the carnage! When the landing craft's ramp was dropped, he was immediately hit with machine gun fire and fell into the water. One of his buddies – apparently one of his closest and dearest friends both in boot camp and later on living in barracks – dragged him into shallow water before being shot and killed. After lying in the shallow water at the edge of the beach feigning death, the man was eventually captured by the Germans, sent to a hospital to convalesce, and then placed in a prisoner of war camp until 1945. The second veteran had been on a landing craft in the third wave, which got to within 1000 yards (910 m.) of the beach, saw firsthand that the battle was irretrievable, and was forever thankful the landing craft was ordered back to the ship! This veteran, although not wounded physically, had been mentally scarred for the rest of his life, after witnessing the slaughter on the beach that fateful day! It had changed his life and at this time in the late 1970s he was not yet 60 years of age! Both men met in a convalescent hospital in a large city after the war, both men had become hopeless alcoholics, both men lived off Social Assistance and Federal Government Veterans Allowance, and both men lived on dog food in this seedy, downtown hotel!

So when the gentleman hockey player finished his story, he noticed I had a tear dripping down my cheek, which I wiped away, and then he said and I remember this distinctly, "I see you haven't lived much of this life, Bud, it only gets better, don't think about the past, think of the future and do your best." But I haven't finished, somehow during the 40 minutes I'd been with this guy and I'm sure influenced by the Admin. Assistants' behavior behind the scene, it got around the office that this particular gentleman was "so and so," a former member of the Montréal Canadiens! In an instant and I mean mach speed, there were three older colleagues coming over to shake the man's hand, one even asked for an autograph and offered to put him up for the rest of the summer in a suite above his garage, at no expense no less! The older gentleman smiled that coy smile, and I burst out laughing. It keeps you young.

VIGNETTE 17

DURING THIS PERIOD, WORKING AS A SOCIAL ASSISTANCE CASEWORKER, I had the opportunity, or more accurately the occasional nightmare opportunity, to sit in on interviews with my older colleagues. These were gentlemen of advancing years for that era, in their late 50s/ early 60s, veterans of the Second World War, who had grown up during the Depression. They were double tough, resilient, often ruthless and very righteous in their beliefs, a dying breed that was gone and almost forgotten by 1990, thankfully I'm sure, for the female employees! But I digress. I would arrive at the interview and the Panel, usually comprised of five personnel from different areas of the Organization, would be sitting behind a long table gossiping, waiting for the prospective interviewee to enter the room. This day as I walked through the door, I could overhear one of the gentlemen saying under his breath, "Here comes the young pup," which was followed by a frustrated sigh and then another comment, again under his breath, "I wonder if he'll ever learn." Inevitably, we interviewed support staff – more specifically, the Admin. Assistants, or as they were called in those days, secretarial staff. These were typically young women 18–22 years of age, who were high school graduates and less often graduates from a bona fide secretarial school, with both typing and shorthand experience. What's the problem with interviewing, you ask? This is a typical responsibility given most staff throughout their years of employment; it's a common, mundane responsibility that everybody hates, but has to do. *Again, what's the problem, Jake?* Okay, okay, here's the clincher – remember in the mid-late 1970s, the feminist movement was barely under way and sexist, chauvinistic comments from males were still commonplace and generally unchallenged. We "young bucks" coming up were at the forefront of a changing attitude regarding equality, respect, and support for our female counterparts. *Jake, we get it, in English, changing professional attitude.* To reiterate: allowing equality for the female gender at the worksite and if the truth were to be told, a wisdom that the women's movement was here to stay and not a passing fad.

To illustrate my point, I present the following interview with trepidation! Please don't gag, this Vignette goes back 35 years and I am not wishing to make anyone sick, but more of a statement of fact of how far we've progressed regarding professional respect and renunciation of gender bias. Before I go on and to help you get a feel for the antagonist Crazy Dave, think of the brilliant character actor Chris Cooper. He has typified Crazy Dave's manner and behavior in many, many of his movie roles, such as the neighbor in *American Beauty*, which should provide a better character transparency to help you envisage Crazy Dave. Thank you, Chris Cooper! Now on with the story.

So here I was, squished between Crazy Dave, nicknamed because of his fossilized, sexist dogmatism concerning the opposite sex, and his peer, the Manager of Human Resources, who was a year from retirement. A lovely older woman, but beyond her depth regarding this newfangled feminist ideology. Once, or is it twice again I state – the Interview was a RECIPE FOR DISASTER! A young woman was ushered in and seated in a chair in front of the panel of five stalwarts chosen to evaluate her for an Admin. Assistant position. Prior to the interview, I had asked Crazy Dave if he would spend a moment with me alone in the corner of the room; he agreed. I then asked him forthright (i.e., man-to-man), "Dave, could you refrain from asking about miniskirts this interview?" Response, "And what the hell's wrong with miniskirts especially if the girl's got pretty legs?" Next question, "Dave, could you refrain from talking about the North African campaign?" Response, "I'll think about it." Next question, "Dave, you've got a habit of ogling the young women if you know what I mean, it could get us in trouble." His response, "And what the hell's wrong with looking at a nice body, I'm not AC/DC ya know!" This point-counterpoint repartee went on for the next couple of minutes. My requests for Crazy Dave to refrain from his candid, inappropriate, and often obtuse comments generally fell on deaf ears. More specifically, "Jake, Jake, Jake, you're still wet behind the ears." My response, "They can't be that wet, I just applied to Med School.". Frequently during the previous year or so I had approached his colleague, the lovely older woman, Manager of Human Resources, regarding his inappropriate behavior, especially when it came to interviews with younger, much younger female candidates! Here comes the $64,000 response and remember this is in the mid-late 1970s, "Boys will be boys, Jake, and Rome wasn't built in a day, but I'll keep in mind what you've been saying." Yeah, right – so much for the feminist movement and women's equality, Heisenberg's principle of uncertainty was being thoroughly tested this day?!

Specifically, any attempt to measure something will have the effect of minutely altering that which is altered. The early/mid portion of the interview went swimmingly well with what turned out to be an uncommonly bright, clever, young woman! A structured interview format was followed, Crazy Dave for once followed the protocol, and I thought maybe, just maybe he'd listened and absorbed my suggestions! WRONG – at the end of the interview, or more precisely when the young woman was asked if she had any questions regarding the nature of the job, its duties, and whom she would be assisting in the Organization, she cleared her throat to respond. But before she could say anything, Crazy Dave intervened. As I dictate this book I shudder to think of the consequences had this interview occurred in 2014 or even 1994?! Crazy Dave spoke in his usual authoritarian manner, "If I could say a few words before you respond, Miss" – remember in the mid-to-late 1970s Ms. had not become completely prevalent – "I'm going to be your boss and a few personal questions will certainly 'clear the air,' or at least let you know where I'm coming from." The young woman nodded and looked down – in those days many younger females would not address an older man in authority, eye to eye; it was perceived as an act of disrespect. HERE IT COMES!

"Do you own any miniskirts?" The woman nodded and I just about fell off my chair! Crazy Dave continued, "That's great, because we need those pretty legs around here to liven up this boring place, feel free to wear miniskirts any time you want!" I was not only stunned, but swung my head over and glared at Crazy Dave and then shrugged my shoulders and looked apologetically at the young woman, who raised her eyebrows, smiled and looked down.

Crazy Dave's next question was equally inappropriate but one I'd heard many, many times before. "Let me tell you a little bit about my background so we understand where I'm coming from – I'm a veteran of World War II as I'm sure your dad was." But before he could go on, she shook her head and stated, "My father was a Conscientious Objector and did not serve." Volcanoes are scary to look at when they erupt on television – that day I witnessed a human volcano about to erupt, who would've committed murder, or at least attempted murder, if I hadn't been in the room! I do exaggerate but it was bad, she'd touched a nerve that replicated yanking an abscessed tooth! "Let me get this straight, your old man was a 'C.O.' – too high and pompous mighty to sign up and DEFEND HIS COUNTRY IN TIME OF WAR?" The young woman's response and without batting an eye, engendered poise, courage, and a love for her parent, "Although you perceive his action as cowardice, he paid for his convictions by receiving insults, threats, and social alienation from his so-called friends; my father stood by his beliefs."

Crazy Dave's response, "AND WHAT THE HELL WERE THOSE"? And remember this is in a formal job interview, four other people on panel, including the Manager of Human Resources. "Sto Pro Veritate," she replied in a barely audible, soft voice. Crazy Dave's response, "ARE YOU TELLING ME TO SHOVE IT" was met with quiet laughter by the young woman! With this sign of contempt, from Crazy Dave's perspective anyway, he STOOD UP and was motioned to sit down by the four of us on panel; luckily he did so! She looked up quickly, "I see you don't understand Latin, 'Sto Pro Veritate' means, 'I stand for truth' and my father is a man of his word and could not kill another human being whatever the cause"!

Crazy Dave was dumbstruck – for the first time in his professional career I'm sure! After a few seconds, he stated, "And what's your old man doing now?" The young woman's response, "If you mean my father, he's a Philosophy professor and his area is Epistemology," was met with an immediate and loud retort, "LET'S KEEP IT CLEAN YOUNG LADY, NO REASON TO GET CRUDE," then a pause for three seconds, "Just remember I've killed better men than your old man in North Africa and we'll get along just fine." Again I was stunned and for a second time nearly fell off my chair, as did one or two of the other panel members. That day, in my mind anyway, the young woman, back straight, eyes dead center totally committed, became the prototype for the feminist movement, "May I call you Dave? Older Dave, or Ignorant Dave, whatever – it doesn't matter. I wouldn't, or better still, couldn't take this job if my life depended on it and my father is worth 20 Daves and 50 interview committees," and with that, got up nodded to the panel and walked out! Pretty impressive for a woman that age in that era!! We forget that girls were socialized to be submissive, demure, and apologetic during the 1950s and '60s in many, many families, not all, but many!

Once again, here comes the $64,000 question. *Forget the question, Jake, what was the upshot of the interview process regarding quality control, quality improvement, customer satisfaction, in other words – total quality management practice?* The answer – the square root of zero! People shrugged their shoulders, looked over at Crazy Dave, shook their heads, gathered up their papers, grumbled, and walked out of the room! Everyone that is except yours truly, not that I'm a hero but honestly thought Crazy Dave needed some feedback. Quite frankly, he looked shocked and stunned – thank God and Jesus Christ for that at least! His response? "What did I do?! Maybe it's that time of the month, you know that crappy pre-menstrual stuff." "No Dave it's not crappy pre-menstrual stuff – women menstruate for a reason, to allow reproduction of humanity, you fool – I can't believe you don't get why she was insulted!" Crazy Dave's response, "So she thought I was an asshole?" summed it up and I couldn't have said it better!

Here it comes again and don't be alarmed – Crazy Dave was in the system ANOTHER FOUR YEARS! When I look back at the late 1970s, his behavior from our current point of view and political correctness was way beyond the pale!! Although still very, very inappropriate for that era, it reflected a lot of enabling and gender inequality on the jobsite that occurred with little to no containment – to put it bluntly, "those were the bad old days!" Thank God for the "Psychologically Healthy Workplace Model," the model that's in place currently in most North American organizations!

There, I've pushed the "Model" for the third or fourth time, but it needs to be pushed! The working environment should not be a "jungle" but a fun experience! Yes, lots of hard work and at times labor intensive, but also a place to look forward to coming to! Equally, if you're going to spend a lot of time every day, of every week, of every month of a very (and hopefully) long life, you should be able to enjoy your work environment! So much for the Crazy Dave story. On to the next one.

VIGNETTE 18

THROUGHOUT MY EMPLOYMENT AS A SOCIAL ASSISTANCE CASEWORKER A few professional "personalities" stuck out in my mind, primarily because of the audacity of their behavior and not so much because of competence, charisma, or bravery in the field, and believe me, you had to have guts to do this job and maintain an objective state of mind. Murray W. had been on the job approximately five years, knew his casework job duties intimately, but was far too intelligent to be working in this job capacity. Several of his peers and family members had been in the medical profession including his grandfather, who had incidentally treated my uncle's spouse on their honeymoon 45 years earlier – it's a small world! Murray W.'s major problem was risk-taking while doing his job, which bored him to tears! During one encounter with a woman suffering from pre-senile dementia, at the time in her early 50s, he literally placed the phone in the desk drawer while she was talking, or more accurately, tangentially verbalizing, shut the drawer, sat back and read a report, then opened the drawer approximately five minutes later to continue his conversation with this loquacious, albeit dementing person! Very professional hunh (eh)!! His musings at the Single Men's Shelter were legendary! When asked simple direct questions by clients, mostly suffering from chronic, long-term alcoholism, remember these were mild to severely demented men, Murray W. always had a quick retort – way above their level of comprehension, which was cruel and unnecessary.

Murray W.'s lack of achievement in life both personally and professionally, caused him to displace his frustration onto the "poor dweebs" as he called them! Once again, here's another colleague that should've been challenged by the Higher-Ups and certainly Human Resources, but of course it never occurred, because Murray W. stayed slightly under the radar. That was until he encountered Dora S.

Dora S. was in her mid-20s, approximately 5'9" (1 m. 75 cm.) and 120 pounds (55 kg.), with dark brown eyes, short bobbed hair, and a propensity, there's that word again, to wear a sheer, see-through blouse and tailored pants. Think of the actresses in the "screwball comedies" of the 1930s and that was Dora S.'s physical appearance. She was bright, articulate, but rather cold and distant with males especially. *That's another one, Jake, what gives?* I know, I know. One day shortly after she began working, she arrived wearing one of her sheer, see-through blouses, this time without a bra! This set all the men astir – especially when she stood full-length in front of the picture window on a sunny day. Nothing was left to the imagination and we looked forward to Dora S. having many lapses in judgment by wearing this most provocative attire as often as possible and especially on a sunny day! I wondered what her clients felt about it. Here comes the problem.

As I said above, Murray W. could be rather brusque when he felt he was talking to an inferior intellect. One day when Dora S. arrived at work, wearing the notorious sheer see-through blouse, and happened to be standing by the equally notorious picture window, and yes, on a VERY sunny day, Murray W. made a "crack" about the formation of her teardrop breasts. Actually, from a technical point of view his observation was quite accurate. But from a professional stance obviously inappropriate, which should have brought a complaint of professional misconduct and harassment, but didn't, it would have in 2014. Once again and I get bored saying this, in the mid-late 1970s the female gender at the worksite received a lot of crap from oversexed, under-laid twenty-something males! Dora S. responded a few days later by purchasing a copy of *Playgirl* magazine, which showed full frontal nudity of males, and placing it on Murray W's desk. That day he was asked by some of the older male colleagues if "He'd gone over to the other side," "Swung both ways," "Was AC/DC," "A Nancy boy," "Enjoying some stray stuff," "Pulling somebody's pud." When Murray W. got back to his desk and saw the *Playgirl*, he put two and two together and conspired to get even. The next day when I came into the office I was told to go to Dora S.'s desk, which I did, and found an oversized dildo with a pink ribbon wrapped around it. Oh dear, what to do, then lo and behold who should show up but Old Joe.

In all his 64 years he'd never seen a dildo and when he picked it up, he thought it was a "blackjack" for self-defense purposes, in case one of the Social Assistance clients attacked Dora S. "I must say well done, that's using her head – look at the size of that knob!" HELLO – someone had to sit down with Old Joe and explain the nature of the dildo and what had caused its arrival – another office

Chapter Two | 53

conflict was "brewing" and would only escalate with time, unless Old Joe "nipped it in the bud"! In essence, Old Joe had come nosing around because he'd heard the rumor that Murray W. worked both sides of the bar, if you get my drift. I reassured Old Joe that wasn't the case, "relax, go have a cup of tea and I'll take care of it." When he left I dispensed of the dildo. To be honest, I put it in one of the female divorcees' office drawers. That by the way is another story, for another book, at another time. Divorce was a big deal 50 years ago and by the mid-late 1970s it was less of a big deal, but still there were no Escort Services and you had plenty of horny middle-age women who needed "a man around the house," or so I was told by one of the horny middle-aged women! I waited until Dora S. and Murray W. arrived at work to sit down with the intention of nipping this thing in the bud. I needn't have worried, something had transpired between these two during the past couple of days and I got the feeling, you know that feeling in the gut that tells you 'there's an affair in the air.' You guessed it, they were an office "item" for the next six months, until she "found the Lord," decided to renounce men, and moved to a convent in Peru, South America. Yes South America, not Indiana, stupe! *Jake, Jake "chill out."* Okay, okay I get impulsive sometimes, sorry.

Am I getting long-winded? Hope not, we're almost through Chapter Two – I have two more stories to tell; then we'll move on.

VIGNETTE 19

ONE DAY TOWARDS THE END OF MY "ILLUSTRIOUS" CAREER AS A SOCIAL Assistance Worker I began wondering what the next decade – the 1980s – would entail? The big new innovation which had "come down the pike" was computerization, which frightened everybody! I mean can you imagine 640K memory in a computer?! My Admin. Assistant at the time stated in no uncertain words, "Jake – I think these machines are here to stay – you'd better learn how to use one," and my response, "They're just a fad – they won't be around for long" went over like a lead balloon. How wrong could I be about a phenomenon that changed the world and how we do business! But on with the story. Old Joe came into my office one day with a Social Assistance problem he found rather perplexing. The person's voice on the phone was male, but stated his name was Suzanne... Old Joe wasn't sure whether to ask if he was male or female, and gender orientation was a little more straightforward in those days – either you were or you weren't. I told Old Joe to "cool his jets" that I didn't care and would take the referral, but thanks for the heads up anyway.

Suzanne's address indicated to me that she lived in "Welfare Row," a horrible moniker that was actually nicknamed by a disgruntled client who was found ineligible for Social Assistance many years earlier. He then tried to compromise the Social Assistance Workers' integrity by suggesting they had a bias because the client lived in Welfare Row. Unfortunately the nickname had stuck during the past 20 years and was used by all the staff. To digress for a moment, one of the first things you learned as a brand-new Field Worker when management divided up the geographical locales and chose Workers to manage these catchment areas was the legendary Welfare Row! "Look out! There are some really strange 'dudes' down there, just look out!" A very professional and clinical attitude – am I right?! But some serious crimes and nefarious activities had occurred and continued to occur throughout the period of time this location was inhabited by vagrants, prostitutes, "down and outers," and "grifters" from other parts of the country. *On with the story, Jake.* Okay, okay!!

I located Suzanne's address, parked my car approximately one block away, and walked over to a run-down building where she lived. I "buzzed" her apartment number and a masculine voice responded, allowing me to enter the building and proceed upstairs to the third floor. I knocked on the door and a male appeared in a T-shirt, with budding breasts. His hair was long, his gait effeminate with the "broken wrist" effect, and his skirt hugged his buttocks – aha, my first transgender client. Throughout the Application process Suzanne was quite open, even frank about the operations he was having to become female and was excited about the prospect of "coming out." He was also receiving ongoing outpatient therapy from the local hospital and due to his funds being reduced from an inheritance was forced to apply for Social Assistance. His ability to look for work, which was a criterion for being eligible for this particular Government subsidy, was compromised during the period of gender reassignment. In conjunction, the bias in society at that time against gender change operations was huge! People were not predisposed to hire someone they felt was an obvious "mental case." In looking back all those years I'm still bewildered at the "hubbub" regarding gender reassignment. As I sat across the table listening to Suzanne tell his life story – I felt like paying him regarding the information gleaned, rather than the other way around. If this had not been a professional relationship and under any other circumstance, Suzanne would've been someone I included in my circle of friends. He had integrity, intelligence, a strength of character and courage that I found truly remarkable! For that era and in this particular geographical area of North America he had a lot of guts! I did find Suzanne eligible for Social Assistance that day and wonder whatever happened to this individual as I dictate this book 35 years later.

Post Script

A number of days passed and then suddenly one afternoon Old Joe entered my office and shook my hand. He'd read my report, was satisfied Suzanne was eligible for "Assistance" under the circumstances, and from his experience and advanced age, this had been a case to remember! Nowadays, this particular situation wouldn't have batted an eyelid of a nearsighted Social Assistance Supervisor, or anyone else for that matter! Society's liberalization and acceptance of individual rights has influenced social justice to aggressively challenge bigoted, prejudice – for the most part anyway. *Pretty philosophical, Jake, you're almost Old Joe's age!* Maybe I did learn a thing or two, I'll let you be the judge. Read on.

VIGNETTE 20

My last story in this Chapter is a bit hair-raising as I was given a referral to see a single, young woman with a two-year-old toddler who coincidentally lived in Welfare Row. Actually just down the street from Suzanne, whom you've just read about. I quickly checked the name to make sure it wasn't the same person mentioned in an earlier Vignette – it wasn't. PHEW – I didn't need any more adrenaline rushes like that one! But it happened nonetheless! The situation was quite different but equally alarming! The individual's name was Harriet H. and her address was in the middle of this notorious part of town. The way in by vehicle was quite harrowing, narrow one-way streets that made turning around to redirect your route impossible. Once you got on a particular street you stayed on that particular street, until the end, which allowed you to complete a severe left or right hand turn to the next street which went in the opposite direction. Obviously you had to have your wits about you, or you could miss the address and go by a string of low-rise apartment buildings, which were nondescript and very easy to miss. Harriet H. lived on the second floor in one of these low-rise apartments with an "open" balcony. What's an open balcony Jake? An open balcony in one of these buildings had two railings going across the balcony longitudinally – approximately two feet (.65 m.) above one another, that was it! Not much structural integrity for safety provided and whoever designed these buildings, which had been built postwar – World War II that is – was not thinking of toddlers! Little human beings who could pass beneath the longitudinal railing, yeah you heard it right, RAILING as in singular, not plural. But let's get on with the story.

I "buzzed up" – Harriet H. answered with a very polite and casual, "Hi there – come on up – hope you're havin' a good day." What a nice introduction from a client! By now after nearly two years as a Social Assistance Worker I was used to a more, much more, perfunctory manner. I walked up to her apartment on the second floor and before I could knock the door opened and there stood a young, "willowy" blond woman approximately 5'8" (1 m. 72 cm.) in height with a lean, well-proportioned physique. But most importantly, she held in her arms one of the most beautiful two-year-old preschoolers I'd ever seen. This little boy would've captured the hearts of even the most callous and cold-blooded felons. The child's love for his mother was transparent and very infectious. His toys and attention to scribbling with his crayons while we talked were a delight. I complimented Harriet H's parenting skills several times throughout the interview, which was a big presumption and one I nearly lived to regret! She was in a clinical depression, or what I later surmised was a clinical depression and had a serious bonding problem with her son. *Stop digressing, Jake – on with the story.* Okay, okay.

Harriet H. was sitting at the table with her back towards the open veranda/balcony approximately 10 feet (3 m.) away. The distance from her apartment to the ground was nearly 20 feet (6 m.). As we talked, her little boy had a habit of talking to his toy, dropping it in front of him, crawling over to the toy, talking to the toy, dropping it in front of him, etc. It was such a subtle motion/movement and he was so small on the floor below us, while we sat talking at the table – you get the picture. Here's the "kicker," unfortunately Harriet H.'s body and shoulders impaired visual contact with the child, keeping him from our view! And because she was facing me and the little boy was behind her on the floor, this was an accident looking to happen! As we talked throughout the Application procedure, I felt she was eligible for Social Assistance as her husband had recently deserted the family and taken all the money from the joint account, which I verified with the bank. According to Harriet H., he was nowhere to be found, or so it would seem. Back to the story.

During this time Harriet H. got up to make some coffee, looked over at her child who was now approximately five feet (1.5 m.) from the balcony entrance, yet Harriet H. did not make a cautionary statement or go over and pick up her child! Conversely, she strolled back to the table in a casual, laid-back manner, sat down, and continued answering questions, once again with her back to her child!? I just about fell out of my chair – I got up, strolled over, picked up the little boy ,and brought him back to play BESIDE the table. I went back to the veranda area, picked up his toys and

58 | Love Your Enemies in Case Your Friends Turn Out To Be Bastards

at the same time made a throwaway statement, "Mrs. H., I'm a little concerned about your child's movement towards the balcony as we talk – maybe we could shift positions." Harriet H.'s response was again nonchalant, "Of course, why don't we" and we changed positions; this time she faced the balcony, allowing her to view the child's movements in the room. You guessed it – during the next five to ten minutes as we completed the final stages of the Application process, her little boy, as I was to discover, had repeated his pattern of play and was by now near the balcony's edge! Approximately two feet (.65 m.) from a 20-foot (6 m.) drop to the ground below! Here's what saved the day, in my opinion: the whistle on the kettle began to blow, indicating that instant coffee could be made. Harriet H. slowly got up and sauntered over to the kitchen sink area and asked, "What d'ya take in your coffee, Mr. Hagerman?" I swung my head around to respond and immediately saw the child – out of the corner of my eye – this time about one foot (30 cm.) from the edge of the balcony, innocently playing with his toys unaware of the impending doom! *Jake, you've got great peripheral vision!* Okay, okay, now on with the story. A lightning bolt couldn't have struck faster as I leapt from my chair and ran to the balcony to scoop up the child! Forget muttering under my breath – I stated in loud, no-nonsense terms that I'd be calling Child Welfare, as I felt the child was at risk in this particular household! Harriet H., Ms. Nonchalant, laid-back, explode-a-grenade-and-it-wouldn't-bother-her lady, was going to receive a visit from the Child Welfare authorities. It was required, nay demanded, as her actions contravened the Child Welfare Act of that region, or any other region for that matter. Specifically, the infant was deemed "at risk" with this Caregiver! My observations anyway and hopefully your interpretation as well!

Once again, in that era there were no cell phones; I had to think quickly and with her boy in my arms made the fateful telephone call that every parent doesn't want to hear – a challenge of their parental competency! I sat for the next 60 minutes, alternating holding the little boy in my arms and then letting him play in front of me. I made small talk with Harriet H. while we awaited the arrival of Child Welfare Services. They would be conducting an investigation which could entail "apprehending" the child – removing him from his mother's care. More specifically, if they felt the child was at risk in the care of his parent and until the mother was assessed as having better parental skills/judgment, they had the mandate to remove the child and be placed "in care." Or, the other option was finding an alternative caregiver – giving the child to a relative or friend to take into custody, while Harriet H. received a much needed parental training program. The tragic fact was observing Harriet H.'s calm demeanor and acceptance that her parental ability was negligent, which could have resulted in catastrophic consequences regarding her son's safety. She was not visibly angry, nor did she shout, or resist the Child Welfare Worker's decision to apprehend her child. Lastly, she was unable to provide the Child Welfare authorities with anyone she knew who could competently care for her child. Harriet H. was a lonely, isolated individual who received help and guidance, which eventually led to her child being returned to her care – approximately 12 months later. This by no means is an unusual Child Welfare situation; the Caseworkers are for the most part a magnificent group of dedicated individuals, who have the care and safety of children as their highest priority!

That's it! The end of Chapter Two – I hope you're enjoying the book and I think it gets better, so relax, put your feet up and continue reading, but PLEASE no beer or red wine just yet!

Of Note: Before reading on take a gander at the following: You will learn a lot about "co-dependency" in organizations that are dysfunctional. OVER-CONTROL is structured into dysfunctional organizations, in conjunction with basic dishonesty of communication, which is often used to manipulate the employees and the public! The following Vignettes describe this dynamic very adroitly. Read carefully and take note, as you could find yourself consulting in one of these Organizations someday. If so, enter this milieu with a healthy skepticism! Keep vigilant and try to defer judgment to facilitate analysis from an objective perspective. Remember, you could be asked to compromise your integrity when all is said and done, and your professional reputation is at stake! Think about it, and now on to Chapter Three.

CHAPTER THREE

VIGNETTE 21

BY NOW I HAD COMPLETED POSTGRADUATE EDUCATION, WORKED IN THE Mental Health profession, and reached the age of 31, but had yet to have any management experience. Eventually I found a great opportunity, a mid-management position that was high-profile but with its share of stressors most of which were politically motivated, but what else is new? I'd moved almost 2000 miles (3200 km.) across the country and had displaced a "shoo-in" candidate who was a staff favorite, which put me at a distinct disadvantage. Alas, I would learn to regret my employment decision throughout the next four years I worked at this job!

When I heard from the Human Resources representative that I'd been chosen as the successful candidate, I was told to place a collect call to a number which she provided and talk with my immediate boss, Steve Z. As it was a long-distance phone call and an important position to be filled, I thought it best to respond post haste by collect call. I proceeded to call the number provided and overheard a deep voice state HELLO at the other end of the line. When the Operator asked if he would accept the call as it was a long-distance reverse billing charge, the gruff voice at the other end stated "NO I WON'T" and hung up! I was stunned to put it mildly!! This was my introduction to the job?! Approximately three hours later I phoned the Human Resources woman back and explained what had happened and she gave me a new number. This time the voice at the other end of the phone was the boss of my immediate boss, Steve Z. I made no mention of the rude and rather brusque response by his colleague towards a virtual unknown, not at this time anyway. This new man, the top boss, Kerry J. was quite experienced and very bright. What a relief I thought – but I wondered deep down if I could get along with the grumpy Steve Z.

I took it upon myself to visit the worksite three days early, don't ask me why. *I won't, Jake, you can be such a boy scout!* Okay, okay. Arriving in this new city, with virtually no friends and one or two relatives whom I hadn't seen in over 10 years and wasn't particularly fond of, was not fun! A warning signal went off as well when I was met with a frosty, to say the least, introduction by the line staff sizing me up and making what I felt was a differential diagnosis of Jake Hagerman. One particular nasty "piece of work" conned me into a debate and in order to win, made a ludicrous and tasteless analogy, "Quite frankly, if you believe that, then you believe there were no Concentration Camps in the Second World War." Once again I was shocked and wondered what I'd walked into! *Jake, I guess he didn't make the "connect" with your name!* You've got a point. The first day of work Kerry J. was introduced to me, then later on, Steve Z., by the Regional Director. Let me describe the two physically and forget about the Regional Director – this time anyway. Kerry J. was in his early forties, approximately 5'5" (1 m. 65 cm.) tall and about 170 pounds (77 kg.). He was a powerfully built man, short, but certainly not small, and with a postgraduate education. His intellect and quick integration of topics pertaining to the field of Mental Health impressed me! Steve Z., on the other hand was in his early sixties, a former policeman with an 11th grade education, 6 foot (1 m. 82 cm.) and approximately 210 pounds (93 kg.). For an older man his body was still toned, in spite of the fact that he was a pack-a-day smoker. What an odd couple; however, of note was that Steve Z. had hired Kerry J. 12 years earlier – remember that as we move along with the story.

The first staff meeting was a "big deal" introduction of four new colleagues to the Organization, myself included, describing to a staff complement numbering 20 people our backgrounds, areas of expertise, general philosophy of practice, and inviting questions at the end. I was the youngest and went last, and to put it bluntly, I got an onerous feeling, "Oh no, what have I done" almost immediately after ending my little speech, which lasted about 10 minutes. You know that queasy, unsettling cognitive dissonance you get in front of a group of strangers with suppressed hostility, who wish you were somebody else but you aren't! If you haven't had that feeling, it ain't nice, believe me! My colleagues who'd also provided their respective autobiographies to this group, appeared to be, at first blush, very well chosen for the Consulting positions at this particular Unit, of this particular Government Organization. I didn't feel as confident, although I acted older than 31, I had a gut feeling I was going to be tested by these 20 staff who were older for the most part and much more experienced! This, as it turned out was an accurate assessment and I aged over the next four years. I really aged, both in wisdom and toughness!

Underlings, and I include myself, often struggle for power, control, and comfort while doing their jobs to the best of their abilities. Unfortunately, it's when you throw in the mix of very strong, experienced personalities who've worked together for many years and DO NOT want change – it gets tough and being a "newbie" authority figure is a target on your back. But I'm sure you've been there – enough moanin' and groanin'!

Steve Z's style was basically a "do as little as you want, or what you can get away with, life's too short" attitude. Not a great role model and as it turned out one of the most passive-aggressive, cunning, and vengeful professionals I've ever worked with! Throughout the next three months every question posed during our famous 60-minute coffee breaks (which I was required to attend) was a ploy to gather information about my background. This included and when I look back I have to smile, "Have you ever had a homosexual experience?" "Nope, I haven't," and instantly the subject was changed to sports, women, outdoor activities, clothing, aftershave lotion, organizational politics, you name it and I was asked it! I had nothing to hide and in turn asked questions and learned a great deal about my immediate boss and future nemesis, Steve Z.

Chapter Three | 63

By the end of my third month of a 12-month probation, yes, you heard it right, a 12-month probation, I somehow offended Steve Z.'s Admin. Assistant one day! This was a DISASTER – a tornado, hurricane, lightning storm combined. Let me put it in perspective: Admin. Assistants can make or break a career! I have come to that belief after 21 years in mid and senior management positions and a further 20 years as a line worker. Something I said, something I did, caused this woman who was possibly five years older than me to HATE MY GUTS and then some for the next four years I remained at that job!! Maybe I shouldn't have debated the merits of tampons versus maxi pads to really infuriate this eizel-moyser,[4] just kidding! Remembering her behavior while I dictate this missive has made me feel cavalier and reckless. Sorry, but I was not provocative, evocative, or any other "ive" in her presence. She simply hated my guts!! Who's this Johnny Come Lately toadstool telling us what to do attitude!!

The next six months entailed Jake learning his job as a midmanager with a multimillion-dollar portfolio, dealing with fourteen shrewd, devious staff who tried and tried to pressure me out of the position and the Admin. Assistant from hell double-, triple-, and quadruple-challenging my authority and correcting my errors in the most humiliating of circumstances! Thank God I had a positive relationship with Steve Z.'s boss, Kerry J. We met once a week, at which time I debriefed Kerry J. with as much "transparency" as I dared. He was, as well, relatively new and very careful around the Admin. Assistant. *Why*, you ask, *he's the boss, Jake?!* In essence, Kerry J.'s "hands were tied." *How so?* Kerry J. had been seconded to this position after a major confrontation with a senior political figure in Government. You guessed it – he had a parallel crappy position like I did, albeit with a lot more power but with the dubious distinction of having to supervise the infamous Steve Z. And who was Steve Z's "pipeline," the eizel Admin. Assistant! *Why not quit or ask for a transfer, Jake?* Because I'd signed a two-year contract for this particular position and was required to finish my probation period before requesting a transfer or quitting. If I quit I had to pay the remaining

---

4   An ass-informer

time back to the Government and was in no position to do so, as I'd amassed major debt while attending school.

Here comes the fun stuff and I say that out of the "side of my mouth." Approximately nine months into the job and after Steve Z. and I had had a minimum of 25 confrontations about you name it – the inevitable happened! As I was walking by Steve Z. one morning in the main work area, which housed approximately six workers and support staff, he tested me with an insulting, ignominious comment/gesture. When I approached him and gave a quick retort equally as insulting, I found myself grabbed by the inside of the thigh and armpit and flung, I mean literally FLUNG! I was airborne approximately four feet (1.25 m.) hitting an office wall head first, which precipitated the Admin. Assistant inside an adjoining room to start screaming hysterically! Talk about limbic system overload, I hit the wall hard, "saw stars," and then saw red! Forget the "Psychological Healthy Workplace" philosophy, which hadn't been invented yet. Before I knew what I was doing, I strode over to Steve Z. and slapped him with as much power as I could muster! Afterwards, a staff member said it sounded like a clapboard on a movie set. Immediately upon hearing this loud, firecracker noise people stood up from their desks, just as I tossed Steve Z. to the ground with a hip throw – as I recall Tsuri-goshi – and being VERY enraged I threw him HARD. His body bounced off the office floor as I jumped on him and raised my fist to fire in four or five "jackhammer" punches! Then WHOOSH something happened, I came out of it. "What the hell have I done" flashed through my brain and I froze! Then HE LOST CONTROL and the rest is basically a blur!

I do remember staff standing around and cheering while we rolled around the floor swearing and attempting to block then counter; elbows, arm locks, palm strikes, kneeing, acting like the stupid fools we were! Suddenly a "sky hook" lifted me off the ground and then the same thing happened with Steve Z. The top boss Kerry J., hearing the commotion, had come in and lifted both of us off the ground, one after the other. "Get to my office right now both of you!" and then, "Okay, folks, the show's over; get back to work!" People sauntered back to their desks, talked in muted voices, and let go with the occasional giggle. I wanted to bury myself, then light a fire and die underground, a long painful death!! The date incidentally was 9/11/82. Nine eleven, nineteen eighty-two, it was the most humiliating professional day of my life and has remained so for the past 30+ years! To prove my point: I'd be at gatherings years later and a stranger would approach me stating, "Aren't you Jake Hagerman? Did you really 'smoke' Steve Z? How'd you get sucked into that one, I heard you were smart – guess not that time" (snicker). Nice hunh (eh)?! But I digress, on with the story.

Kerry J. sat between Steve Z. and myself smoldering and then quietly asked to hear both sides of the story. I won't bore you with the details, needless to say I was worried that I wouldn't make my probation! In 2014 or for that purpose 1994 I would've been fired on the spot, escorted off the premises by two security guards and my personal effects sent to my residence, all within the space of two hours! Back in 1982, at this particular locale such was not the case, although I was chastised and told a decision would be made in the next two business days regarding "consequences." Incidentally, I did the most logical thing I could think of under the circumstances. I went down to the local bar and started drinking "boilermakers" from four in the afternoon until two in the morning, staggered home, "hit the sack," got sick, hit the sack, got sick, and then was awakened at nine in the morning by the ungodly sound of my phone ringing off the hook! Oh my aching head – what a hangover! For a split second I thought it was my mother phoning long distance to say "Hi" and get caught up with my new place of work, new city, and geographical area, any dating prospects – you know parents. This wasn't the case. The gruff, blunt voice at the other end of the phone reminded me why I had a hangover that was destroying my brain. "Jake, Steve here, sorry about yesterday, I guess things got out of hand, I apologize." This idiot apologizing? I couldn't believe it, nor fathom the nature or meaning of this token gesture of remorse! You know when you feel you're being "taken for a ride" and you balk for a second, but then you want to hear more because you're still in shock? That's the way I felt! "Yeah, Steve, things certainly did get out of hand and I'm going to have to think about your apology."

Steve Z.'s response was as I recall, "Okay – I just thought I'd call, I'll see you on Monday" and he hung up. Several months later during a period of respite between Steve Z. and myself, I stated how impressed I was that he'd put "the best foot forward" regarding the fight incident by phoning me to apologize. In a microsecond he responded with a sly smile, "I thought you'd sue me for assault and an apology would look good." That about sums it up regarding Steve Z. and Jake Hagerman's relationship for the next three years and by the way I did make my probation. Now on to the next story.

VIGNETTE 22

CHRISTMAS CAME QUICKLY THAT YEAR; I ENJOY THE HOLIDAYS AT CHRISTMAS time but don't embrace the Christmas spirit like many of my colleagues in this field – it's just one of those things, and upbringing has a lot to do with it as well. But nonetheless, we had our annual Christmas party and it was a doozy!

Steve Z. got so drunk he ended up arguing with a former staff member about one of his bigoted baseball opinions, something along the lines, "black players in the Negro league according to many people were better than their white counterparts, but I totally disagree and by the way Ty Cobb was the greatest impact player of his era." If you know anything about baseball you will know that Ty Cobb albeit a GREAT player was by all accounts a Southern racist, who was despised by many white and most black baseball players! When this fact was pointed out to Steve Z. by somebody we know, he picked up a bottle of Jim Beam whiskey and threw it, yes threw it through a thousand dollar office picture window – I know, I saw the bill, a lot of money in 1982! Needless to say this drew attention from the hundred-odd partygoers – one of whom was the Senior Administrator of the District. He stated later on he was in the bathroom and "didn't witness anything untoward." Yeah right?! A number of weeks later and this stands out and was witnessed by many, many staff, Steve Z. came to work with his Christmas present, a brand new .38 Smith & Wesson revolver but

Chapter Three | 67

as he stated, "it's only got a four-inch barrel"! Freud would have had a field day with that one! Steve Z. started moving around the office playing a hide and seek/bank robber routine behind the desks, the staff running for cover, while he clicked the empty gun and made KAPOW sounds – aiming and shooting his imaginary victims and roaring with laughter when the women started to shriek! By the way, would you like a lethal weapon pointed at you?! All of this done with the understanding that it was in good fun (yeah right) and before I forget, knowing full well that Kerry J. was out of the office on vacation for the next two weeks! You think I'm kidding?! Not one syllable of this statement is false! Ah those good old days in the early 1980s, I'm being facetious and you're not stupid. Nowadays with people "going postal," a staff member would've phoned 911, the SWAT team would've arrived, and Steve Z. would've been the "late" Steve Z.

Two of the most serious drawbacks of working in this den of iniquity were the lack of transparency by many staff in order to survive in this very antagonistic work milieu and the blatant cruelty and narrow-mindedness that were a common, day-to-day experience! To highlight these dysfunctional symptoms, which were a sickness throughout the entire Organization, the following anecdote is provided. *Jake, cool down!* I will, sorry about that.

A dubious situation occurred with a colleague and myself when we were faced with the obvious dilemma of not only chastising a staff member, but having to provide a severe reprimand, tantamount to termination of employment, if a particular "conduct" occurred again. Human Resources was involved, Senior Management had been debriefed, and my colleague and I being the "newbies" were chosen at the last moment to be the bearers of bad tidings! The recipient took it well under the circumstances and asked if we wanted his resignation? We both stated "No" but vehemently suggested that because of the circumstances of his recent professional misconduct, it would be advisable to "toe the line" in the future! REALLY, REALLY TOE THE LINE (if you know what I mean) – he nodded, shook our hands and then verbalized, "This must have been very hard for you guys," turned, and left the office. Both of us felt we had saved his dignity, although he had to return to the "pack of wolves," his statement not ours, that he worked with, to offer a debriefing session. Yes, it was that serious! I say this with no animosity but with deep regret that those "colleagues" who felt the disposition and consequence assigned to this particular staff person too lenient were hell-bent to get even!! People, remember it's not a perfect world! *We know, Jake, we know, on with the story.* Okay, okay.

Two days later having parked my truck in the underground parking lot one block from where I worked, I returned to find a seven-foot (2.5 m.) key scrape along the length of the driver side of my vehicle. The truck was only three months old! I returned to the office, "faced down" five or six staff members who looked, sideways, at the floor, at each other, or simply walked away. Guilty as sin I thought as I phoned my Insurance agent! A further two days after my incident the other mid-manager and co-bearer of bad tidings, and generally a good guy, went out to his vehicle after work to find the trailer attached to the back of his SUV spray-painted with a mild obscenity! What it said I can't recall, but do know it was meant to "wound," which it did and then some! A little warning from a group of generally hard-working staff, who despised a particular member of the group and as a result of our directed efforts to give this person a second chance, were in a hard way to get even! Life is not fair and people judge harshly – if the collective whole finds a singular faction out of order, the "law of the jungle" kicks in! The cruelty and despicable conduct people play at the worksite, it keeps you young, right? I don't think so! Needless to say, investigations occurred, interviews and downright interrogations, but nothing came out of the inquiry that was worth a damn. *Jake, you're getting "down."* Okay, okay. I can't remember what happened to the staff member we disciplined, but I'm sure he survived and is collecting a big fat pension somewhere. I think we're ready for the next story.

VIGNETTE 23

ON ALMOST A DAILY BASIS MY TWO SUPERVISORS, STEVE Z. AND KERRY J., met with me for extended coffee/supervision, like an hour and a half each day!? I learned many things from the dialogue between these two, as one glorified the good old days and renounced the modern ways and changes that were being imposed – like treating women as equals! The other challenged the irascible, strong-willed, prejudiced personality across the table. A continuous fight ensued, troglodyte warfare – Joe Frazier versus Muhammad Ali again and again and again, over a four-year period! They attempted to draw me into their respective, philosophical camps, but I would have none of it and paid for my convictions in spades! The staff, numbering about 20, observed the vitriolic "battles" going on, which they exploited to the hilt. What I learned and never forgot was the meta-communication, *the message behind the message*, which you needed to learn in order to survive in mid-management. PLEASE TRY AND REMEMBER THIS LAST STATEMENT – it is sacrosanct and an important *must* to survive in most political ecosystems. This is discussed at length in Section Two of the book.

More specifically, you had to become fluent in this style of communication, with its hidden agenda, double entendres, rapier wit, and prolonged discussion regarding the Mission/Mandate of the Unit vis-à-vis the Organization. The political ramifications of decisions made were then and ONLY then evaluated for potential promotion to the ranks of Senior Management! The usual set-up, and I use the phrase accurately, was a request made by my four consulting colleagues discussed earlier in the Chapter, for help in resolving political problems with Kerry J. and once in a blue moon, Steve Z. What's the big deal you ask? The big deal was being triangulated by both sides and used as a middleman and more often than not forced to make a contentious decision, which would undoubtedly infuriate the other side! Three of the four consultants were from geographically distant urban centers, which had a myriad of collateral services available a phone call away. The fourth Consultant was from points unknown up north, who sat back and watched impassively the "goings on."

Unfortunately, the consulting group tended to bring up "the town and gown" comparison with the city's cultural simplicity too many times, which antagonized BOTH Steve Z. and Kerry J! More specifically: "This place is retrogressive, its service provision is 30 years behind the times." "I've always considered myself an intelligent person but I must have taken a stupid pill to end up in this hole." "My expense account is never paid on time and I want a raise for mileage expenses – it's about friggin' time don't you think!" Subsequently Kerry J. would listen, have a "conflab" with yours truly, and then Steve Z. would get involved and the fur would fly!

Here's the downside, as the four consultants were often used by the 20-odd line staff for consulting purposes and human beings being human beings, there was the occasional breach of confidential information that should never have been disclosed, regarding the consultants' battles with Kerry J. and Steve Z! The consequent ripple effect was the staff often misinterpreted or took out of context the complaint disclosed by one of the consultants. This invariably had a negative effect on the morale of the Unit. With time the "higher-ups" heard about the chronic, political problems that reduced the morale and subsequent performance ability of the line staff and guess what happened to this high-profile Unit!?

One day, the second or third year into my job and after a particularly harsh meeting with the consultants, guess who came for a surprise visit? The Regional Director and I'm sure you figured that one out a paragraph ago. This man being from the Continental Northeast, that is, very verbal and highly educated, very ambitious and highly intelligent, listened to the same old redundant complaints from the consultants and in one fell swoop ELIMINATED the Consulting Unit! *Good,* you say, *that decision eradicates crappy professionalism and a lot of dysfunctional communication!* Wrong, it had taken five years for Kerry J. to battle with the Regional Director over a budgeted amount of money that was realistic and apportioned, earmarked in common language, to this unique clinical adjunct for the line staff to utilize. In one fell political swoop the Consulting Unit was disbanded, much to the chagrin of the line staff who'd played quasi-therapists with the consultants to meet vicarious needs, and lost out big time! Within three months, three years' worth of hard work upgrading professional standards, increasing quality control, quality improvement, internal and external customer satisfaction went up in smoke and was gone, poof just like that! The Consulting Unit's clinical impact had been metaphorically speaking, a stone thrown into a pool of water with a positive and very beneficial "ripple effect," then sadly becoming a neutral, flat ambience in a short, very short period of time! Who's to blame? I could go on and on – I had attempted many times to mediate but was doomed in this initiative. I was told I was too close to the problem! Apparently there was no money in the budget to bring in an external mediation expert and the inevitable became a reality, it was that simple; the Consultant Unit was history!

VIGNETTE 24

A FEW MONTHS LATER I SAT DOWN AND HAD COFFEE WITH KERRY J. AND stated how upset I was at the turn of events regarding the Consulting Unit's demise. In an effort to cheer me up Kerry J. told me a worse scenario, a factually true story that had been in the newspapers years before. Here goes – ten years previously, back in the early to mid 1970s, a foreign individual had successfully competed for a clinical position at a not too distant rural hospital. In those days Human Resources was more lax than currently and did not thoroughly investigate foreign qualifications. The person in question had placed on his wall an advanced degree from another country which was written in Latin as was his license to practice his discipline. People simply presumed he was as competent as his Curriculum Vitae had stated and oh that fancy diploma must mean he's an important person!

Within three months, the "jig was up" as the multidisciplinary team had witnessed blatantly incompetent individual and group therapy sessions through the one-way mirror and realized they had been conned, duped, manipulated, you name it! This individual's report writing, if you want to call it that, was storytelling at its minimal best. What to do? The person's licensing body was contacted, a complaint lodged by the Administrator of the Hospital and Director of Clinical Services, which was taken very seriously!

An investigation of sorts was held at which time, due to the individual's country of origin being halfway around the world and the legitimacy of information being sent in question, a decision was made to forgo a long and tedious investigation, which most likely violated the person's rights. Whatever, he was terminated "without just cause," provided a six-month severance, and escorted off the premises – see ya – NOT QUITE! The man was disallowed from ever practicing in this particular jurisdiction again. *It's over, you say, the good guys won,* WRONG!

Approximately 18 months later, Kerry J. stated his colleague, who had known through collegial connections the outcome of this clinical disaster and potentially dangerous situation, happened to be walking down the main floor of a hospital 300 miles (480 km.) away, when he thought he saw the person mentioned above walking out of the Human Resources Department! As this particular office was still 50 yards (45 m.) away, Kerry J.'s colleague couldn't catch up to the man in question, who was almost out of sight. Kerry J.'s colleague arrived at the door of the Human Resources Department, entered the office, and proceeded to fabricate a story about the person being an old friend from many years earlier – but unfortunately he couldn't remember the man's name. The Admin. Assistant stated, "The guy who just left?" "Yes, you got it, I forgot his name and want to surprise him, he'll be so happy to see me." Her response and brace yourself! "John Davis, his name is John Davis and his office is down the hall and to the right, room 228."

Kerry J.'s colleague literally raced down the hall and as he approached room 228 rehearsed what he was going to say in a robust, prosecutorial Hamilton Burger voice, as in the 1950s *Perry Mason* television series. He then mustered his resources and knocked on the door! A familiar foreign, clipped accent responded, "Just a moment," and a second later the door opened. Without going into detail regarding the subsequent diatribe, Kerry J.'s colleague read this phony gazlen[5] the "riot act," more specifically, misrepresentation of a professional title, fraud, intention to commit fraud after the fact, etc. He subsequently and in front of this profes-

---

5   thief

sional miscreant, or more accurately, bogus professional miscreant, telephoned the Licensing Board and then the police, at which time Mr. bogus professional miscreant confessed that he had legally changed his name. He "Westernized" it because of his "inability to successfully compete for gainful employment in this country!" I beg your pardon – not mentioning the fact that he'd ALREADY lost his professional license to practice in this jurisdiction using his original "real" name!? Talk about denial, rationalization and minimization, unbelievable! The story hit the newspapers; however, no one, at that time mind you, took the next step to aggressively evaluate the protocol of the National Examining Board's assessment of Professional Equivalency! It was many, many years later that a reciprocal agreement, linking geographical regions of the country was ratified by the various licensing bodies of this Profession! How many fraudulent professionals slipped undetected into North America in those days and how many continue to practice today AND at the public's risk is anyone's guess! *Jake, calm down, chill out.* Okay, okay, on with the next story.

VIGNETTE 25

TOWARDS THE END OF THIS PARTICULAR JOB AND I MEAN THE END, THE staff's behavior towards me was on a continuum from disdain to hatred – this antagonism and alienation was meant to erode my confidence and began to wear on me by the second year, and by the fourth I was ready to say adios and move on! During this period two particular staff persons offended me by the "gadfly" nature of their personalities, combined with questionable professional deportment. I ain't no saint but their behavior and disrespect for one another was something to behold! If you attempted to intervene in their frequent skirmishes you were drawn into an enmeshed "chopping block" repartee, "no quarter asked no quarter given"! Absolutely no quarter was given in their quest for superiority between each other and attempts to crush their respective egos. Stay away if you valued your professional dignity because if Human Resources was called, the backlash of your apparent invasion of their range war could be career ending!

They tended to play dirty, "back stabbing" games and did so on many occasions! A good Samaritan was gutted and left to wilt and die on the proverbial career vine. *Sounds like the "tail wagging the dog," Jake, what gives?* You are correct, and Management let this morale devastator continue for at least the four years I was employed at this job and then some, but on with the story.

Unfortunately, a major "trigger" of this hate campaign was a beautiful young Admin. Assistant who, due to her previous "live-in" overspending their joint bank account, moonlighted as an exotic dancer to pay off an enormous debt. When I asked what in God's name would make her think exotic dancing was an appropriate way to get out of debt, her response was, "I make approximately three times your income per month, Mr. Hagerman," and she walked away. She must have been a good exotic dancer! I'm not sure as I think back to the early 1980s, regarding this particular scenario anyway, who said what to whom exactly to precipitate the "hubbub." My sources tell me one of the antagonists was at a Bachelor Party being held at a local strip club and the rest is history. Males will be males and boys will be boys and somehow the twain always meet, because quicker than you can say "Jim Beam, Jack Daniels," the gossip spread like wildfire around the Unit and then the Clinical Division of this huge Government Organization. The Admin. Assistant/Exotic Dancer, or as my mother cryptically coined, practicing, "artistic tableau in the nude" had to know her reputation would be ruined! What transpired involved one of the antagonists attempting to defend the honor of this young, aspiring grisette! Apparently his nemesis had "shot off his mouth" about the Admin. Assistant "sliding off the rails," or "down the poles" to be more accurate, and in current vernacular "was a friggin' d-bag." "Them's fightin' words" and the battle was on!

Here comes the basics of what happened next; I will leave out the intricacies, the "whats and the wherefores," because it doesn't matter. The antagonist challenged his nemesis to a three-set tennis match, the loser having to "streak" down a back alley – his choice – in the downtown, moderate sized, North America city where we worked – yeah right!? To say the least this was a scary proposition – remembering of course if the police became involved and charged the loser with lewd and lascivious conduct, it could spell the end of a career! In Mental Health Services one cannot have a criminal record – your career and ability to make a living depend on licensure to practice! Nevertheless, both parties shook hands regarding the bet and the game was on! The publicity of the imminent match spread like a tornado throughout the Clinical Division! Everybody talked about it and the two antagonists went into training like nobody's business. The first set went six – three for the antagonist whom everyone hated, a brawny ex-athlete who was very intelligent but displayed a malignant, predatory personality with most colleagues – his clients loved him of course! He had obviously played tennis or at least racket sports for many, many years and was laughing at his opponent with every serve. At one point I actually thought he was salivating; drool appeared to drip from his lips between serves and drop onto the tennis court – that's how much he despised his opponent! On the other hand, it could have been the hot weather and overexertion. *C'mon, Jake, get on with the story!* Okay, okay.

Unbelievably the next set went to his nemesis, who was not going to go down without a fight!! He barely beat Mr. Malignant Personality, I can't remember the score, but everybody cheered and thought, "Okay, he's got a slim chance to win, but a chance nonetheless!" His serve was okay, but his backhand totally stunk. Consequently, Mr. Brawny/Malignant personality consistently served to his opponent's backhand, much to his chagrin. The third set was tied, I'm not lying to make a good story, it literally ended in a tie, both men too tired to continue to play, one suffering from heat exhaustion as the temperature was in the mid-high 80s (30° C). The other, using the opportunity to "play up" that he was a good sport and would allow the game to end in such a fashion, caused pandemonium! Here's the problem – the staff members, which numbered approximately 50, came out to see blood – metaphorically speaking of course, there's that "m" word again. In clinical jargon it's called "substitute gratification" and anyone who's been to a blood sport such as boxing, wrestling, or mixed martial arts tournaments has seen your average Joe turn into a raving maniac! Wanting his side to win and psychologically speaking, transposing himself as a spectator into his "idealized other" in the ring, or in this case, the antagonists in a tennis match.

People started to howl, even heckle their outrage, yelling at one of the antagonists to "start Hebraist studies or get the hell out of Dodge!" "How could a Jew give in?" Fight to the death ya coward, you're better than that!" "Remember the '67 war, goddammit, what the hell kind of a schlub[6] doormat are ya anyway?" "Meshugener N'goy mamzer,[7] you should play better, I'll never talk to you again!" And those were the "niceties"; I won't repeat the obscenities! The cops were phoned and when they arrived and were told the nature of the problem, they started to howl with laughter! I don't blame them; most of the people in the stands were highly educated professionals, some with international reputations. Their appearance, age, and attire acutely separated them from the standard, mixed crowd of spectators at a game. Without a doubt a blind man could see the difference! Here they were carrying on with their vitriol at two formerly angry men, one of whom required first aid for heat exhaustion. From my point of view, everybody needed "their heads read." Thankfully no charges were laid, the police told the spectators to head home, and the two antagonists, well they just stood around, talking quietly in their dissipated states. The Admin. Assistant had had her honor defended, kind of anyway, everybody came out to cheer on the respective combatants and things went back to "a dull roar" at the office. One more story to go and then it's on to Chapter Four.

VIGNETTE 26

DARYL B. HAD A SECRET – A VERY SERIOUS PROBLEM THAT SHOULD HAVE been challenged vociferously during his training fifteen years earlier,

---

6   jerk
7   crazy bastard

but alas, as in many industries it was pushed "under the rug" so to speak – the less said the better – yeah right? This happened more times than I wish to remember in the bad old days, but I digress. When he qualified in 1970 his mentors "red flagged" certain proclivities, which if dealt with in therapy, would have resulted in no just cause for concern regarding his personality match with Mental Health Services. Unfortunately, it took a broken relationship to precipitate emotional problems that took a turn for the worse affecting Daryl B.'s professional reputation and the Unit's morale to its core. For a period of time anyway and yes, there was a happy ending but eventually – very eventually!

Jake, you're getting morose, kick back and tell another funny Vignette. Sorry, but this story has to be told and being that it occurred over thirty years ago, I feel obliged to disclose the general issues, changing, or more accurately masking details so as not to sully "someone's" reputation. It happened like this.

Daryl B. lived on/off for approximately five years with his girlfriend, "who provided him with sustenance" whatever that means. For reasons not clarified by the staff gossip, Daryl B. was unceremoniously "dumped" by this woman. *So what,* you say? Aha! That's what you know! Here's the positive stuff about Daryl B. – he was a damn good therapist! You name it he was competent at it and I'm referring to Individual; Group; Couples and Family therapy. A very, very competent professional who UNFORTUNATELY went into crisis in front of our eyes!

How so, you say? For approximately two weeks after the breakup there he'd be – not saying much, coming into work punctually, doing his job and being the good guy, albeit a bit anal-retentive but nevertheless, highly respected for his ability to do his job well! One day he showed up with mascara on his eyelashes! How do I know this? A patient he was seeing, a "blue-collar" tradesperson left the interview room in a highly agitated state exclaiming, "Is this guy AC/DC or what!?" Remembering in the early/mid-1980s gay pride, "outed" homosexuality that is, was not readily accepted and in the particular geographical area I was employed, that certainly was the case FULL STOP! Simply put – I worked and lived in a conservative, "right wing" reactionary, political milieu. People were extreme right of center, that is, rural, hard-working and suspicious of "outliers" including – dress, music, profession, type of car/truck driven, it was that conservative – get the picture? More specifically, professionals in the field of Mental Health were considered "left wing," "pinko," "bleeding heart liberals," "economic scavengers," "shrink jerk-offs," now d'ya get the picture?

    I walked into his office some time later AND at the request of Senior Management, after Daryl B.'s patient had left in a huff. This particular "situation" had gone around the office like a house afire. And yes, Daryl B. was wearing eyelash mascara which was overdone – making him resemble a 14th-century Druid or the rock star "Marilyn Manson," take your pick. Without going into detail, Daryl B. did not want nor appreciate my feedback! The next day another patient left Daryl B.'s office in a huff – this time stating, "I ain't 'spilling my guts' to a weirdo wearing nail polish!" AND yes, once again at the request of Senior Management, I went in and talked to Daryl B., who was in fact wearing nail polish – cherry red actually! Daryl B., it appeared, was making a statement! What to do? Actually the cowardly thing that anyone would do in that era – NOTHING. The next day Daryl B. "sashayed" into the office with a purse/handbag AND with an exaggerated wiggle that left everyone wondering what the hell was going on, as in, was he "all there" pants that were so tight that I worried his testicles would explode? Typically, over a month period, I was approached by three to four support staff per week saying things like, "Jake – you're his boss do somethin'" "The guy's havin' a friggin' 'break-down' and you're doin' nothin' about it, what the hell kind of boss are ya?" "What are ya, 'asleep at the switch' or somethin' – you gotta 'hurtin' unit' over there – get with the program!" Nice hunh (eh) and those were the "support staff"! Don't even ask about my peer/professional group, which fed me malicious complaints like, "Your conduct or lack thereof, is an expression of poor leadership and is deleterious to the morale of this Unit." Yeah right! *Jake, they sound pompous and pretentious!* You got it right, they were, they were!

Subsequently and over the next three to four weeks Daryl B. refined the feminine gait! No more exaggerated wiggle, but rather a more enticing glide/saunter. This time a smooth and I mean liquid smooooth gait, wearing spray paint pants as they were called in the day – they were THAT TIGHT! The women started to complain – there was staff dissension, client dissension, management dissension – everybody dissension! I received three different complaint letters from female staff who threatened to go to their political representative if nothing was done! I had several meetings with my bosses about "this crazy situation." Here was my response to the high muckety muck, senior management inquiries. Yes – it was my opinion that Daryl B. was involved in transvestite fetishism. He was a heterosexual male, he had been under clinically significant distress recently and there was impairment (for that era anyway) in social but not occupational functioning. He enjoyed "cross-dressing" so the hell what!! And NO – I didn't think he was involved in gender dysphoria because he didn't verbalize persistent discomfort with gender role or identity. And no, I didn't know whether he was having recurrent intense sexual fantasies or behaviors and I didn't feel it was my place to ask! I was his Manager not his therapist! I did remember what a wonderful therapist he could be and that he was in a period of crisis (which was to last many more months). In truth and I have to be honest – I can't remember exactly how long it lasted! The long and the short of it (no pun intended), Daryl B. enjoyed cross-dressing!! It was provocative for him to dress up in female attire and imitate female behavior. And no, he wasn't interested in having gender reassignment. Unfortunately, his need to dress up and show off in a feminine manner was in the wrong era and wrong geographical region, but such is life.

Here's what came down and it's a happy ending! If you can believe it, he was transferred to the Single Men's Hostel – counseling homeless men – providing them support regarding their finances, overseeing structured programs for them to attend, and generally being the good guy that he was! He accepted the new job with vigor and appeared to enjoy the total acceptance by this new clientele. And yes, he got teased at the beginning and had to prove himself which he did and when he died in the late 1990s, there were over 400 people at his funeral! An interesting story with a dilemma at first, then at last a nice, happy ending, and now it's on to Chapter Four.

Of Note: Here I go again, before starting the next Chapter, take a gander: Dysfunctional organizations often project problems to external sources rather than taking ownership. This is institutionalized thinking at its worst and most basic level – not taking responsibility! There is also distorted thinking – taking their problems and blaming them on an "external factor." When/if you frequently encounter this defense mechanism in an Organization of which you're consulting or working, BE WARY. You could become the object of derision for no other reason than being the "newbie," challenging the status quo, talking to a rival unit, organization, politician. NOW, on to the next Chapter.

CHAPTER FOUR

VIGNETTE 27

Before I begin with the next story, let's recap to this point. By now I was 34 years old and ready for a new challenge. I was tired of working in Government and decided to move into the nonprofit sector – this time in Senior Management. I spent 18 months looking for the "ideal job" and thought I'd found it in a neighboring city with approximately the same population. The interview went well, actually very well! Two weeks later I received a call confirming that I'd been chosen as the successful candidate! I gave notice, went through the normal exit interview "hoopla" with the two gentlemen from the previous Chapter AND an additional interview with Steve Z., my immediate boss, and his staff – a helluva hazing actually. Thank you very much, Steve Z – quite frankly, what a d-bag! I'm sure he felt the same about me! I'd never lived down our little "tussle" during my probation period and over the next three years paid for my lack of judgment in spades and then some! His staff worked me over pretty good as they say! But that's life and who said it's fair – I learned many things from that job – much more from my mistakes than my successes by far!

I met with my new boss on Monday morning, went over my portfolio, which included overseeing eight supervisors with approximately 20–40 staff each. He also showed me the Administration Chart, you know the old "pyramid" on the wall routine. A nice looking pyramid as I think back, impressive even – but at the same time deep and daunting, as it depicted pictorially my responsibilities, which were immense to say the least! Easily enough work for two Administrators in this position let alone Yours Truly. After a few days I was quick to ascertain that five of the eight supervisors were militant feminists, two of whom had misandristic tendencies – quite frankly a pure hatred of males AND hair under their armpits too, just kidding. Yes, the good old days – needless to say an interesting situation, for even the most seasoned professional. Who cares, I thought! This is a great opportunity to learn Administration at a senior level with one of the largest portfolios of that particular geographical region. My, we're so ambitious when we're young and eager for challenge AND I thought if I mind my "p's and q's," I should get along with my new staff – Dream on McDuff!!

Not one Supervisor under my leadership was weak; they were all very adept at their jobs, instrumentally at least. Some were better than others with the empathic, interpersonal nuances that should become routine when overseeing staff on a day-to-day basis. My boss was much beloved and very intelligent! He had molded this team of professionals through sheer will, determination, drive, and expertise. Externally he made some enemies, but he never betrayed his desire to make things better for his subordinates and they dearly loved him for that! Here's the problem that I uncovered during my first six weeks on the job, and to make a long story short, and it's a very long story, I determined my boss, who was emotionally involved with the Controller, from my observation anyway, had misappropriated funds from the other Divisions' budgets and transferred them to his Division's budget! This done to ameliorate, so to speak, the quality of work life in his particular Division, that is, "my Division," which he administered. I won't go into detail, but this finagling of the Organization's finances alienated my Division from its counterparts within the Organization – are you surprised? To defend, or more actually rationalize the contempt by the other Division's leaders, my boss tended to project an antagonistic attitude towards his peers, their respective Divisions, and the quality of their Divisions' accomplishments. Some of my boss's observations were bang on, but unfortunately his highfalutin' attitude was assimilated by my subordinates and on and on did this merry-go-round of point-counterpoint accusations, diatribes, and vitriol continue! Nice place to enter hunh (eh) – what d'ya think? *I think it stinks, Jake, get out while the going gets good!* Okay, okay, on with the story.

HERE WE GO AGAIN, I thought and ALSO within the first six weeks was the arrival of the new Administrator, who was to put it bluntly a very skeptical and shrewd judge of character, as shrewd as my boss and then some! He became acutely aware of the goings-on in my Division in no time flat. My boss had been able to bamboozle the previous Administrator with the old "B.S baffles brains" approach when providing budgetary feedback at the weekly management meetings. This was of course backed up by his very good friend, the Controller of the Organization. Once again to make a long story short, the new Administrator after attending two or three weekly management meetings concluded "something stunk in Denmark" and began pressuring these two schlemiels[8] for accountability – like accurate budgetary statements reflecting the expenditures and rationale for expenses of this particular Division. The details of these meetings I was not privy to – I wasn't there, so basically there is conjecture on my part – but what I do know is the following!

Both men were gone within eight weeks – approximately two weeks apart! Here I was barely four months into my new job and handed my colleague's position, which I felt was way beyond my level of management percipience and niche of comfort, what a set-up! At that point I should've quit, but pride took over and bit me in the ass! The eight supervisors demanded an explanation of why my boss had been impugned and treated in such a dastardly manner by this new "Dictator." Oh dear what to do? I told them in no uncertain terms and without a good night's sleep, that there had been financial irregularities and it was determined both gentlemen should "pull up their socks"! Both felt otherwise and quit with little notice – and with that disclosure, lots of venom spewed from my subordinates' mouths! You guessed it – Jake's cadre of

---

8   clumsy bunglers

supervisors went ballistic on Jake and then some! The let's behead the messenger routine prevailed. More specifically, they alleged I was in cahoots with this Dictator Cretin, Paskudnik,[9] "how could I let his behavior go on without a fight," "why don't you wear a dress," "if I was married to you, you wouldn't get any tail," etc., etc. Incidentally, my former boss, I found out later, had two years previously threatened to resign, but the Board had urged him to stay on! This time however with carefully crafted maneuvering by the new Administrator, or should I say a carefully "rigged" demise, the Board heartily accepted my boss's resignation!

It gets worse, my new job required attending the same weekly meetings with the newly arrived Administrator as my predecessor had and without "pussyfooting" around I began to realize this new boss-fellow was a VERY seriously disturbed man! The Directors of the three major Divisions agreed with my assessment! Initially they'd been happy because he'd squashed my former boss and his accomplice, but very quickly ascertained this was just a political ploy to get rid of corporate memory and "make his bones" as a tough, no-nonsense administrator. The expulsion of these two shlens could have been just as easily one of my counterparts who were not perfect in their jobs. They also found out very quickly how politically ruthless and conniving the Paskudnik, boss-fellow could be! Oh yes I nearly forgot, another point of contention – his propensity to manifest FOUR different personalities!

Yes, you heard it right – four different voices – four distinct patterns of speech to match the tone, vernacular, and character of the voice used at that particular time! You guessed it, the guy was a histrionic personality disorder with a narcissistic overlay, a nasty, malignant piece of work – try working for one, it ain't fun or easy! We, as a group, nicknamed his "personalities" the administrative voice; the normal voice; the sexy voice; and the hybrid voice. Yes it was that bad! Over the next 20 months our lives were made miserable, especially when this Paskudnik hired a former colleague to be the new Controller and became the boss fellow's pipeline of information regarding Organizational gossip and intrigue. We, the

---

9   revolting, evil person

Directors, began having clandestine meetings offsite at the local "watering hole." Nothing ever got accomplished but we certainly drank a lot of beer and stroked each other's egos. Ideas of retribution were conjured up but never acted upon; unfortunately, we as a group had learned helplessness, in layman's language an inability to act, as in frozen tag/second-guessitis.

Basically we feared for our jobs, professional reputations, standard of living, professional mobility. We were, or more accurately had become, entropic delinquents plain and simple. And then you've got to look at yourself in the mirror – a sickening veil of nauseous contempt pervades when you look at that reflection! You hate going to work, you're generally agitated, quick to temper, sleep deprived, fearful in the worst possible way because you want change to occur but it never does, you have learned helplessness – it ain't nice! There, I used that expression again! Anyone who attempted to challenge the Administrator/Dictator/Autocrat was ruthlessly eliminated!! This occurred just frequently enough to reinforce the fear that permeated within the Senior Management ranks and encourage entropy.

One day my phone rang and the extension number 57 shone brightly. No God not today! YES, it was a phone call from the Administrator/Dictator/Autocrat. I picked up the phone with hesitation, wondering which of his four voices would come over the phone. His "normal" voice this time – great, he's in a good mood. He was wondering if I could come down and attend a meeting at 11 a.m. I stated I was free and would be there promptly at 11; he thanked me and hung up. Not 15 minutes later my phone rang again and extension number 57 popped up. No problem, I thought, picked up the phone and in my best voice stated, "Hi, can I help you?" "GET THE HELL DOWN TO MY OFFICE NOW," the "admin" voice boomed. I was down there in a "flash" and this time, as I sat in the chair opposite his desk, listened to him ramble on about what he was going to say at the 11 a.m. meeting. Slowly he got up and started walking past me and then around the room BEHIND ME. I found this very disconcerting, as the chair I sat on was not a swivel chair so I had to sit straight and look ahead. I was damned if I was going to twist my neck to give him the respect and attention he felt he deserved. Twice he leaned over from behind my back and talked into my ear – his head approximately three inches (7.5 cm.) away. What he stated I can't remember, as his style of communication and invasion of my space was VERY unnerving and seemed somehow rehearsed. And so it was! *But, Jake, isn't that harassment?* No kiddin', just keep on reading; you ain't heard nothin' yet!!

This pattern of interview-interrogation behind closed doors occurred frequently with my colleagues as well, some of whom were emotionally tough and could take this form of interrogation. The confrontational ploys used by this chameleon boss-fellow to intimidate and influence decision-making precipitated staff to take time off and even complain to the Board Executive, which didn't get them anywhere. Then, with time, the learned helplessness paradigm and exogenous depression of the management group increased in severity and in one person's case, became a full-blown adjustment disorder. Others loaded up on mild tranquilizers such as zopiclone, or self-medicated with old-fashioned booze, in order to maintain the semblance of stability! What a joke and I don't mean a "ha ha" joke, but one out of the side of your mouth in the back room of a darkened building kind of joke. Not good for morale, mental health, esprit de corps, you name it. The demise of the Organization, which was over 30 years old AND with a national reputation, was in the hands of the Administrator/Dictator/Autocrat! He was attempting to break down and eliminate the corporate memory, and done in a very logical and preconceived manner – no doubt about it! What to do? *Leave, Jake, just leave, your mental health is at stake!* I know, I know, but I couldn't leave – it was that g... damn pride thing biting my ass and learned helplessness hamstringing my ability to take action effectively! Fear does that to you – a paralytic fear of reprisal and retribution that impeaches your dignity and self-worth.

To digress for a moment, the staff and I mean the line staff organized a clandestine group which began sending hate mail every month to the Executive Board, the Administrator/Dictator/Autocrat, his cadre of professionals in senior management, including Yours Truly, you name it! This monthly dialogue of contempt and accusations was well written and impugned the leadership, its ineptitude and reduction of quality of work life in the Organization, blaming everything on the Administrator/Dictator/Autocrat. These monthly critiques for the lack of a better descriptive went on for almost one year! The local newspaper got involved, Senior Government officials REFUSED to become involved, stating it was an internal problem, and finally the television media became involved! A further three months went by and this clandestine guerrilla warfare still continued. All of us were amazed at the Teflon ability of the Administrator/Dictator/Autocrat, who had the guts of Dick Tracy, the calculating shrewdness of a Bengal tiger, and the IQ of an astrophysicist! Nothing seemed to bother him – his defense mechanism, ostensibly, intellectualization, denial/rationalization supported his ability to maintain poise, clear thinking – that is – kind of clear thinking and exactitude! *A lot of big words and fancy phraseology, Jake!* You're right, in English, it was a "Friggin' Zoo" and yet my pride wouldn't let me quit unless it was under my terms – not his terms! You've been there – you know what I'm talking about and life can be a "can of worms" with some fudge candy once in a while but this was ridiculous; I was living a lie! What to do?

One morning as I looked in the mirror nursing a hangover I realized I was coming to the end of my rope. My eight supervisors routinely ganged up on me at our weekly meetings, and looking back, I don't blame them. My energy, stamina, and goal directedness had diminished during the past 20 months under the sleight-of-hand, crush your gonads, take a pounding management style of the not so new Administrator/Dictator/Autocrat. At work a few days later my phone rang with the extension number 57 and my hand trembled! Yes, me, Jake Hagerman, a tough guy, my hand was trembling! The "sexy" voice was distinct – "I just want to say how enjoyable it's been working with you the past 20 months – I'd be interested to know your feelings on this matter?" I almost fell out of my chair and bit my tongue before responding – here it comes, "It has been an interesting and at times difficult 20 months but we're still here."

A PREGNANT pause for three one hundreds before he responded with, "Why don't you come down and spend some time with me, it appears we have to talk and clear the air." My response "How 'bout 2 p.m. this Thursday"? – was all I could muster – "See you then" was his response. The affectation, with a 1960s Ann Margret/Joey Heatherton-like voice or should I say "purr" was both disingenuous and seductive in his attempt to be disarming. But if you look at the meta-communication, a threat imperative was there, most definitely it was there!

To top it off not 10 minutes later at my staff meeting, I was provided with a list of complaints from my eight supervisors – all of whom had signed a letter of non-confidence regarding my management ability and leadership. UNBELIEVABLE I thought to myself!! Those rat b.... what I'd done for them, shielding them 9/10 times from this Paskudnik's illogical demands, reckless and contrived directives that appeared to make sense, but didn't make sense, if you can understand the juxtaposition. When they pertained to maintaining power – aggression, ruthlessness, degradation – the whole lot was used to promote his leadership and "took the cake" in nerve and guile! As I dictate currently, a brilliant movie comes to mind with the actor portraying two roles – the son of Saddam Hussein and his double. I don't know why this picture didn't receive more critical acclaim or at least an Academy Award – the direction, screenplay, and acting brilliance was superb. That movie in many ways was a template of the living nightmare of this job/work milieu and I GET A VOTE OF NON-CONFIDENCE?! That hurt – to this day I still bear a grudge that is not buried deep – but what the hell, life is not fair, as I was told many years ago by my old man – you remember Dad's statement to me earlier in the book. It's true, but on with the story.

Three days before Christmas/Happy Holiday whatever, I had a letter shoved under my door, once again reiterating the eight supervisors' "listed complaints" about my inept leadership behavior. Basically, their diminished job comfort and inability to perform their roles as they were used to doing when under the tutelage of my predecessor, etc., etc.! Thanks for the Happy Holiday card, folks! I

Chapter Four | 89

went home very depressed. Yes, still single at the time, I bought a bottle of malt whiskey and drank myself into oblivion! *Not a very mature way of handling stress, Jake!? What the hell's going on!?!* I'll tell you what's going on, the stress was getting to me and this was the last straw! I had felt the staff's frustration, contempt and disrespect for 18 months and the Administrator/Dictator/Autocrat was winning the war of attrition, that's what's going on!

The night before our Thursday meeting I thought long and hard about what might be its general theme. You just never knew with the Administrator/Dictator/Autocrat – it depended on which voice and characterization of that particular personality was portrayed. I arrived at his office door approximately five minutes before two – quite frankly prepared for the worst! I summoned up my courage and knocked on the door. "Come in, come in, can I get you a coffee?" Ah, the "normal" voice I'm in luck! WRONG – "I just want to say how much I appreciate your support throughout the past 18 months – it has not gone unnoticed." Damn, the "sexy" voice, I think I'm going to vomit! My response was short and to the point, "We are in a dreadful state of affairs and I'm wondering if we're on the same page administratively?" A ballsy thing to say to a malignant narcissist and I felt I was in the "mind's eye" of what Hitler's generals must've felt when they confronted Hitler during an operations meeting and were not just met with a rebuff, but open hostility and irrational rage! This despotic side did not happen throughout most of the meeting with the Administrator/Dictator/Autocrat. Not at the beginning and middle portion of the meeting anyway, and I quickly perceived he had few allies and needed support from anywhere and anyone! Perhaps the Executive Board had had enough – all of this ran through my mind by 2:07 p.m. "I appreciate your frankness and yes it has been a very difficult and perplexing arena to work in, hasn't it" was his response. Ah, the "normal" voice; maybe it's going to be a good meeting after all! WRONG, the choice of one particular word, "arena," gave it away!!

Remember what I said earlier about meta-communication – but I digress! For 30 minutes he pontificated and then stated abruptly, "I'm thinking of amalgamating two Divisions into one, which will entail eliminating a Director's position – I'm interviewing two Directors – you happen to be one of them." Damn, the "hybrid" voice, a highly manipulative ploy to foster both fear and entitlement. Cognitive dissonance, the approach-avoidance paradigm, the valence of power rests in the manner with which you respond to such a "loaded" question! KEEP THAT IN MIND.

Specifically, a Director placed in this position has to be very careful about the nature and quality of his/her response because it will be remembered down the road and possibly used against you in spades! I gave a direct response because at that particular time I felt I had the upper hand – the worst he can do was ask for my resignation, which I was prepared to give! "Before I could take on such a role and the responsibilities incumbent in this new position I would want to see 'proof of practice' – in common English, a style of leadership coming from your office that is less formidable and more approachable for all involved." He almost went across the desk at me!! The "admin" voice came through loud and clear, "WHO THE HELL D'YA THINK YOU'RE TALKING TO? YOU INSOLENT SACK OF SH...AND TO THINK WHAT I'VE DONE FOR YOU THE PAST 18 MONTHS – I CARRIED YOU." I sat quietly and felt in control for once during the past 18 months – I felt truly in control – it was a wonderful, almost sensual feeling to respond in the following manner, "You're probably right in your comments about my lack of loyalty but a forthright answer is better than a sniveling..." I was cut off and then some! "IF YOU THINK YOU'RE GOING TO PLAY JOHNNY ROCCO THE THIRD IN MY F.... OFFICE YOU'VE GOT ANOTHER THINK COMIN' AND BY THE WAY I COULD HAVE YOUR LICENSE REVOKED." I stood my ground, "that is your prerogative but I'm wondering what statute in the code of conduct and practice standards of my profession have I contravened during the past 18 months? And by the way if I've contravened a practice standard I never received a challenge from you, the client constituency, or my peers. Be very careful how you proceed!" I couldn't believe my ears and my behavior and still can't 25+ years later – I was drunk with power, or perceived power and it felt great!

This time the Administrator/Director/Autocrat, with blazing eyes, a vicious "sneer" and a broken nose which he chose not to fix, got up from his desk and very slowly, very methodically, strode over to where I was sitting, walked behind me, and started to speak – once again his head less than 6 inches (15 cm.) from my head. "Malignant narcissist, does that ring a bell, Mr. Big Shot?" "Leading with impunity is like raping without conscience, shall I go on Alpha Big Shot?" In a microsecond I had processed what I'd feared the most during the past year – that I'd been taped by a colleague and this information passed on to Mr. Administrator/Director/Autocrat or his collaborator, the Controller! I'd been "busted"! Yes I said those statements in a fit of frustration and rage and they'd been taped and were now being used against me! They could be very easily transcribed, witnessed by a Notary Public, then sent to the Registrar of my College, whose action could be anyone's guess, depending on how my defense or lack thereof was interpreted.

As I sat there with his head still uncomfortably close, and behind me, the thought of the past 20 months flashed by in a microsecond, the "siege mentality" that we'd been put through, this "snake pit of vampires and goblins" was the way I'd described the Organization to my friends and I still stand by that statement! The "admin" voice broke my concentration, "Your balls are in a vise, Mr. Big Shot, and there was never an option regarding your future in this Organization, NEVER AN OPTION." Before he could continue I got up and stated in a matter-of-fact voice, "Do what you have to do, I'm through," and walked out the door. In the background I heard him shout, "YOU'LL LEAVE WHEN I SAY YOU CAN LEAVE!" I kept on walking.

I wrote a resignation letter and left it on my desk, gathered up my personal belongings, had them boxed by the time the Security Police arrived to escort me from my office, and was surprised with my behavior! I was very exhilarated. No more tremor, fatigue, anger, frustration, condemning self-hatred!! No more marriage by convenience for him, hell on earth for me. It felt great! Approximately seven months later the Board Executive bowed to the myriad of complaints and voluminous evidence that indicted this man! He was fired on Friday, given a severance package that was totally unrealistic in my professional opinion, and went back to his old job, which he'd left 1500 miles (2400 km.) away, THREE YEARS earlier!? How the hell did that happen!? He'd been gone three years and he gets his old job back!! What gives here?!! But it happened and life's not fair! By the way nothing came of his threat regarding the College, he was too smart to risk a scandal this far along in the game and didn't want to risk a severance that would choke a horse! As an aside, almost to the month 10 years later, one of my former Supervisors at this job asked me for a reference, which I stupidly gave, don't ask me why! She got the job, was trained in a new field, and provided me the opportunity of a business deal which she felt I couldn't live without. Bygones be bygones I thought; against my better judgment, I agreed to the business terms and ONCE AGAIN got the "short end of the stick"! Only goes to show, "once a sucker always a sucker"! I'm tired, on to Chapter Five.

CHAPTER FIVE

VIGNETTE 28

IT TOOK ME APPROXIMATELY THREE MONTHS TO MOBILIZE EMOTIONALLY after leaving that particular job! Thank God and Jesus Christ for the mental toughness I'd developed during the previous 10 years. Regardless, as it turned out I wasn't going to return to Senior Management for another eight years. The next job was a Director's position in a newly formed Agency that had recently been provided "start-up" funds. I'd been recruited by its Board President who thought I'd be ideal for this "brand new position" as it was described over lunch. "Nice touch" you say – after the hellhole existence of that last job! *TAKE IT, Jake, this is a dream come true – TAKE IT!* That's what I thought too and it should have been that way – but it wasn't! I updated my resume, had what I thought was a positive interview, considering the emotional upheaval I'd just been through, and was offered the job. The funny thing was – as I was lounging against the wall waiting to be interviewed, a previous candidate who I presumed was interviewing for the same job left the interviewing room and nodded at me as he walked by. I'm not a tall man but I dwarfed his size and then some. I estimated he was less than five feet tall (1 m. 52 cm.). As it turned out, the Interviewing Panel decided to have two Administrative positions, an Executive Director and a Second in Command "Director" position. The former was strictly administrative with no direct clinical responsibilities, the latter, a line supervisor position overseeing all clinical casework. The ED position, I found out much later – approximately three months later in fact, had already been earmarked, yet as Director, the other senior position of the Organization, I was now being asked had I seen the "new" Executive Director! I beg your pardon, this "new" position had been filled and the incumbent was starting the following Monday morning? To be honest, I'd already been told, kind of anyway in the preceding weeks, that a new ED position was being developed but what the hell was this? Something unsettling rang in my head and not the tinkle, tinkle of champagne glasses celebrating life, but the clang, clang, clang of siege guns laying down a barrage before a frontal assault. Relax, I thought, you're still suffering from emotional trauma, you're a survivor, a tough guy, nothing and I mean nothing will equate with your last job's stress load! Hold that thought while you continue reading.

Monday morning arrived, sooner rather than later. Unfortunately I'd tossed and turned the previous night, ruminating and catastrophizing. No amount of CBT coping strategies/technique worked and I arrived at my job "hung over" with worry. I was not to be disappointed – I'd worried for a very good reason, guess who walked through the door? Ned, "the lead pipe cinch," that's who! He was a well-known Administrator in this particular geographical area and had single-handedly downsized a rival Organization the previous year. This action had caused a mini revolt at that organization amongst the "old guard" staff, who had gone to the press and bitched their case but to no avail. Was it a good move? I have no idea, I wasn't there; some people thought the downsizing drama was exaggerated. Getting back to the story, it seemed he was here to stay and I'd better get used to it! *On with the story, Jake, on with the story.* Okay, okay.

Ned, "the lead pipe cinch," had been a rival and unceremoniously terminated without cause from his last job! Rival in the sense of marketing for money, competing for funding – which had been given to us at this brand-new agency I had just joined and not his old Agency – dun da dun dun! And yes, he was the man who had passed me in the hall during the Interview process. He remembered me and I remembered him – the chemistry wasn't there and to say the least I wasn't impressed, nor was he as it turned out! This individual had a brilliant mind, not as formidable as the Administrator/Dictator/Autocrat's but nonetheless a very shrewd, conniving individual whose modus operandi was the "bottom line" – always the bottom line! To reinforce what I'm talking about – we'd reviewed the Vision and then Mission/Mandate of the Organization, this document developed by one of the most intelligent Boards I'd had the privilege to work with during my (by now) 10-year career. In short, they had impressed me during the short period of time I was involved with them! Then Ned "the lead pipe cinch" came out with one of his "pearls"! "Jake, I don't really like what I'm reading, do you?" My response, "How so?" was not taken well as he retorted, "Jake, I'm not always right but I'm never wrong; I need dialogue not conjecture," and walked away with a snort of indignation! Now what the hell was that supposed to mean!? ONCE AGAIN, dun, da, dun dun!! Oh no, here we go again, another malignant narcissist. Now you can release your thoughts.

    Over the next several months a number of staff members were hired for the clinical program which I oversaw, in addition to several support staff. Of course Ned "the lead pipe cinch" felt it necessary to demonstrate his authority on a regular basis, which inevitably backfired. More specifically, people were left wondering, "who the hell does this guy think he is?" The comments were not kind, "Why doesn't this guy zone into the '80s?" "Is this guy for real; I thought servitude went out with segregation," "What's his license plate number I feel a road rage coming on," etc. What to do, are you thinking what I'm thinking? *Jake – get the hell out while the going gets good* – I couldn't, I'd just begun the job!

    Unfortunately Ned "the lead pipe cinch's" ego was twice as lofty as his short stature and then some! After approximately three months on the job, he decided on Monday morning, which was his appointed time to have staff meetings, to announce over a loudspeaker he'd had installed that he would forgo the regular meeting in the Board room and have the staff assemble in the hallway instead. What gives? His office, which incidentally was twice the size of mine and the other recently hired mid-manager's combined, was at the end of the hall. Approximately 10 of us heeded the message and stood in the hallway outside our offices waiting for him to emerge from his office. He did so, DRAGGING A CHAIR behind him! He placed it in front of his door, proceeded to stand on it to give him additional height and from my perspective, authority over the "hoi polloi." You can guess the reaction from the staff and the negative correlation between stated message and credibility – his purpose and intent became a silly spectacle and then some! This Administrator of great intelligence no doubt, less than five foot tall (1 m. 52 cm.) stepping onto his chair then speaking to us about a subject that was as mundane as watching paint dry! People tried to keep a straight face, bit their tongues, looked at the floor, looked at the ceiling, looked sideways – we were embarrassed, to put it mildly, for him, not for us poor plebes. After approximately 15 minutes Ned "the lead pipe cinch" finished his soliloquy, stepped down from the chair, gave us a quick bow, reentered his office dragging the chair behind him, and shut the door. People reentered their offices and then began the gales of laughter! People laughed so hard the Security guard knocked on doors to find out what was going on. Oh no, here we go again, a different manifestation of management dysfunction with narcissism grossly interfering with insight/self-awareness. Jake, I said to myself, as deja-vu flooded my cortex, are you again going to play "Jingles" to this guy's "Wild Bill"? Do you have the energy, fortitude, and courage to be a standup guy ONCE AGAIN?! No, I said to myself, I'll sit back on my laurels and let him self-destruct! But it didn't happen, not on my "watch" anyway!! I'm no hero but PRIDE, that silly g…damn word, entered the picture and bit me in the ass – ONCE AGAIN.

Approximately one month later, as I attended a weekly staff meeting, I noticed an agenda item that puzzled me and subsequently enraged me! It read, "Standardizing Annual Reviews" – sounds innocuous doesn't it? If you can believe this, Ned "the lead pipe cinch" had attached the unabridged, Annual Review of a colleague of mine WITHOUT eliminating the identifying features – like his name! YES – WE WERE PRIVY TO MY COLLEAGUE'S ENTIRE ANNUAL EVALUATION. I was dumbstruck and tried to articulate my vexation to Ned "the lead pipe cinch," whose response was equally unfathomable, "Jake it's okay, calm down he's moved to..." which was 2000 miles (3200 km.) away, but nevertheless! He then stated, "I'm sure he wouldn't mind – we're all professionals here." The silence in the room was deafening! By the end of the week two more staff members had submitted their resignations and left without notice. Without notice was unheard of in the mid 1980s, when there was still some semblance of work ethic, loyalty, and commitment to the worksite! This I might say did not get back to the Board Executive and should have been an immediate priority, but it wasn't because we were hoping that Ned "the lead pipe cinch" would change or soften his behavior, or better still leave! NAIVE HUNH (eh)? "Twice burned 50 times shy," Jake sat in his office and queried his fate!? A long-term working relationship with this man meant total abrogation of integrity. This was a "bottom line" guy? B.S. guy you mean! "The end justifies the means!" "He who survives wins!" "Never say die, I'm going to win at all costs!" You get the picture! I felt he would start making demands on all of us individually that were totally unacceptable, AND HE DID.

One day while I was pondering my fate, a pretty female head popped into view at the doorway. "Do you know where the ED's office is?" My response, "Yeah, down the hall at the end is his office," and went back to reading an article. She smiled, said "thank you" quietly, and a few seconds later I heard her knock on Ned "the lead pipe cinch's" office door. His response jolted me back to reality, "Hi, honey, come on in." A few moments later they passed my office and with my door slightly ajar I noticed they were holding hands. My God, he actually had a social life?! I wasn't the only person who observed their liaison and the gossip quickly spread around the office, some matter of fact, some quite malicious, "She's much bigger than him." "He should buy some stilts he's going to get a crick in his neck." Staff can be cruel but then that's life. We found out very quickly (how I don't know – it's been too many years) that this lady friend co-owned a business with Ned "the lead pipe cinch" AND, get this, less than two blocks from the Agency – hold that thought! She was an accountant by training and very intelligent;

in a nutshell here's the problem that arose very quickly. It's called conflict of interest; Ned "the lead pipe cinch, began spending more and more time at their business and less and less time at the Agency. I won't bore you with the "goings-on" over the next six months, you've already listened to my bitching in Vignette 28, but from my perception and everyone else's, and that's a lot of people at the Agency, there was immense fraud being perpetrated, BLATANT theft of time! Individual Board members were carefully selected by the staff and asked out to lunch, at which time Ned "the lead pipe cinch's" behavior was described in detail. Unfortunately for me AND once again I found out lightning does strike twice in the same place, or it did in this circumstance! The respective Board members could not believe someone would have the audacity to, by this period of time, after approximately six months on the job, work at most and I mean this without any exaggeration, TWO HOURS PER WEEK as an Administrator of an Agency! In conjunction and also factored into their hesitancy, was that Ned "the lead pipe cinch" had already come to our Agency with a cloud over his head regarding the downsizing of his former Agency, which had a "national reputation," this along with his subsequent termination without cause!? Why would that cause hesitancy/dissonance in taking action from a Board Member's perspective? It should have been a giant "red flag" but it wasn't; this is circular logic at its best! I'll continue my story, it gets better!! BUT before I continue, go make some popcorn, drink some beer, pour some wine – red not white, and listen to this yarn!

There was no union at our Agency, too bad, because a Secret Staff Committee was formed after Ned "the lead pipe cinch" in his infinite wisdom, decided to combine two Units thereby expanding the range of service provision, but at the same time finding redundant three "line" positions. Obviously he felt the caseloads, which were already high, could be further expanded and dealt with competently by the remaining BUT reduced staff complement, BAD MISTAKE!! The place went "bananas" and that marked the beginning of the end for Ned "the lead pipe cinch"!

The Secret Staff Committee brought forward an innocuous agenda item at the weekly staff meeting entitled, "Time Management Issues." Ned "the lead pipe cinch" fell for it hook, line, and sinker! From his perspective and this was a very narcissistic perspective, the staff were finally coming around to a more clear understanding of Total Quality Management Practice. The Japanese system of management: quality control; quality improvement; internal and external customer satisfaction was his baby, his raison d'être! He grinned and grinned when he shook my hand at the end of the meeting, which I tried pulling away, feigning a sore finger – *yeah the middle one, Jake* – I know I'm a mind reader. But in reality I was worried that my colleagues would think I was in "cahoots" with this miscreant. In clinical vernacular it's called "anosognosia" or lack of self-awareness. This particular affliction is one of the main presenting problems with survivors of brain injury and was mimicked by Ned "the lead pipe cinch"!

Narcissism will do that to people! I bring this up simply to convey how totally removed he was regarding any insight into his personal behavior. A self-absorbed narcissist! For such an intelligent man, ambitious with a capital A, this behavior was self-destructive and a career killer, astounding to say the least! But on with the story, actually it gets quite interesting!!

The staff, in a very nice way, suggested devising an "In-House Longitudinal Study," comparing a control group with another targeted group whose behavior, that is "job duties," would be "compared." The variables analyzed entailed: time management ability; work to rule behavior; cost effectiveness and cost benefit analysis of completing casework. The nitty gritty, transparency of this project tweaked the interest of Ned "the lead pipe cinch"! Here comes the old anosognosia again, neat word huh (eh) ANO SOG NO SIA – he simply didn't realize he was being set up. Obviously the outcomes between the two groups would be compared. That is, the control group and the identified treatment group's respective outcomes would be compared over time and statistically analyzed. Based on the results of the quantifiable data, a logical progression of recommendations could be made AND with the possibility of a publication! The ED's eyes sparkled; someone thought he was physically aroused at one point! Actually a lot of gobbledygook, the project, which looked great on paper, was simply a ruse to collect data to evaluate Ned "the lead pipe cinch"! Specifically, his time at and away from the Agency, on a day-by-day basis, for a period of six months. This was the only way the staff felt the Board would listen. Quantifiable, objective data as evidence of the ongoing misuse of power and authority – because no amount of discussion thus far had achieved a damn thing!

In the meantime, the over-burdened caseworkers with the increased case numbers began "falling like flies"! My job as Director became more tenuous as the number of resignations – caseworkers who were succumbing to burnout – increased exponentially. No amount of reasoning worked with Ned "the lead pipe cinch." Remember his motto at the beginning of this Vignette – that's right, spend a second – look it up, no don't, just kidding! His code of conduct "I'm not always right but I'm never wrong" rang inside my tiny brain. I began to free associate and up popped the following phrase – "Post hoc, ergo propter hoc" – after this, therefore because of this error. This statement of fallacy was in fact being played out at our Agency! Ned "the lead pipe cinch" had a psychological need to downsize everything. "I want a lean mean fightin' machine" was his mantra. Unfortunately, his ruminative manner and very rigid, concrete thinking about what he envisioned was right and very wrong included little, if any insight into his own predatory behavior! This was influenced in part by his upbringing, a home-life described by him in his weaker moments as devoid of demonstrated love, caring, and empathy. Every child wants and seeks approval. His attempts for approval and success had been stymied by two very competitive parents; it seemed unconditional love was not one of their strong points! As a result this neglect translated into the "smaller is better" theme, which was being played out at the Agency. Guess who was smaller and better!? Resolving personal conflicts was one thing, but acting them out at the expense of staff morale and job security was an entirely different proposition! I beat myself up trying to figure out what to do and finally said to myself – who the hell knows!

What I do know is Jake was under close scrutiny and began to feel set-up for a big, big "fall." I was by now "corporate memory," which could have been dangerous, as in potentially destabilizing, if the Board Executive requested my opinion of the current Organizational dynamics under this person's leadership. And Ned "the lead pipe cinch" was ruthless, "gutting" anyone he felt was disloyal to his management style. There I go again – my tendency to over-evaluate but what d'ya think? Don't worry, there was no need to catastrophize because I wasn't approached by anyone in authority regarding this organizational dilemma! NOT ONE PERSON. Conversely, I did the approaching and got nowhere!

HURRAH, I'll say it again more softly (shush) Hurrah!! The Secret Staff Committee came back with enough evidence to choke a horse and certainly put the kibosh on Ned "the lead pipe cinch." There were even photographs of him standing beside his girlfriend, taken at "his" place of business TWO BLOCKS AWAY, with times and dates placed underneath and stamped by a Notary Public. Unfortunately for Ned "the lead pipe cinch" they coincided with when he should have been working at our Organization! Remember those were the days before, much before, the high-tech "snooping" gadgetry we have now! The caper had worked, now the Secret Staff Committee set its next task to develop a cogent, "crisp" document that was not overstated, but demonstrated the extreme malfeasance that was being perpetrated! At one point during the investigation and it is a laughable recollection even today, Ned "the lead pipe cinch" suggested to the Board Executive during a monthly meeting that they should hire his girlfriend to be the Controller of the Agency – "Of course you know she's a qualified Accountant." They almost took him up on it!

At about this time I was at a luncheon with two of my staff, one of whom was "dear friends" with a member of the Board Executive. My critical comments I readily admit were emphatic to say the least and were taken by this cretin "Benedict Arnold" and subsequently disclosed IN TOTO to his "friend" on the Board. The following day I was called into the Board room where three members of the Board Executive were waiting. They proceeded to interrogate me – my "reckless behavior" vis-à-vis professional code of conduct, as further undermining the shaky morale of the Organization. Give me a break! The inquisition began on Friday morning and ended Monday at noon. Now in 2014, it would be deemed harassment and by the end of this "he said she said" diatribe and I say this with great deliberation, I quit the job – or more aptly described, the *Gong Show*! That's it, I'm finished – no more B.S.; I'm outta here! I was 37 years of age, with two crappy jobs under my belt and two very crappy experiences in both mid and senior management. But damn I learned a lot and then some, those experiences were worth a double Doctorate, triple M.D. The laugh was when I went to my office to gather my belongings – who came and helped me? The informer! Why I don't know – yes, guilt was probably "rearing its ugly head" as I didn't see any gloating. But at the same time, and it was a strange sensation – I didn't have the energy to reject his kindness! I'd been victimized by my own mental fatigue, letting down my guard. After this experience and in all future jobs I tried to think in three dimensions – organizational dynamics, positioning, meta-communication, and I'll throw in a fourth – guile, that is, Ganef[10] – a thief's cleverness without his criminal intent.

But Jake you haven't finished your story – what ever happened to Ned "the lead pipe cinch"? Okay, okay, I owe you this one. As I recall, the Board in their infinite wisdom incurred another six months of staff resignations, phone calls from beleaguered ex-staff waiting for their overdue records of employment, clientele complaints, and even a politician complaining from the local riding – before real action was taken and not by the Board! The Secret Staff Committee requested a special Board meeting which was granted "in camera." They brought along the trusty document, the so-called "In-House Longitudinal Study," which blew the socks off the Board Executive, two of whom were academics. From what I was told the gales of laughter – actually howling by a number of Board members – could be heard on the street below! The Secret Committee members had very calmly and methodically explained the ruse from beginning to end! Two hours later Ned "the lead pipe cinch" was tracked down, at HIS place of

---

10   thief

business of course, and in person two of the Board members told him, in front of his girlfriend, "To get his ass back to the Agency NOW." He looked bewildered, at least according to the gossip mill, and of course anosognosia reared its ugly head for the last time – at the Agency anyway! He simply did not comprehend what was going on during the two-block walk back to the office! Both members of the Board remained quiet in spite of his attempts to engage in conversation. *Jake, he must've known the jig was up!* Nope, my sources told me he didn't – in fact quite the opposite! He thought it was some kind of a deliberate sham to camouflage a Surprise Party, at which time the Board Executive was going to congratulate him for his brilliant-brain leadership regarding the "In-House Longitudinal Study." Sorry, Ned, not this time or any time soon! They gave him a "tongue lashing," vowed he would never receive a reference, and in very short order, like two minutes or less, terminated him with "just cause"! Two Board members accompanied him to his office, gave him five minutes to collect his personal possessions, which he did and then left forthwith never to work in the Mental Health Industry again!! At least not during the past 25 years since this occurred as far as I'm aware. There is a God and Jesus Christ and for once I felt justice had been served and corruption vanquished! How time flies when you're having fun, now on to Chapter Six!

Of Note: Pause for just a moment before reading on: Most dysfunctional organizations operate from distorted thinking paradigms. Many of the problems occur when employees carry forward unresolved problems from outside of work (e.g., adult children of alcoholic parents) and use the organization milieu to work out their personal problems, agenda, and conflict on their colleagues! This damaging behavior creates chaos and havoc amongst the unwitting staff with a negative effect on work productivity. Think about it. Now on to Chapter Six!

CHAPTER SIX

VIGNETTE 29

MY NEXT JOB I OBTAINED THROUGH A FRIENDSHIP WITH TWO VERY BRILliant practitioners who'd "run the gauntlet" like myself and were sick and tired of being "played." We got together over a bottle of wine or two, or three, then decided to formulate a Consulting business – bidding for contracts with the Regional Government and occasionally with Private Enterprise. Everybody's heard of transformational leadership – a person who characterizes charisma; a sense of mission; inspiration; intellect – someone who stimulates his colleagues and subordinates. Aligned with and occasionally opposed to transformational leadership is transactional leadership, which is generally considered a leader who can maintain the "quality" in programs. Back in the day – mid to late 1980s, everybody wanted to be a transformational leader. The problem was not many people had the ingredients for this difficult and often perplexing role.

One other thing I forgot to define – "expert power," which according to the experts around 1960, defined a person with "unusual knowledge." Someone with "legitimate power" had the authority to make decisions over others, but for the most part had been granted this position of authority. *Jake, where are you going with all this stuff?* Basically this, what started out as a collegial friendship, ended disastrously after 10 months, for me anyway! My "friends" carried on for a further five years, ending their business and personal relationship, hating each other's guts, and then some! Along the way, at least during the 10 months I worked with them, each of us tried to impose our respective styles of transformational leadership on the other two, which ended in dismal failure! In conjunction, all of us were highly educated professionals with the egos to boot and thought we were experts and legitimate power brokers. What a "load of hooey"! We were generally pompous and pretentious "nitwits" pretending to be big shot professional Consultants smarter than everyone else or so we thought!

Please, please, please, if you're going into the Consulting field, regardless of your training, you'd better make sure you have the right temperament, knowledge, expertise, and toughness to get ahead and survive over the long haul. Just ask Donald Trump – he knows! We presumed like the idiots we were that everything would fall into place, a couple or three successful contracts and we'd have a national reputation. Yeah right – once again I was humbled, but learned a hell of a lot along the way. Enough foreplay if you must, let's get on with the Vignette and some funny anecdotes. *Please, Jake, anything!* Okay, okay, sit back, make some popcorn, crack open a beer, have some wine, red not white, it's been a long day!

One day we received a phone call from a colleague, who had finally, at age 38, become pregnant and was going on maternity leave. This person was very well regarded and qualified in a specialty area that was rare to say the least. Finding a replacement for her would be hard! Her employer asked us "Big Shot" Consultants if we knew of anyone who would be able to fill in for a year or so? Unbelievably, my business partner stated, "Yes that should be no problem" and the hunt was on, as stated by my colleague. I, on the other hand "sweat bullets," kept a straight face, and afterwards went out for drinks with my two business colleagues and dropped the "What the hell did we get ourselves into – what were you thinking of?" question. "No worries, Jake, what's your problem?" was the answer, so I shut up, finished my drink, went home, and had a good night's sleep. One week later my office door opened and my colleague rushed in exclaiming, "I've just talked with a contact in ABC Country who knows of a person who is qualified in the subspecialty area we need and would be willing to emigrate!" I couldn't believe it, and was overjoyed, as the consultation fee or more accurately the "finder's fee" would be astronomical!! The Company employing our friend had "deep pockets" and the money issue to retain the replacement individual was a trifle, or so it seemed! Again, I said to myself, this is too good to be true Jake, and it was, IN THE BEGINNING.

Three weeks later the incumbent arrived – after an incredible amount of work to complete reference checks, process passports, work visas and have contracts signed sight unseen, remember we needed a body post haste, hence, the regular protocol to fill this position was compressed. Dun da dun da, we lived to regret this decision in spades by the way! My colleague picked the gentleman up at the airport, parked him at a five-star hotel, had an expensive lunch after which our new recruit left briefly to shower, prior to meeting us at the office. My colleague with our star acquisition arrived in good spirits and I was introduced with my other business colleague to the incumbent, whose name, or as I present it here as a pseudonym, was SHAMEEB ABEEB. Unfortunately, his future nickname would be tagged, "Abeeb the Boob." My job, which I thought was basically a second-level advisory role, was in fact "Chief Liaison Officer" with the hiring Company! That is, running interference, making the transition as seamless as possible for the incumbent, as Mr. Abeeb was from a different culture and professional orientation and unfamiliar with the protocol of work requirements in this country. Yes he had foreign training, qualifying in the same specialty and subspecialty areas as our colleague on maternity leave, and had excellent, no that's too mundane, exemplary work experience, according to my colleague's research. Yes indeed, a very rare combination and not to be trifled with! Unfortunately, what transpired in the ensuing months, specifically, my designated duties with Mr. Abeeb, was another experience, believe me! Reader, from here on in forget your appointments and enjoy the Vignette. Please, read on.

There was a problem, and it was a doozy! Let me digress for a moment, as mentioned earlier, a cultural phenomenon occurred in March, 1971, when Germaine Greer's book *The Female Eunuch* was published. Women in North America encountered the Feminist

Chapter Six | 107

movement but not for the first time, as Betty Freidan's seminal work *The Feminine Mystique* was published in 1963 on the same subject. But this time something was different and whatever that something was it "clicked" – the marketing strategy/cultural tapestry of the "hippie" era, whatever, influenced *The Female Eunuch* to become a gigantic hit! It had been written for the layperson and turned up at exactly the right time, the right moment, and people, more specifically females, found a political platform that defended their rights as an oppressed minority. *On with the story, Jake!* Okay, okay – Shameeb Abeeb was not aware, nor for that matter, the least bit interested in the feminist movement, which got him and us in very hot water very quickly! About three weeks into the job, during which time I thought I'd "hand held" Mr. Abeeb through every step of his job duties, work protocol, anticipated Company politics, as he was a foreigner – the whole shebang – I found out I was deluding myself! All of this consulting stuff came tumbling down one Tuesday morning when I got a call, or more specifically a "blast," from the Director of Human Resources of the Company that employed Mr. Abeeb. "Where the hell did you get this schlub?"[11] No pleasantries from this Chutspenik![12] "I beg your pardon" was my answer, a rather meek response but a response nevertheless. "Just get your ass over here; we need to talk!" I was there in 20 minutes, sweating bullets (once again) while I swerved through traffic, exceeded the speed limit, and generally wondered what the hell was going on. I got to his building and forsaking the elevator, raced up three flights of stairs, two steps at a time, knocked on the Director's door, and was told, "Get the hell in here; you've got some explaining to do!" I shut the door behind me and for the next half hour the Chutspenik Director debriefed me on the "goings-on" with "this boob Abeeb," or as the staff preferred to call him, "Abeeb the Boob"! It seemed that the first order of the day when Mr. Abeeb was settled in was to call a staff meeting. That was fine and dandy, but here's the problem and it was a great big problem even in 1986! He was standing there in front of approximately 20 women, no males, and proceeded to

11   jerk
12   brazen fellow

explain how he wanted them to respond to his "directives"! He then proceeded to inform them of the "snapping cadence" he expected them to learn!! And if they did so quickly, things would go swimmingly well! HERE IT COMES AND DON'T BUY A GUN! He proceeded to snap his fingers once – which meant come to his work area immediately; he snapped his fingers twice, which meant follow his directives, whatever they might be; snapping three times meant get him a coffee. Are you still sitting in your seat? How's that for your first staffing problem as a brand-new BIG-SHOT CONSULTANT?!

While this "problem" was being parlayed by the Director of Human Resources of this "very prestigious Company with a national reputation," I was trying to keep a straight face, but at the same time realized the depth of a cultural problem that was being presented and shuddered at the prospects!

I then proceeded to sequester the afternoon to interview all the major players of this scenario, before approaching Mr. Abeeb. This request was granted and then some! More specifically, and this was a directive coming from the Chutspenik Director of Human Resources of this "very prestigious Company with a National reputation," and went something like this, "Get your ass in gear, change things immediately, I've got a feeling we're going to be in the papers!" Damage control was the order of the day. *But, Jake, you ask – JUST FIRE THE GUY!* It wasn't that easy, his skill-set academically was very, very rare! It would take from my perspective three months of intense, laborious work contacting colleagues from around the world to find a replacement for this particular position and for this particular period of time. A maternity leave "cover off" is not very attractive by any standards, let alone at this level of job qualification! Remember, there was no Internet in 1986, most communication was by "snail mail" – slow, pedantic transmission and fraught with problems, especially when dealing with communiqués from abroad. No – forget about firing the guy, I was in the thick of things and had to CAREFULLY think my way through this! The interview with Mr. Abeeb's female subordinates was "high-octane"! The women were enraged at his demeaning behavior, the Company for hiring "the Boob," and the Consulting firm hired to contract "this asshole relic"!

Without going into detail, it was a long, a VERY long meeting that afternoon, at the end of which three very competent professionals quit without giving notice! Ostensibly, the old "he goes or we go" ultimatum. They left! I had requested additional time to speak to Mr. Abeeb prior to any decisions being made by them, but this request fell on "deaf ears" and why the hell shouldn't it? Rightly or wrongly they left stating, "you'll have to accept the consequences of hiring the boob," uh-oh! *Uh-oh, Jake, that's it? Uh-oh!?* Okay, okay, I was in a jam!! I contacted Mr. Abeeb and made an appointment for 9 a.m., bright and early the next morning. "For what purpose may I ask?" was his retort! I placated his request with a simple, "Just to make sure there is a seamless transition with this new job; I need to hear how you're doing from your perspective." *Jake, you lying bastard, why didn't you have the guts to tell him why you really wanted the meeting?* I don't know quite frankly – but what I do know is that I was tired and frustrated! More importantly, I needed more time to think and if I'd been confrontational on the phone, I could have jeopardized a resolution of this very serious personnel problem. Or so I thought. Wrong again, Jake!

Mr. Abeeb arrived at my office bright and early 9 the next morning, a bit perplexed to say the least, as this meeting, which he felt was "impromptu," was interfering with his workday and pre-arranged schedule of activities, which were "very important"! I quickly cut to the chase explaining the nature of the problem, which was snapping cadence out and verbal repartee in! I requested his feedback and hoped for the best and here comes a major understatement – throughout this tenuous interaction I was very conflicted! To be perfectly honest, while growing up around an oppressed minority, I had experienced, on a continuum of slights to munificent insults, post-war bigotry to speak in plain English! But the critical acuity of this problem "trumped" anything I'd ever encountered and then some (no pun intended Donald)! Before I forget and you think I'm a complete dunce, I was picking up that Mr. Abeeb had a very high opinion of himself and his competence in his rarefied subspecialty and DID NOT take lightly to critical feedback! Are you also getting this feeling? Just kidding, now listen to his response to my request for change. That is, from an obvious disregard for professional protocol to better working relationships? Hold onto your hats because this was his answer, "What is the problem here? The situation is very simple, however I will repeat myself VERY S L O W L Y this time so you may comprehend my expectations." I beg your pardon?! At this point Mr. Abeeb snapped his fingers once and stated, "one snap means come to my work area immediately." Mr. Abeeb snapped his fingers twice, "two snaps means follow my directives whatever they may be, most often going to the file cabinet, providing feedback about an error, clarifying work that is being done, qualifying a result so as to provide me information to do my job better – is this so bad?" He then snapped his fingers three times, this time with a very bored expression on his face, "Three snaps means bring me a coffee." *JAKE, GET RID OF HIM, I can hear you saying, "He's from the 17th century!"* Sorry, it ain't that easy! This man's upbringing, with a very educated and brilliant mind, had not IN THE LEAST included an understanding of equality or professional decorum with the opposite sex!

Hmm, what to do? Here's what I did. "Mr. Abeeb, you must immediately cease and desist any further snapping commands at this place of employment or you will be terminated forthwith!" Here came his response, and this guy when he stood up was approximately 6 foot one (1 m. 84 cm.) and 240 pounds (115 kg.) – a big dude now, a much bigger dude in 1986 when males grew smaller, from my viewpoint anyway. "Who in God's name do you think you're talking to?" And that's with a scowl and menace I won't forget and those static glaring eyes, deep brown, liquid glaring eyes, which provoked my rather meek attempt to sound tough, "A man in very serious trouble if he doesn't abide by my request!" At this point Mr. Abeeb pushed by me – I felt like a postage stamp, *Jake, where is your 6 foot 4 inch (1 m. 91 cm.) bodyguard?* Mr. Abeeb got to the door, swung it open, strode out and slammed the door with a BANG. I phoned the Chutspenik Director of Human Resources immediately and debriefed him of the meeting with the women, the three resignations, and my meeting with Mr. Abeeb! Here comes his response, which reflected a penchant for transactional leadership – quality control/quality improvement! "You and your asshole Consulting Company are going to get sued if this situation is not contained; DO I MAKE MYSELF CLEAR?" "Clear as mud," I responded, which was followed by a click, his click not mine! Not one hour later back at the office I waited for my two business colleagues to finish their respective meetings with clients, who were hopefully easier to deal with than Mr. Abeeb. I won't bore you with the histrionics that went on for the next three hours. Unfortunately if you work in the Consulting business, "Murphy's Law" prevails – expect intangibles to rear their ugly head. Specifically, what you think is never going to happen g...damn well does happen and usually in spades! The three of us decided to contact Mr. Abeeb and have a conference call, which had become VERY in vogue during that era. *Yeah right, Jake, you sound like an old guy!* Okay, okay. Initially he refused to have anything to do with "bandit charlatans" and referred us back to the Chutspenik, Director of Human Resources, who redirected him (thank God) back to us. A meeting was eventually set up at his office, as he would not come to our CIRCUS MASQUERADE as he described our office, to discuss the matter with ERSATZ LOSER TYPES as we were described. Are you getting the picture? *Jake, I don't think he liked you very much!* No kidding, Ace. But on with the story (Ha – got you back)!

Prior to the meeting, each of us in turn debated the finer points of transformational leadership, that's how popular it was in the mid-'80s. It was hailed as the panacea of leadership and management practice. *Of course, Jake, we've heard that one already; get on with the story!* Okay, okay, we rehearsed our respective roles prior to the impending meeting. What a laugh; the long and the short of it was, "If we don't think of something fast we're going down the shitteroo!" A very sophisticated response from the team of "Big Shot Consultants," one of whom had an MBA, don't ask me from where! Nevertheless we rehearsed several scenarios that might occur and hybrid scenarios that would probably occur as in Murphy's Law. A good thing we did because as we were about to find out, Mr. Abeeb was not stupid and some tough cookie!

We arrived and knocked on his door. Mr. Abeeb was alone – we were surprised that he hadn't brought legal representation! We entered his office and sat down ready for battle. We'd decided that I'd be responsible for the opening statement, or more accurately, "indictment" of his conduct towards his female subordinates. He sat quietly taking notes, looking disconcerted but at the same time waiting patiently while the three of us, quite adroitly I might add, presented our concerns and the concerns of the Company, by which he was employed. When we finally completed our presentation, which lasted over an hour, he stated, "then are you finished?" We nodded in unison and he proceeded to carefully craft a defense of his behavior that was bordering on delusional. A fixed, idiotic array of falsehoods, inaccuracies, and most important of all, a total misrepresentation of Management's concerns about his conduct with his female subordinates! Were we on the same planet? My colleagues sat in suspended animation throughout Mr. Abeeb's carefully crafted network of lies, mostly understatements and deceit. But the "cobwebs," if there were ever any, quickly vanished! One false step verbally and you could be eaten alive, in Court that is; I was even suspicious that Mr. Abeeb was taping our meeting!

He finished with a flair, stood up, and was prepared to walk out. It was evident by his behavior that there was no room for discussion, mediation, you name it! We need ya, Jake!? I stood up quickly and off the top of my head came, "Please, no more snapping cadences at work; that has to be understood"! His response was chilling, "I will do what I do – in my Country you would be collecting trash," and walked out SLAMMING the door behind him! We sat there and I wish I could say we laughed our heads off but we didn't; we just sat there in total shock and disbelief! We returned to our office disheartened; who wouldn't be after the audacious behavior we'd just encountered! Then came the inevitable condemnations from my two, very professional business partners! "Didn't you see what he was like, Jake?! What kind of an asshole Consultant are you?! Jake, I thought you were smart but I guess you're stupid! This was a stupid BULL...mistake – thanks, Jake." Oh yes I forgot one, "I'd like to drive a stake through your f...eye!" Don't worry. I gave back

Chapter Six | 113

as good as I got, swearing a lot along the way, "You groyser dimwits are very f... stupid. You couldn't land an account or screw a dead frog if your lives depended on it. I was in the trenches with this miscreant while you were f... the dog. I hate your f...ing guts, again in English F... YOU, now do you get it?" This diatribe of contempt went on and on until finally I stated, "I've got a meeting" and left in a daze! I rushed back to the Company, ran up the stairs 2 x 2 and arrived at the Chutspenik Director of Human Resources office "lickety-split." I knocked on the door, heard the response ENTER, and walked in, shutting the door behind me. "So what happened? I'm all ears and it better be good or you're in shit!" Brilliant, just brilliant, I really appreciated all the support I was getting!

I debriefed about "you know who" while the Chutspenik Director sat impassively listening to my comments and making notes. His response was incredible in its simplicity but right on! "Monitor the bastard – keep tabs on everything he does and report back to me in the next two weeks. If this guy tries his snapping cadence one more time, he'll be terminated without severance, lawyers be damned; we've got him by the 'short and curlies'!" The next two weeks were fraught with Jake setting up an office directly adjacent to Mr. Abeeb's work area. Luckily, because of the nature of the business, there was a one-way mirror in the room where he worked. You guessed it, over the next four months I camped out in the room with the one-way mirror taking copious notes, actually setting up a functional analysis (oh yes, I forgot – Mr. Abeeb was not pleased)!

More specifically, identifying the A – B – C of Mr. Abeeb's behavioral repertoire. "A" – the antecedent events that occurred just before problem behaviors; "B" – the behaviors to be modified, obviously the number one priority was cessation of his tendency to use the snapping cadence; and finally, "C" – identifying the consequences of the events that followed the problem behaviors. A major problem was the subordinate staff, who were intimidated by the man to put it mildly, and their acquiescence to his aberrant behavior, being in fact a reinforcer, or in layman's terms a reward. Here comes the problem with this paradigm. I had decided on continuous event recording, more specifically, recording every occurrence of behavior during a specified period – his workday of approximately eight hours! I had to decide between recording frequency of behavior, duration of behavior, intensity of behavior, latency of behavior, form of behavior, or some combination of these variables! Without boring you with details, I manufactured a very cogent study of this man's day-to-day behavioral responses. He was fully aware that I was there to supervise his conduct, that was in part due to a direct, no-nonsense Letter of Warning sent to him by the Chutspenik Director of Human Resources. It required Mr. Abeeb's signature indicating that he'd read the letter and understood the consequences of deleterious conduct toward staff, or in the day-to-day operation of completing his job duties.

    Yes, I got tired and frustrated, wondering whether my analysis was in fact credible, or if we'd end up in court on a harassment charge. On and on this evaluation proceeded, throughout the better part of four months! My business partners were by now not talking to me, the problem had been contained, but obviously I couldn't be in two places at once. My partners were carrying the burden of the work and in their defense our little Consulting business was taking off – this due in part to our contract with the "very prestigious Company with a national reputation." However, little did outsiders know that I was the little Dutch boy with his thumb in the dike! The stress of worrying about Mr. Abeeb during that four-month period was incredible. I collected data, interpreted it, and presented it to the Chutspenik Director of Human Resources every two weeks. He was satisfied this "monitoring supervision thing" as he called it was working out and maybe just maybe, Mr. Abeeb would be able to complete the "cover off" maternity leave. The length of a maternity leave in those days was typically six weeks; however due to the expertise and superlative work done by my colleague taking the leave, the Company had graciously allowed her a one-year leave of absence! Quite frankly I would've been dead before the year was up, I was that stressed-out! *But what about Mr. Abeeb's behavior, Jake? What about his behavior – was he towing the line?* I know I know, I'm getting to that.

Needless to say and I use that expression a lot, Mr. Abeeb hated my guts, hated the Company, and was trying like hell to get another job in North America. It appeared he didn't want to go back home. Aha, maybe North America wasn't so bad after all! And I must say, his behavior with his subordinate staff improved better than a teeny bit. But again, this was under very controlled circumstances; he knew he was being monitored very closely – his behavior scrutinized to the nth degree and any deviation from standard working protocol as we know it in North America would have been immediately challenged! In short, a termination would jeopardize any lucrative opportunity for future work in this country. Here comes the anticlimactic ending, sorry, nothing out of left field, folks. One day in the middle of the week I got a call from the Chutspenik Director of Human Resources to come to his office forthwith (i.e., like yesterday). As you've probably noticed these calls were not to be trifled with and this man had "legitimate power," expert be damned.

He had been granted this power by the President of the Company, who happened to be his brother-in-law! You did not, if you were smart or the least bit intelligent, challenge the veracity of the directives given by the Chutspenik Director of Human Resources! When it came to the well-being of the Company's reputation, standards of practice, quality control, and quality improvement, this person was a one-man wrecking machine. If anyone challenged his authority the culprit was a "nudnik"[13] or a "moyser"[14] and dealt with post haste as in, "there's the door you dumbass…get the…outta here!"

I got to his office once again without taking the elevator and knocked on the door, "ENTER" boomed from within and I did so nervously. "Sit down, Jake, how ya doing taday?" "Okay I guess" as I turned to my file folder, taking out the files with the graphs, the data, and my narrative summary of the information collected during the past two weeks. "No need for that crap, we can fire the guy!" I was stunned, really, really stunned, my response and a rather meek one, "I beg your pardon," was met with a loud guffaw which progressed to hysterical laughter and continued on and on for

13   nuisance, obnoxious person
14   informer

what seemed like almost a minute. It was contagious and I started laughing as well, not knowing what I was laughing about! When the laughing subsided the Chutspenik Director of Human Resources' response almost knocked me off my chair, "I just got a phone call less than an hour ago from Abeeb's predecessor – SHE WANTS TO COME BACK – SHE'S BORED!" I couldn't believe it; it was too good to be true!! I leaned over and shook the gentleman's hand and asked when she would be returning exactly? The response was a bit startling, "a week tamarra morning" – "I beg your pardon, one week from tomorrow morning?" "Yeah a week tamarra morning; as we talk Abeeb is being paid out and escorted off the premises – Jake, you did it!" What did I do, apart from alienating my working relationship with my business partners, potentially jeopardizing my professional reputation with my peers, infuriating a professional in a subspecialty who would undoubtedly shoot his mouth off about how crappy he was treated, anyway it was over! After a few minutes of small talk and politely declining an invitation for a business lunch with the Chutspenik Director of Human Resources and the President's brother-in-law I got up and left. LEFT in the real sense I might add! I got back to the office, telephoned my two business partners for a debriefing meeting, which was also strangely anticlimactic. I found out later from a disgruntled former secretary that a Letter of Non-Confidence had been crafted behind my back, ostensibly an impeachment of me! The document absolving them of any responsibility or "fallout" in layman's terms of the Abeeb Shameeb affair in case he sued for damages. Thanks folks, it was nice working with you, or as my mother used to say, "Love your enemies in case your friends turn out to be bastards!" Yeah right, and *whatever happened to Shameeb Abeeb, Jake?* Who the hell cares – on to the next Chapter.

Of Note: Before you read on please review the following: Co-dependent colleagues often say "yes" hoping you will go away so they won't have to bother with the time, energy, whatever, with what they've agreed to do. They frequently say "yes" when they mean "no" because they want to be approved of and also to avoid conflict! They haven't learned that in "normal" working relationships people agree to complete projects they are capable of doing and plan to do and then they abide by their word. In a co-dependent's frame of reference, promises are made to be broken and are made countless times at the expense of credibility and smooth working alliances. THE PROCESS of perpetual agreement with no intention of following through becomes an unfortunate working paradigm, creating problems at an exponential rate! Dysfunctional organizations have their fair share of co-dependent employees – BEWARE of the "nice guy approach"; it's often followed by a paucity of action or inaction. Now you can read on.

CHAPTER SEVEN

VIGNETTE 30

WELL THAT WAS IT, I QUIT MY JOB, TOOK A QUICK THREE-WEEK VACATION somewhere to clear my head and restore my faith in myself. I had always thought I was a responsible professional and competent judge of character, but the conflicts at work were undermining my confidence and I was beginning to wonder what lay in store for me in the future. Wouldn't you?! I was not to be let down, so please, read on. When I got back from my holiday, semi-rested, I embraced the unenviable task of hunting down a job. Three months later I sat down in the Boardroom of a Major Care Facility somewhere in North America giving what I still maintain is the best interview of my career! Lo and behold I got the job and started almost immediately, I was still only 37 years old but a "shop worn" 37! Relative to the general population I was very well educated and made an excellent salary, but something was missing – you guessed it – the wife, the picket fence, the two mischievous "rug rats"? I'll touch on that later.

I was purposely demoting myself to a mid-management position with approximately 40 staff and 12 disciplines to oversee. The budget was okay, my boss, the Executive Director, was a right-wing bureaucrat who played favorites like nobody's business. Of major concern was her marked fear of her immediate subordinate, simply one of the most ruthless, calculating and "cold-blooded" individuals I'd ever met! She loved, no she bathed in power and control, a master of the double entendre, the "cut and thrust" of senior management repartee! Somehow I admired her ability to wield this extreme authority with little, if any fear of retribution – people were truly intimidated by her coercive power!! No one during the four years I was her subordinate directly challenged her behavior, NO ONE. At my first meeting she addressed me formally by last name, asking me twice to remind her what my first name was, which she immediately forgot. She set down the modus operandi of her supervision expectations, which included the following: Her two cohorts, not as bright and metaphorically speaking two thugs really, would visit me every Friday afternoon from 1 until 2 p.m. I was to present them with a pre-arranged document detailing and itemizing my staffing strengths and needs, budgetary updates, short- and long-term goal achievements vis-à-vis the Mission-Mandate of the Organization.

In reality, this information could be used as an indictment against any Manager who did not perform aggressively, nor could not or would not align themselves with her philosophy of "doing business." Oh yes, I almost forgot, I was informed that I would be asked about any nefarious activity which I'd encountered from my staff – made up of 12 different disciplines! That's a lot of different philosophical approaches to address! Get this one – if I refused to comply with this "request," I would be perceived as insubordinate and negligent in my job responsibilities. "What would happen to me under these circumstances?" I asked timidly; can you believe my servile behavior? But are you surprised after my previous work experiences? "That depends" was the terse response! The "nefarious activity" part was in her mind the biggest and most important aspect of the one-hour interview held weekly between Yours Truly and the two "Rottweiler twins," as they were labeled. This request for disclosure, in reality a potential noose to hang yourself, was to all intents and purposes, a directive and not to be taken lightly! In my head I reminded myself that I was a competent Manager and a better leader than most of the geshtrofters[15] in my position of authority at that Organization; that was my ego talking and pride, that deadly word PRIDE.

---

15   cursed people

So what you say – Jake, she's a "hard-nosed" administrator, so the hell what, you're a tough, no nonsense guy you can take it, again and again – yeah right, by now after 15 years in the field I was getting a little punchy! The problem lay in the two Rottweiler twins and the accuracy and honesty, or lack thereof, when conveying my debriefing session at their weekly meeting with the boss-lady. Our boss, the Second-in-Command, was given my written document with quantitative information, but she also depended on the "twins" debrief of the verbal information I provided them each week. The Rottweiler twins were very used to "dodgy" Managers and would zero in on these poor, defenseless shmendriks[16] whom they maligned and simply drove out of the Organization in time, which they had plenty of! No, if you wanted to survive you had to be fairly straightforward at these weekly meetings, attempt to develop a rapport with the Rottweiler twins while biting your tongue, giving them accurate data and then getting back to the business at hand. Jake, we need ya!

Nomothetic methods of evaluation focus on statistical probabilities that compare the individual's response to normative data. All this means in English is the Second-in-Command had amassed over the 17-year period that she was ostensibly (via coercion) the legitimate power at this Organization, an inordinate amount of data! She completed regressive analyses on behaviors to get statistical probabilities on the likelihood of a particular behavior or set of behaviors occurring in the future. Any management personnel who were statistical outliers in this woman's comparison of their responses in the one-hour meetings, the so-called "supervision sessions" and data provided, would precipitate doomsville for the poor unfortunate umglik![17] *Why, Jake, speak English, why?* Because if their behavioral responses and data from their respective clinical programs did not match with the normative data this woman had compiled over the years, regarding that particular behavior or set of behaviors, this was a big scary "NO NO"! The woman covered her ass and then some folks! *But Jake, we need a concrete example, just give*

---

16   nincompoops
17   born loser

us an example! Okay, okay, I think I said it right but enough academic exhibitionism. Here goes an example.

A colleague who worked for me on a consulting basis attempted to define during a weekly clinical meeting a very rare form of cognitive deterioration, a type of dementia, called Wilson's disease. Because of its rarity a medical practitioner in family practice might come across this specific dementia possibly three times in a 30-year career, if that. I'll give you the good stuff first; this was a highly intelligent man with an undergraduate credential from Stanford University – obviously not a slouch by any stretch of the imagination! He and I often crossed swords because of bad chemistry, a mutual lack of respect and cognitive dissonance, when we found ourselves in general proximity from each other, like 25 yards (23 m.)! We got to be pretty feisty, including some "low blows," but I did respect his intelligence and ability to articulate knowledge – but that was about it! Sorry, I digress, halfway through the meeting, in walks another colleague, with a double specialty in medicine and an international reputation which was much deserved! He sat across the table from my nemesis and down two or three colleagues. Before I forget – this was a weekly team meeting with approximately 15 people in attendance. After listening to my "best friend" spout off about the very rare Wilson's disease for maybe five minutes maximum, Dr. IQ waved him off with a gesture of contempt and simply took over with a 20-minute discussion of the minutia of this very rare neurological illness!

Here comes the bad stuff, the minutes of the meeting were transcribed and a comparison of the responses of both individuals compared, by you know who! This, I presume while holding a text in neurology or at least neuropsychiatry in one hand, while reading a text on teaching ethics with the other, all used as normative references, who the hell knows – I wasn't there. A regression analysis on the areas discussed throughout the meeting was then completed, by comparing a tabulated format (matrix) of the textbook information with both colleagues' statements regarding Wilson's disease, which was plunked into a computer and analyzed. Guess who won? A few weeks later I got a call from the Second-in-Command to come up to her very large, ostentatious office. This appointment was not at our regular, pre-arranged meeting time but rather, above and beyond the weekly "supervision session" with the Rottweiler twins and at a brand new time – her convenience not mine, not even a compromised "our" time. Dun da dun dun!

I won't bore you with the details of the meeting, but the bottom line or at least my impression of the bottom line and the interesting discussion that ensued, entailed Wilson's disease. *I'm not surprised, Jake, don't be coy!* Okay, okay. More specifically, the obvious disparity in knowledge and factual accuracy that both parties conveyed while discussing this very rare disease. Give me a break, that's like comparing a Webster's dictionary with a hunk of papyrus along the Nile River! This simply was not a fair comparison and for once I did stand my ground and defended both sides, specifically, their pros and cons as professionals in a clinical setting. What a laugh, it went nowhere! She'd made up her mind and in so many words told me to think up some pretense to use to defend a decision NOT to renew my "best friend's" consulting contract. Quite frankly from her perspective that was the end of it; she had a busy day and my presence was no longer needed! As I recall she literally waved me off!? I couldn't believe it, the ignorance of that gesture was appalling! *Were some cracks in the armor starting to show, Jake? All those previous blows to the head precipitating pre-senile dementia – a sign you've been in the shootin' gallery too long?* Sorry, I just wandered off for a second reminiscing about the incident. But you get the picture – of course you do, you're bright, intelligent people with a clinical orientation. I hope I clarified the way she did business and didn't make a mistake or leave anybody behind. How do you "action plan" with an individual like this? Here goes. Believe me, going to her immediate superior would have exacerbated the situation and then some! That person was in the Second-in-Command's back pocket, made a very generous living and had the typical ruthless streak most cowards possess and will utilize if the status quo is challenged. Nope, that option was definitely out!

Yes, the staff got together and yes, we developed another "longitudinal study" as was described in Vignette 28. She was far too savvy and not quite as grandiose as Ned "the lead pipe cinch," you remember him! On this occasion it was decided to bide our time and meet regularly, clandestine meetings of course, to address what appeared to be marked traits of obsessive-compulsive behavior cloaked in micromanagement stratagem and perspicacious intuition. *That's a lot of big words, Jake, we get the picture, she's damn smart!* You got it.

For the time being let me flip to a subplot of the story. A "ripple-down effect" had begun to occur throughout the Organization, ostensibly mimicking the idiosyncratic management practices of the Second-in-Command. Not copying her practices exactly, but in fact utilizing her draconian methods to ensure "consistency, efficiency and effectiveness." Her three favorite words that I heard repeatedly throughout my four-year tenure under her reign! Let me provide an example: A colleague with an equivalent sized program to mine ran staff meetings like a drill sergeant. During weekly case conferences he demanded that each representative discipline, which numbered about a dozen, utilize the same presentation format. That is, the same headings, areas to be covered, sets and subsets describing those areas to be monitored, etc., etc.! It sounds practical but it wasn't workable and for a variety of crappy reasons, too many to discuss at this time (or any time) to be blunt. Subsequently, the ANXIETY – the rigid, anticipatory anxiety exhibited by this insecure Manager, my colleague and generally a good guy, if the various disciplines did not adhere EXACTLY to his directives! This contre-coup, "ricochet" effect tempted fate big time as in reprimands and outbursts from Mr. Generally a Good Guy person! I guess you could call it osmosis, as he began to reflect the Second-in-Command's neurotic exactness and "standard of excellence," her words again. Superficially this authoritarian, command style of management bastardized a Total Quality Management approach by attempting to copy its tenets of quality control, quality improvement, internal and external customer satisfaction! Unfortunately, the ingredients of this ersatz approach caused rigidity and reactivity amongst the staff, the antithesis of creativity! In English the presentation format was stifling, promoted animosity, staff dissension, and militant opposition to change. The "blinkers" were on and stayed on for a long, long period of time!

Another example was a "Centralized Referral System," which was put in place by the Second-in-Command "to combat duplication and wastage of staff time." Specifically, a triage team was developed to manage and vet the referrals coming into the Center. On paper it sounded good; these individuals would match the referrals and level of estimated attention they required with an appropriate clinical program/unit. The Managers of the respective programs in this Centralized Referral System became aware very quickly of favoritism regarding easier case referrals going to the friends of the triage team and if you were on the "outs" with this team or a member of the team, you got stuck with the more difficult and demanding referrals! The obvious result – the burnout rate was much higher on a per capita basis on a team that consistently obtained referrals needing moderate-high care requirements! Forget about the criteria that were set up for referrals to be dispersed appropriately and took upwards of a year to develop and standardize! Yes, the Second-in-Command had developed on paper a very "consistent, efficient and effective" intake process! But in practice it was bastardized, sodomized, and all the other "ized" that have a pejorative context! I fought for four years to have an individualized intake system due to the nature of the specialized program I ran, but to no avail. In these situations you start to resent BIG TIME, I know I did! The Managers of all the Care Units met once per week, Monday mornings from 9 to 11 a.m. There were approximately 15 managers representing 12 different disciplines at this meeting, chaired by the Second-in-Command, whose slapdash "cut and thrust" scathing vitriol was actually quite pristine in its cruelty! Think of the actress Glenn Close playing a refined Don Rickles sprinkled with Bob Newhart mannerisms/quips and you've got an idea of what transpired in those weekly, two-hour meetings! No one could match her acerbic nature during the meeting, but afterwards was another story, as her behavior influenced some of the more insecure Managers to try copying her style. Unbelievable but true and who got it in the end? You guessed it, the "grunts," who else, the poor slobs that do all the work, that's who!

The line staff wondering what the hell had gone on this week and the next week ad infinitum, because inevitably there was some newfangled idea brought back to try out on "the Units," which set in motion an emotional continuum ranging from the doldrums to dysphoric haze! A steady supply of "technique" for lack of a better word was manufactured to "improve working conditions on the Units"!? It was thought up and packaged by Senior Management, headed by you know who, the rationale being to promote staff morale! Trials were initiated to standardize these various techniques and they all failed. More specifically, the malignant animosity stated earlier began to rear its ugly head! Staff would purposely sabotage data and the junior management (that's me) would turn their proverbial heads and take a "blind eye"! *Why, Jake, why, that's not you!* A good point, it wasn't me! We were simply too overworked to bother attempting to make things better, that is, completing additional work – which we hadn't bought into in the first place! That's when the staff decided to form a "committee," secret of course, to address the situation. Here's what happened.

One day my colleague from the second floor approached me with news that one of the Rottweiler twins was transferring to another Organization and the Second-in-Command had chosen as her replacement a strong, capable, even formidable individual who was shrewd, cunning, a chameleon in fact, AND very intelligent. Here's the good thing – she was one of us! She hated the Second-in-Command and would stop at nothing to have her transferred or fired. Aha, the good guys have a chance for once! But before I continue I can't go on without bringing up something important. Around this time I met my lovely wife, became engaged, and got married, all in the space of seven months, and we're still together 23 years later. The commitment of my relationship and love for her kept me going and does to this day, as I work in this oft-times oblique and demanding Industry! *On with the story, Jake, this mushy stuff is wrecking the plot!* Okay, okay, keep your shirt on! *What to do, Jakey, what to do?* I'll tell you what we did – we had a classic, passive-aggressive action plan – a clandestine meeting of course! This included all the junior managers we could trust, which was approximately a dozen, including the replacement for the Rottweiler twin who transferred to another job in another Organization. We schemed and schemed and basically came up with a strategy – to assess the Second-in-Command's "attitude." *I beg your pardon, Jake?* You got it right the first time!

We formulated an assessment paradigm, "Comparative Analysis of Attitude" against norm-referenced criteria. We developed a definition and interpretation which we examined against the methods/procedures, or array of procedures, that the Second-in-Command used against us individually and as a group during our weekly meetings.

We developed "norms" for her methods/procedures and appropriate validity and reliability estimates, which looking back were a little "dodgy" to say the least. However, the inter-rater reliability was excellent, everybody knew exactly what to look for and did so very accurately throughout the duration of the evaluation. I know because I cross-validated their responses to assess accuracy. Subsequently we developed a "criterion measure" which we tested; her behavior or performance against what we thought were absolute standards of performance used by such people as Edward Deming, the father of Total Quality Management practice. In essence, her behavior was coded and then matched in form and content against an absolute standard and then given a rating on a Likert Scale (i.e., 1–4). We included performance objectives which entailed an acceptable level of performance. Scores regarding attitude/method/procedures were tallied on a weekly basis. In the Second-in-Command's case we determined five areas of attitude which we defined in behavioral terms to be assessed. A predetermined percentage/number correct was developed, in regards to achieving a predetermined level of acceptable performance attributed the five types of behavioral responses, reflecting attitude.

In essence, we were assessing attitude performance with behaviorally stated objectives. That is, five areas of attitude which were assessed and prioritized regarding areas of concern. Lastly, the percentage of correct items regarding attitude as presented on a weekly basis was calculated. We were then able to give an "estimate interpretation" of the Second-in-Command's ability to improve. We even had a section at the end stating, "Attitude Interpretation," where we could tally up on each of the five areas of assessment of attitude, a response such as, "you have performed at 90% accuracy as measured against an absolute standard X Y Z so we estimate that you will behave about nine out of ten times in a similar manner." Then we would state for each of the five attitude factors assessed, how a person should respond ideally which, as stated above, was measured against an absolute standard.

Not bad hunh (eh), once again it took about three months to develop and put into action and here's how we did it. *Wait a minute, Jake – why didn't you guys just go to her Superior and put the "goods" on the table?* Answer – back in the 1980s it didn't work that way. It wasn't that easy, or in most of the places I've worked anyway. Management opinion was sacrosanct and their attitude was very unforgiving when challenged! *Gee, Jake, maybe you worked in crappy work environments?* Maybe so, but then so did an awful lot of other people I've talked to in the Industry! Okay on with story, the data started rolling in and the results, from our point of view, were very positive, more specifically, the Second-in-Command was NOT making the grade! The behavioral dimensions of attitude being assessed were indicating a big negative valence "across the board." Someone's brilliant brain idea to compare each of the five attitude factors with an absolute standard did the trick! After approximately six months of investigation, an indictment of information regarding the Second-in-Command's failure to manage appropriately in a number of work performance areas was received. A great many areas actually, which reflected markedly inferior work performance! Aha, her proverbial "goose was cooked" or slightly parboiled at this point, but on with the story. *Good idea, Jake.* Okay, okay.

There is no other way to put it, we had her by the short and curlies, but what to do with the data? What to do with the data? While we pondered this dilemma at the local "watering hole" one week, suddenly in walked a friend from Martial Arts, by name of

Billy O. "Havin' an evenin' meeting are ya, d'ya mind if I sit here?" There was a pregnant pause of about 3/10th of a second and then somebody said (actually it was me), "Billy I want you to meet some friends," and that's how it all began. Billy O. was a very successful entrepreneur, multimillionaire, two-time divorcé with a string of girlfriends and a "countryfied" manner that was very disarming. He knew within 15 minutes we were a dissenting group and by the end of the evening after a few too many cocktails, people had disclosed much too much about our caper regarding the Second-in-Command. That was the upside and with Billy there was no downside, thank God and Jesus Christ, because if he'd ratted us out we would've been totally vulnerable to a variety of retaliations and none of them nice! That's how much trust he engendered by his manner, actual gentility, and extreme insight into our problem. He returned the following week with an answer and I bet you want to know what it was. *Spit it out, Jake.* Okay, okay.

Billy O.'s suggestion as he held court at the watering hole was very simple and quite plausible. Here it goes almost verbatim, "Take the information, 'mask' the identity of the Second-in-Command and send a representative from the clandestine management group to meet with the local politician with ties to the funding body of your Organization. Request an interview, then do a presentation on 'Effective Evaluation of Management Protocol.' At the end of the presentation with the report that you submitted to me, which is an indictment, he will ask the inevitable question, 'I would love to know who this phantom Manager is? But I know you can't breach confidentiality – ah shucks.' Being the crafty, 'slimeball' politician that he is, my bottom dollar is that he'll address the situation. Why you say? If there's potential for scandal, which in this case is inevitable, he will want to feather his bed politically. You watch, he'll invite the leader of this group, or who he perceives is the leader, for a business lunch/liquid libation in an effort to source the Second-in-Command's identity." And with that little speech he stopped as quickly as he started and ordered a drink – a double scotch and soda. What happened to Billy O.'s good old boy accent – it was gone like yesterday's news. There was a pragmatic, ruthless side to this man – the end justifies the means, he who survives wins, kill or be killed, etc., etc. People sat there stunned, literally speechless! There were a few mild rebuttals such as, "But this would cost her her job." Billy O. nodded and went back to nursing his brand-new scotch and soda. I jumped in, "Billy, we'll have to think this over." Billy O. nodded and went back to ministering his drink.

Jake – what the hell happened? Wait a second and you'll find out – Yes, the inevitable phone call came from the slimeball politician with "deep pockets" with the funding body of our Organization. At that point we decided to send, or should I say more accurately, requested to send, not the Rottweiler twin replacement – who was too aggressive and hated politicians. She was behind us 100 percent, don't get me wrong, but for this mission, forget it! She would've flunked miserably! No, we sent Ms. R. instead, a 31-year-old librarian who was a former soldier and Martial Arts expert, with a penchant for justice and if it had then existed I'm certain a "tea party" Republican! *A Black Belt, Jake!? You sent a Tea Party Republican Black Belt to meet with the slimeball politician?* YUP, you got it the first time!

She liked to drink and when she drank she got mouthy, "potty mouthy" if you know what I mean. Just the person we needed to disclose our little secret and get us all in "trouble" – *yeah right, Jake, we get the picture!* We had to figure out after she accepted the mission, of course, what ingredients of the plan of action against the Second-in-Command we didn't want her to discuss with the slimeball politician. Reverse psychology, we knew after three or four "highballs," Ms. R. would disclose big time and she did just that! Everything Billy O. stated came to fruition and I even think Ms. R. ended up spending the night with the slimeball politician! I'm not exactly sure if this happened, but I do know from the "gossip mill" that she didn't come home until the following morning. *What a stretch, Jake, maybe she visited her Aunt Isabelle?* Okay, okay.

But Jake, what happened to the Second-in-Command? Actually and very quickly – I mean within three weeks, an external body of Examiners investigated the management protocol of our Organization. The paper we developed was brought forward with the identity of the Manager masked, but used as "Exhibit A" on how *not* to run an Organization. Actually in spades how *not* to run an Organization! If it hadn't been for the Second-in-Command's 17-year tenure she would've lost her job – probably the very day the Examiners gave feedback regarding their findings! Nope, unfortunately the scapegoat was the Second-in-Command's cowardly Superior who "got the axe." And that's the way it goes in Senior Management! Don't worry, the Second-in-Command got hers, kind of! She was given a lateral transfer within a year to a much smaller portfolio, a big slap in the face for that cruel, demeaning human being, poetic justice be damned! *Jake, you're getting "heavy"!* Maybe a little, but I remember the wake of talent that was lost at the Organization because of the Second-in-Command's egregious behavior – totally appalling! Unfortunately nothing was done until the staff had had enough and took matters into their own hands. Yeah, I guess I'm getting heavy, on to the next Vignette. But before I go, I must celebrate the passing of the late, great Billy O.! He died a couple of years ago; I was told a business deal went bad, and he was done in. Who knows what the real story is, maybe he got wise and "went missing." I do know I will miss his good-natured humor, easy-going manner, and that lubricious, carefully cultivated rural charm! That's the way it goes, here today gone tomorrow, and life is not fair; now on to the next Vignette!

VIGNETTE 31

THE EPITHALAMIUM IN VIGNETTE 30'S ORGANIZATION THROUGHOUT OUR time of troubles involved a couple of "cagey" veterans, jerks actually, whom I forgot to mention. These two colleagues, we nicknamed "Chip and Dale" after the pair of ground squirrels on the weekly Bugs Bunny *Looney Tunes* cartoon show of my childhood. Each rodent had a distinctive manner of responding to the other's question in an overly polite, nonconfrontational "sing song" fashion. An inspired dance of co-dependency, to use modern schtik.[18] I believe the dialogue and repartee invented by the Warner Bros. writers of

---

18   piece, bit of acting

this cartoon series was written on two levels. At work my pair of professional miscreants observed, evaluated, and heard everything, then commenced an extended diatribe on company time which exhausted all within earshot!

After the downfall of the Second-in-Command, approximately three months after our campaign to undermine her authority, the new "Sheriff" arrived in town. Let's call him, not her this time, Maccabeus "The Hammer." This guy was a "Mr. Grant" caricature from the Mary Tyler Moore show of the 1970s. A no-nonsense, "redneck," right wing reactionary approach to everything! A guy with a functionary mentality when it came to work, recreation, and don't get in my way or I'll run you over, philosophy of living – apart from that, generally a good person – just don't cross him! But that's exactly what happened! Well, kind of anyway, because he took an instant dislike to Chip and Dale and vice versa. They may have got away with their obsequious, servile crap by humoring the Second-in-Command, but not this guy! I can state quite frankly that he did not have a narcissistic bone in his body. He achieved everything by hard work, diligence, and political guile to survive in the senior management "jungle" but not at anyone's expense, unless they crossed him – then look out and I mean look out! Here's what happened and it's quite humorous in a sick, ignominious kind of way! Reader, don't laugh too hard! Sit back and enjoy the Vignette!

One day Chip and Dale happened to be having a few drinks, cocktails to be more accurate, at a local "watering hole." Guess who rolled in "loaded" after a football game but Maccabeus. He was alone, minded his own business, sat at a booth and began ordering boiler-makers, that is, doubles with beer chasers. Both gentlemen, "feeling no pain," strolled over and made the mistake of imposing their lubricious charm on Maccabeus. A stupid, stupid mistake!! He hadn't invited them, he didn't like them, and was wise enough to figure out their motive in talking to him was not genuine but untoward. Devious in English – they were up to no good and he put a stop to it forthwith! More precisely, GET THE F... OUT OF MY FACE, which they did, and he went back to drinking and getting hammered, or even more hammered to be accurate. A few weeks later after all of this had seemingly blown over, Chip and Dale made a big mistake at a local business consortium. This organization hosted monthly Venture Capital meetings at which time our nudnik[19] pair chose to "shoot their mouths off." They belonged to this "Opportunity Palace" because in their heart of hearts they wanted to be very successful entrepreneurs – at what I can't say! Anyway, after a few cocktails someone asked them where they worked and they stated our Organization's name, which ended up being a VERY bad thing to do! After a few more cocktails, you guessed it, they started to disclose, no that's too polite, they double- and triple-shot their mouths off about the politics of the Organization!

In their precise words, "we have this stupid windbag boss with a brain the size of a pea, a micro dick so small he needs a magnifying glass to urinate, which is often 'cause he has a serious drinking problem, etc., etc."! Dun da dun dun! They shouldn't oughta done that?! Because guess what happened? Someone standing nearby who overheard Chip and Dale was the sister of a Board member of our Organization, who happened to be very, very rich and very, very influential! Chip and Dale returned to work on Monday and entered the Board room for our weekly management meeting. It was of course chaired by Maccabeus "The Hammer" who happened to be the lover, or former lover, of said Board member! Yes, Maccabeus had many sides we didn't know about, his personal life being one of them! Conversely, we did know this about the man, his ability to "wield the sword" when he had to and this particular morning he welded his sword into Chip and Dale's respective skulls, metaphorically speaking of course.

Prior to the meeting, I had passed Maccabeus in the hall and he winked at me! This man did not wink at anybody and to my knowledge had no proclivities towards same gender colleagues. He kept his distance, did not gossip, expected you to do your job to the best of your abilities, and hated "whiners" and cowards, which fit the bill of course for our two friends! Another interesting fact was after everyone had entered the Board room and sat down – everyone except Maccabeus, that is, he subsequently entered the Board room

---

19   nuisance, obnoxious person

and asked for a volunteer to help him push a very large and heavy desk over to the door. No, let's be completely honest, he and the volunteer pushed half the desk ACROSS the doorway. What was this all about? People didn't say anything because we just didn't! The meeting proceeded as per previous weeks, Maccabeus asking questions, demanding answers but rarely reprimanding mistakes in public. He didn't have to, he had weekly one-on-one meetings with his management staff and that's when you saw his keen intelligence towards accuracy, competence, and vision! Vision of where he wanted the Organization to go, how he wanted to get there, and how we had to work as a team with him as the designated leader quarterbacking his team.

If Maccabeus liked you, he allowed you a lot of latitude to do your job, the "dignity of risk" to initiate action/projects when sometimes you succeeded and sometimes you failed! He liked "gutsy" people on his team. Conversely, those staff he disliked, or in Chip and Dale's case DESPISED – he rode and rode and rode their respective asses into the ground! Brutally into the ground, empathy be damned, it was not in his vocabulary for those poor unfortunate staff he wanted out! He was more than pleased when they announced, as most staff did that he brutalized, that they had resigned and were leaving! He made a point of cruelly degrading them – not in front of a group, but one-on-one in his office! Many a time, at least five or six times anyway, I saw staff leave his office after one of those meetings "in a state." This guy could be an emotional bone crusher! Let me expand and see if you think I'm exaggerating. Reader, be forewarned, this is scary stuff!

Nowadays this kind of behavior is simply not tolerated, but in the late 1980s–early 1990s it was still around but thankfully not for long!! Maccabeus, out of the blue, started to question or more accurately interrogate Chip and Dale, and I began to cringe! They looked at each other and I truly believe they knew "the jig was up"! A most interesting thing happened in this power-play by Maccabeus – he strolled over without losing the cadence and articulation of his condemnation of the pair, sat down on the desk which was halfway across the doorway and began swinging his legs – back and forth, back and forth. Finally with a bang of his heels against the drawers of the desk he stopped and glared at Chip and Dale. Out boomed "HAVE YOU GOT THE BALLS TO SAY ANYTHING, YOU BACKSTABBERS?" They didn't and we just sat there; a few of us smiled but most of us wondered what was going to happen next! Both gentlemen shook their heads and got up to leave – yeah right! Here's the problem, Maccabeus decided THEY would be the chosen two to push this immensely heavy business desk away from the door, in order to leave the Board room. He wasn't going to and if they wanted to leave the meeting before the rest of us they'd have to move the desk themselves! Guess what, no one and I mean NO ONE, offered to help them move the desk! This was Maccabeus's test of the group dynamics, nothing was stated but everything revealed itself, in this one last act of cruelty with this pair of nudniks!!

Both gentlemen were not large physically and would be called "Metrosexual" in current shtik. Perfect hair, perfect teeth, perfect shoes, perfect jacket, perfect tie, perfect aftershave lotion, perfect diction, perfect vocabulary, perfect grammar, and, lastly, sharing perfect recipes. Try as they might, the desk wouldn't move – once or twice they lost their footing in their efforts to move the desk and slipped, falling to the floor. They started to swear and Maccabeus, by now sitting at the head of the Board table adjacent to the desk that was halfway across the door –smiled and smiled, while he made notes and looked scornfully at the rest of us. I think a lesson in humility was being taught that day. *No kiddin', Jake! Is that what you call it, what d'ya think we need, a roadmap and an apple? C'mon!* Okay, okay.

Chip – or it could have been Dale – voided in his pants! Not a nice thing to see, a metrosexual with a pee stain on the front of his beautifully pressed pants! That was it for me; I got up and was followed by two colleagues and helped Chip and Dale push the business desk over to the wall, allowing the door to open. Both men left the meeting totally beaten and humiliated – they resigned the next day! Are you stunned, shocked, surprised even, by the "Hammer's" method of retribution? Certainly you are – at least if you've got a heart you are! In current management practice and even then, his behavior was appalling, but remember in the early 1990s brutal power politics, although rare in this field, did happen and not infrequently – *no kiddin', Jake?*

Lastly and as a postscript, Maccabeus was transferred shortly thereafter in a less than dramatic fashion. No one knows whether he asked for the transfer or it was imposed, but one day he was gone, WHOOSII, just like that, gone! In retrospect, for that 18-month period we had an old-fashioned "standup guy" at the helm, albeit beyond the pale by today's standards. But what the hell, he was a step up from the "Second-in-Command." Remember her!

VIGNETTE 32

ONE DAY A FEW WEEKS AFTER MACCABEUS HAD LEFT AND I WAS HAVING A quiet lunch pondering my future, a colleague, let's call him Fred, came over and sat down. Fred was a watered-down Maccabeus. At work he was a task master, with a "my way or the highway" approach to his particular profession. His staff were genuinely fearful of his brusque manner but respectful of his knowledge, champion heart, and organizational abilities. From my point of view, they could have had a much worse boss. Fred's main failing was his ability to rub people the wrong way and without the slightest inclination to appease, or in any way apologize for his manner. That behavior did not win many friends and in fact made quite a few enemies! But what the hell, I liked lonely old Fred in the same way I like strawberries, a little bit at a time, otherwise, run for the bushes or have an accident?!

On this specific day Fred wanted to talk about a mutual colleague whom he had "the hots" for, and me being me, thoughtful, empathic, Jake – that day anyway – listened to Fred's heart-rending meanderings of attraction for this particular female co-worker. She was an equestrian, owned two horses, and from my point of view could have been a horse herself, or at least a Shetland pony. She wore casual, unpretentious garb, neat, but very often odoriferous. There was always or seemed to be always a distinct farm odor that permeated her attire. The females at work and some of the metrosexual males made reference to her miasmic oddness, but who cares? She was a lovely, down to rural earth individual who I thought could be in the running as a significant other for lonely old Fred. Fred who was going to be dead if he didn't bed Ruth, the rural "hotbox" – his words not mine. I encouraged Fred to contact the rural hotbox for a date and he did what I bid 'cuz it led to bed and not dead, with Rural Ruth! *Jake, I'm gonna get sick!* Okay, okay.

Believe me, he got a lot of action in a short period of time from this very "hot" but mono-dimensional, uncompromising person. *Jake, why the hell was she intransigent?* Hold your horses, I'm getting to that part, a very BIG part, so be patient, defer your gratification for five minutes!

A few weeks later, once again I was sitting having a quiet lunch contemplating my navel, when who should show up but Fred, lonely old Fred. This time he had a whopper of a story, no pun intended. Fred would visit his inamorata every few days for some "nookie", which was fine and dandy, it couldn't have happened to a better man. However, there was a minor problem, that being a big black stallion named "Tombstone" who stood in the field and became gigantically aroused, as in a three-foot (i.e., 90 cm.) erection when viewing lonely old Fred's car arriving! To further elaborate, emphasizing a different perspective – listen to the following! Rural Ruth made mention that the black stallion "was the best stud on the ranch – look at the size of that wang and those balls, he's sired eleven colts with that six gun," etc. She was so proud of her animal's virility and the fact that her horse became aroused SO QUICKLY and SO OFTEN! *What'd'ya expect, Jake – stallions like to get it on.* I know, I know, I guess Rural Ruth's matter-of-fact description precipitated a basic insecurity in lonely old Fred. Because from that day on and being a shy city boy, he couldn't get past the horse's member, its size and proportion, regardless of the fact that Tombstone was a stallion, "the best stud on the ranch, etc." What transpired every time lonely old Fred visited his girlfriend was the black stallion, who stood in the middle of the pasture, would spring an erection coinciding with Rural Ruth strolling over to meet lonely old Fred.

After a while, Tombstone would trot over to the fence, which was approximately 20 yards (18 m.) away, somehow maintaining this giant erection while the two "lovebirds" embraced, kissed, and proceeded to walk arm in arm back to the house, where they did their own breeding. So what you say, you've got a horny horse who is either in love with lonely old Fred, Fred's car, or Fred's paramour Rural Ruth. Well it obviously bugged lonely old Fred, who couldn't erase the size of the horse's gigantic member from his brain, which consequently interfered with quality lovemaking, more specifically the foreplay stuff, which shut down big-time. On to the next paragraph! Speaking from a male perspective, this is scary stuff!

Lonely old Fred asked my advice about his problem! Specifically, "I'm pretty well hung, eight inches (i.e., 20 cm.) at least, I shouldn't be insecure, but Jake this horse thing is gettin' me down" (no kidding). H'mm, what to do? Remembering approximately five percent of males have an eight-inch (20 cm.) penis when erect – that puts the problem into perspective, if you know what I mean, guys! Why don't we put it into an operant behavioral paradigm? To the best of my knowledge, I described what I interpreted was going on, whether it was right or wrong I'll throw it out there for your critique. Operationally defined, a positive reinforcer is any stimulus that increases the probability of the response it follows. Lonely old Fred arriving in his black car became a discriminative stimulus. His arrival, or his automobile's arrival, aroused the stallion, who became sexually stimulated as a primary reinforcer and the arrival of Rural Ruth embracing lonely old Fred, then walking arm in arm with her lover, became in the horse's mind, a secondary reinforcer. The closeness and level of affection the two human beings demonstrated had a consanguineous paired association, which imitated the courtship behavior between the black stallion and his brood mares. Needless to say, he was a horny horse who wanted some action but displaying his talent, or more aptly stated, the SIZE of his talent provided conflict! As in cognitive dissonance for our hero, lonely old Fred, whose human-sized member could not compete! Every male should have lonely old Fred's "problem"! Ai yi yi!! Oh dear, there I go with another interpretation – what a trial and just when our hero was embracing intimacy and attempting to have a better, more enriched sex life!

Lonely old Fred decided to share this problem with Rural Ruth, who saw the horse thing as no big deal – simply a physiological release. The animal is male and males get erections – what's the big rural deal? And by the way, "he's the best stud on the farm"! That was the worst thing she could have stated! Obviously our hero had a different opinion of what the horse represented symbolically, even his name Tombstone spelled disaster! Lonely old Fred had become quite phobic, to a point where he couldn't become aroused in the presence of Rural Ruth, which frustrated the woman to the "nth degree." I mean come on, she's a 30-year-old female with a raging libido who likes sex! Even worse, at work lonely old Fred's staff started to complain about his reduced frustration tolerance and increased agitation! They looked to me for advice; what was I supposed to say? He's fixated on a horse penis, which has made him phobic. I don't think so! It got worse, Rural Ruth thought she could desensitize lonely old Fred's problem by having him watch Tombstone copulate with a brood mare! ARE YOU CRAZY – it made him even more phobic! This could've had disastrous consequences on our hero's future sex life, let alone his current one, which was in the "dumpers" big-time! Not once but nine times she enticed lonely old Fred to come out after work, on the weekends, in the evenings, to watch the goings-on between the black stallion, the very BIG, virile black stallion, and his brood mare, getting "knotted." Subsequently Rural Ruth would demand the same kind of action as in standard of performance, in lonely old Fred's mind anyway, which caused his phobic response towards sex to worsen!

To end the story on a positive note, here's what happened. The brood mare, surprise, surprise, became pregnant and no longer would accept the black stallion's advances, if you get the picture. He no longer became aroused when lonely old Fred visited Rural Ruth, who by this time was threatening to buy a vibrator if her human black stallion didn't get his stuff together. Sensate focus is what saved the day. I suggested they visit my colleague, who could work with lonely old Fred and Rural Ruth. This treatment intervention was used as a means to regain our hero's confidence in the lovemaking department and eventually, with lots of practice and reassurance from Rural Ruth, his mojo working as well! Specifically, lonely old Fred was taught progressive deep muscle relaxation, systematic desensitization, and other coping strategies to reduce his phobic response. That is, reducing anticipatory and performance anxiety regarding sexual activity. As a byproduct to desensitizing his fear of sex, lonely old Fred's behavior at work improved. His frustration tolerance increased, his agitation reduced, his deportment became more friendly, and his latitude for mistakes from his staff softened. Finally, actually it was quite anticlimactic, lonely old Fred was transferred to another facility, so I never found out if his phobic response to black stallions and sex returned. As you know, female animals go into "heat" and the old pattern of sexual responding from a stallion returns year in and year out. But that's lonely old Fred's problem right, not ours, now on with the next Vignette.

But before I continue, I did bump into Rural Ruth upon occasion and actually liked our infrequent connections. Her down to earth, transparent manner was quite a change from most of my boring, competitive collegial relationships. If my memory serves me correctly, she compromised her lifestyle and moved to the city during the week – to be closer to lonely old Fred. But that's all she would say, interesting – very interesting! Now we can go on to the next Vignette! *But Jake, what ever happened to the black stallion with the big wang?* Who the hell knows, he got more brood mares pregnant, that's rural practical stuff, on to the next Vignette!

VIGNETTE 33

BY NOW I'D BEEN AT THIS PARTICULAR JOB FOR ABOUT EIGHT YEARS AND much to my chagrin Senior Management made my job redundant, in conjunction with ten other mid-management positions. Prior to this happening I'd made an acquaintance with a colleague/

mid-manager, who was possibly the most technically knowledgeable person I'd met to that time – a man whose numerous talents and propensity to compete whether it be socially, intellectually, or physically was unparalleled. Lunch time found him playing intramural basketball with other managers. Two evenings a week he played duplicate bridge; weekends were golf and horseback riding. It went on and on and on, he had to prove to himself that he was better than you! This gentleman talked AT YOU rather than with you. Specifically, and if you're old enough, think of Joe Friday on the weekly 1950s and then '60s television series *Dragnet* and that was his manner. Very little inflection in his voice, it was sparse to put it frankly and the "antennae" were always up looking for vulnerability, weakness, and ineptitude, which to a certain degree we all have regardless of the milieu in which we find ourselves. The man's behavior was bordering on pathological! But I'll let you assess that one after reading more about him. He had few friends or associates, nor in my mind needed any close relationships, which would I think have reduced his competitive edge. *Get on with the story, Jake, we get the picture, a tough, competitive no nonsense prostak,*[20] *we get it!* Okay, okay, Christmas time, the holiday season caused many an office protocol to be challenged, thrown out the window, forgotten, misused. That was it in a nutshell – people like to party and so did Mr. Competition – in spades! Think back for a second, remember the Second-in-Command a few Vignettes ago and the weak, cowardly boss whom she intimidated. This nebish[21] boss individual, who held the reins of power at the time of this story, liked, even admired Mr. Competition's guts, intelligence, bravado – you get the picture. Around Christmas time she allowed people latitude in completing job duties with – well how shall I put it, greater "flexibility" – *what does that really mean, Jake?* A laxity in quality control, job performance, and quality improvement, does that answer your question?

Around the first week of January the screws began to tighten again. But back to the Christmas story – I get a phone call three days before Christmas just as I'm going on holidays to the Caribbean.

---

20   boor
21   weakling, nobody

Chapter Seven | 141

Guess who from? You got it, Mr. Competition, who else, wondering if I'd like to come down to his office in the basement of this huge Organization conglomerate for a Christmas/Holiday drink after work – as in singular drink did you catch it, yeah right! "Sure, why not ,but I go on vacation tomorrow." I arrived ten minutes later, his office door was open, and there sitting having "Christmas cheer" was THE cowardly boss who admired Mr. Competition. *That's some "drag" as in political connection, Jake, what did you do then?* I went over, poured myself a double or even triple rum and coke, I can't remember, sat down and joined in the conversation. What d'ya think I did? A couple of drinks later the cowardly boss stood up, quite suddenly actually, said her goodbyes, turned and left. I think she was angry I was "stealing her fire," as in diverting Mr. Competition's attention. By that time I couldn't give a hoot; after two or three very powerful drinks, the alcohol was stimulating my brainpower. In little bits and pieces I would challenge Mr. Competition and he rose to the occasion and then some! Please, read on.

Let's leap ahead three hours – I was totally s...faced and Mr. Competition was just getting warmed up! This guy could drink and drink and drink! He had three hollow legs, three hollow arms, and a hollow chest. I was staggering when I made my way to the washroom for periodic "pit stops." Not so for Mr. Competition, he would stand up, walk straight as an arrow, and return the same way with nary a change in voice inflection, which was no inflection, gait impairment, or visible intoxication! After the fourth hour we had finished a quart (1 L) of rum then started another one, my God and Jesus Christ, too much sugar! By now I was closing one eye to focus with the other and then changing eyes. Mr. Competition had not changed his composure one iota in four and a half hours!

"C'mon Jake, let's go get some food; I know just the place," and with that Mr. "C" stood up, walked over, got my jacket, which was slung over my chair, and motioned me to get up. No problem, I thought – wrong, I used the arms of the chair to push myself up and literally fell over! Here's the amazing thing: Mr. Competition, anticipating that I would fall and with the reflexes of a cat, grabbed me and held me up as easily as a postage stamp – some power, some coordination and stamina, and after all that booze, it was quite extraordinary! Then came the barbwire exegesis, "Jake, Jake, I thought you could hold your booze, guess I was wrong!" Why that insufferable snob, he outweighed me by forty pounds (18 kgs.)! What an ego and it appeared not a charitable bone in his body for a colleague in distress!

Of course you know this means WAR (I said to myself)! I wasn't going to take this crap sitting down and I sure as hell couldn't walk very straight either! What to do? "I need some time to clean up, help me to the wash room and I'll be okay." Mr. Competition's response, and I shouldn't have been surprised, put everything in perspective, "The problem, Jake, is you're out of practice, when you finish cleaning up we'll have one for the road!" Are you kidding, another drink? I could barely see and was looking forward to puking my guts out into the washroom's "great white mother." To Mr. Competition's credit he helped me get to the washroom, shut the door behind me, and probably listened while I vomited. Once done, I stood up, felt 10 times better but was somewhat hesitant to get into that state again, as anyone who's been in my condition can attest! I cleaned myself up, gargled with mouthwash, which happened to be near the sink basin – *how fortuitous, Jake*. Okay, okay. Splashed some water on my face and returned to combat. As was stated many years ago, "In war, the main thing is to win the last battle, not the first." Call it the "Masada Complex" but I was determined to be the last man standing. Pretty macho hunh (eh).

Mr. Competition was awaitin', with that s...eatin' grin a mile wide. "Jake, you gotta drink yourself sober, that's the only way we can lick this problem." I stood there dumbfounded, trying to bend my head around this most recent idiotic statement. Keep in mind I was in his domain and felt I had no choice as he had unsheathed his sword metaphorically speaking and was baiting me; ergo, I had no retort! By the way, has anyone out there heard of drinking yourself sober? If so, I guess I've lived a sheltered life. Mr. Competition scooted over to the drink table, poured a couple of double rum and cokes and returned with a toast. "To Jake, may this evening be the beginning of the end of a crappy tolerance for alcohol," and clinked his glass with mine – again with that s...eatin' grin! What to do? I was NOT going to take this sitting down, or was I? "We've had a lot to drink, why don't we walk to the restaurant?" And this is where Mr. Competition's elephantine ego placed a noose around his big smug, elongated, foolish neck! Poor, stupid kibitzer[22] and I say that matter of factly, twenty-odd years later!!

"Jake, I own a nice comfortable, warm car, why the hell would I wanna walk?" Once again I reiterated, "We've been drinking all evening without a break after a hard day's work and with no food in our bellies, are you sure that's a good idea?" This response was NOT a good idea and caused a major "narcissistic injury" to Mr. Competition's elephantine ego. His retort said it all, "Jake – what are you trying to say – I'm too drunk to drive? And here I thought you're one of the good guys!" "Sorry, but I'm just bringing up the facts as I see them," I responded. I now saw intrinsically a potential avenue to win my vendetta against this "windbag" competitive, egomaniac. *Jake, you're so ballsy!* Yeah, well I'm also human; wouldn't you retaliate? "Tell me which restaurant you wanna drive to and I'll meet you there, I need some exercise." This response precipitated a gesture of contempt from Mr. Competition. "You probably walk like you drink, Jake, but if that's what you want, okay, how 'bout some Mexican food – Jose Diablo's down on Pine Street?" "That's okay with me; I'll be there in 15 minutes," I replied. *But Jake, why didn't you go with Mr. Competition?* An obvious answer, Ace, his drunken-driving, which I couldn't accurately gauge because I was also very intoxicated. Get with the program, aren't you reading the Vignette? That being stated, on with the story, Mr. Competition's stupid retort I expected by now and so would anyone else with two neurons to rub together! His immense ego and grandiosity p.... me off big time – sorry for the vulgarity, but just thinking about this windbag upsets me as I dictate the Vignette.

I arrived punctually 15 minutes later at the pre-arranged Mexican restaurant, Jose Diablo's, down on Pine Street. Of course, waiting for me in a small booth at the end of the restaurant was you-know-who! This time Mr. "C" was drinking double rum and cokes with

---

22   meddlesome spectator

beer chasers! Dun da dun dun – boilermakers! But once again, absolutely no indication of impairment, he articulated well, as well as I could comprehend in my own drunken state. His gestures and body posture were relaxed; I simply couldn't believe how much this man could consume and not look intoxicated! *On with the story, Jake.* Okay, okay. Mr. Competition's next remark, "Let's get rollin', Jake, what's your fancy – Singapore slings?" And with that comment Mr. Competition started to giggle, GIGGLE, this big shot, kibitser "blowhard" giggling? It didn't fit, it simply didn't fit! "How 'bout a double Jamaican rum, 151 proof?" I retorted. "Jake, Jake, now there's a man after my own heart," he replied and went back to drinking his rum/beer chasers. In my mind the only way I could compete was nursing a powerful drink that Mr. "C" respected, at the same time deflecting his insidious comments about my prowess, or lack thereof, in the drinking department – which in those days was considered a manly thing to do – and of course, not show the effects!

Lo and behold, as I surmised later on when sober, two police officers entered the restaurant, went over to a booth near the door, and asked for menus. Here's the problem, which I didn't know about. Mr. Competition, while driving to José Diablo's, was pulled over at a "check stop" and given a warning by the police. The same two police officers who were sitting not 25 feet (8 m.) away!? Initially startled, then more relaxed, our hero started surreptitiously, without my knowledge of the recent police situation, covering his drinks with his huge hands. Then, while talking to me quietly, began sliding the drinks one-by-one to the side of the small, by this time very small, table. Then, slowly and methodically bending forward and placing each drink on the floor beside or under the table using one hand, while he continued to talk to me, not moving his torso a fraction. When I questioned him about this odd behavior, Mr. Competition muttered something about the service being crappy and wanting more room. Of course my back being to the police, and his ego so fragile that he couldn't disclose the real reason why he was moving his drinks to the floor, made me think he was starting to crumble. I was winning our little battle, or so I thought. Then it happened, the waitress seeing that our table, his side anyway, was empty of drinks, came over and with a loud voice, at least in my drunken state it sounded loud, declared, "Are you through with those DRINKS – do ya want ANOTHER ROUND?" You guessed it, the cops overheard the waitress, recognized Mr. "C," then one of them got up and approached the cashier's till to intercept the waitress when she returned from our table. All of this I was unable to see, but did witness Mr. Competition decompensate big-time! He stopped all communication with me, turned a sickly, pale color, and slowly stood up to go, I presumed to the men's room. Too bad so sad Mr. Competition, FOR ONCE YOU LOSE! But I can't feel sorry for him – Karma had bit his arrogant ass! The next thing I observed, or more accurately overheard, was the police officer by the cashier's till requesting Mr. Competition to come over and look at the bill! Odd I thought, where is this discombobulated voice coming from and I turned around just as the second policeman stood up from the booth and also approached the cashier's till. The two of them together – oh dear!

Mr. "C" made a silly gesture with his finger to his chest indicating "Me?" Then I overheard him say in a stage whisper, "I'm screwed, I'm totally screwed, I'm going to get arrested!" I was dumbstruck; Mr. Competition never admitted weakness, never ever! He was done and he knew it; his luck had finally fallen on hard ground – AND he was screwed!! Mr. Competition then strode over to the cashier's till and got into an animated discussion with the police, who by this time had counted up the number of drinks ordered at the table by this windbag. I presume they subtracted my double, Jamaican 151 proof rum. Further discussion ensued, then some begging, which fell on deaf ears – and then Mr. "C" was led away in HANDCUFFS!

What's the moral of the story, Jake? Quite frankly and I say this so many years later, KEEP YOUR EGO IN CHECK. That's it. If you "push the envelope" too many times, Karma will bite your egotistical ass! *But Jake, whatever happened to Mr. Competition?* Answer: He was charged under the criminal code with several violations of the law, almost lost his credentials to practice his profession, but because of an understanding judge only received a suspended sentence! Luckily Mr. Competition had befriended, and I use that word loosely, a number of powerful, influential people who spoke on his behalf, or at least sent Letters of Reference that eliminated any jail time. He continued to work at the Organization where we were employed, but kept a VERY, VERY low profile! As for me, I guess I got the last laugh but somehow it was bittersweet, so maybe just a chuckle out of it. You can rest assured Mr. Competition changed his drinking habits big time after that one!!

Well, that's about it for this Chapter. By this time as stated earlier in the Vignette, I'd received my notice of job redundancy, which to all intents and purposes meant an eight-month severance. Senior management in their infinite wisdom had decided to downsize the Organization by reducing mid-management positions. What else is new? Rightly or wrongly I was on the way out and after eight years I was tired and wanted a change. What's the expression? A change is as good as a rest? I got the change but didn't get the rest in more ways than one. Settle back and enjoy the next and last Chapter of the book!

But before you read on, let me digress from dictating this stuff – I need a break. I hope you've enjoyed reading the menagerie of Vignettes thus far and haven't been too bored! I wanted you to have a few chuckles after a hard day's work!! That's the whole reason for writing this bleepin' book. Some of the Vignettes were mendacious, I admit it, but I warned you early on at the beginning of this undertaking! Some of the Vignettes were "spot on" in accuracy – they really happened exactly as stated! Believe me, exactly as stated! So now we're "down to the wire" – I'm a little fatigued and need to hit the wire rather than…There I go again, forget my whining, I still have a whole slew of stories to talk about but not now. I'm going to end this book with Chapter Eight, which takes us up to the year 2000. Any more recent stories will cause me some worry about retaliation – it's just too close for comfort timewise. So 'rev up your engines and enjoy the last Chapter! Better still, make some popcorn, crack a beer, pour some wine, red not white – then you can really enjoy the LAST CHAPTER "half snapped"!

Of Note: Before you start imbibing please read the following anecdote: Dysfunctional organizations place Power in the control of a few manipulators. Coping with the incessant "games" orchestrated by these few cagey manipulators wastes time and energy that could be otherwise spent making the organization more effective. In dysfunctional organizations planning can be used as a source of control. Planning can be perceived by the higher-ups as a prediction, and prediction is control. Planning in a "healthy" organization is not an outcome, but rather a description and NOT a prescription. Planning in a dysfunctional organization is illusionary; the leaders of these organizations rarely sample widely from both inside and outside the organization. As a consequence, future plans at some level perpetuate the status quo, however giving the impression that change is occurring, but believe me it's NOT!! Often you may see a few cosmetic alterations but POWER is maintained in these facsimiles of work efforts by giving only PARTIAL information to the employee constituents. Informed decisions are difficult to make as only partial information has been given by the higher-ups. A perpetual slow to fast motion *Gong Show* occurs as people begin to leave the organization – then escape in droves as their patience is worn thin and they hit the critical mass of frustration/burnout. Keep this in mind.

Lastly about Chapter Eight, its stories are possibly the most interesting of the 37 Vignettes – but you be the judge. BE THERE OR BE SQUARE (an old sixties expression). Now get back at 'er and begin reading the next and last chapter of the section. *Aye aye, Captain.* Okay, okay.

CHAPTER EIGHT

VIGNETTE 34

SO, THERE I WAS SITTING AT HOME OUT OF WORK, CONTEMPLATING MY navel once again! And then it happened, I got a phone call from a very highly placed professional who had an international reputation, wondering if I'd like to discuss a joint business venture/proprietorship. Would I!? It couldn't have happened at a better time; the cash register sound went off in my head. "Sure, we can get together and have a business lunch at your convenience." The individual, in her late forties, received immense deferential treatment from her colleagues, which I observed when I had an opportunity to share a table with her during a professional conference. Her book published in the mid-1980s helped make her international reputation, not to mention an immense skill in her chosen profession! I was thrilled to put it mildly and then some insecurities began to fester! What if I couldn't meet her expectations, which were exceedingly high. She was a driving, "Type A" personality with an inquisitive mind, an IQ through the roof, and did not "suffer fools gladly." As I lay in bed thinking about my limited options, as by this time I was in my mid-forties with a young family, I really had no choice and in fact this opportunity could be the "icing on the cake" career-wise! Think again, Jake, life is not that simple – think again!

Jumping ahead a couple of weeks – we finally negotiated a mutual time to meet for an extended lunch and talk business, mutual philosophies, likes and dislikes, strengths and needs, you name it. The strengths were many and because giant egos prevailed, hers in particular, our weaknesses were assessed as few. Okay then, "let's get the ball rolling" and we did! Very quickly we developed a business plan, identified mutual job interests of both convergence and divergence, a Vision and Mission/Mandate for the business, cost benefits and cost effectiveness were also examined with investment optics in mind. All of this occurred over a nine-month period. Then, sliding right along, we co-signed a five-year lease, moved into our joint offices, put our respective "shingles" on the door, and through my colleague's immense reputation – had an eight-month waiting list in 10 working days – not bad hunh (eh)! It seemed to be working like a charm, but somehow and I have to admit this, I felt like I was being "played," a little bit anyway, especially when her former husband stated, "Now I can live in peace – you can take over the babysitting role!" Kachunk, the antennae went up! I approached my business associate, or more accurately business proprietress, and disclosed her ex-husband's comment, "Jake, Jake, he's jealous of my career and reputation – I can't really defend myself, can I?" In my head I agreed, but in my heart a danger signal went off! However, on with the story, and "it's a good un," as Walter Brennan used to say in the old John Wayne westerns. I'm only going to mention three or four Vignettes, but over the five years I worked with this "creature," there were at least 50 Vignettes that I still shudder to think about, even at this point at the end of my career. Why I didn't have a breakdown babysitting this CRETIN or in more clinical vernacular, "enabling" her, I'll never know! I still kick myself for allowing pride and ego to displace practical sense and integrity! *Get on with the story, Jake, enough pontificating!* Okay, okay, hold your horses, I ain't Tombstone; a period of senescence is hitting me these days!

So, the business was started, the clients began arriving in droves, and from a modest point of view, things were going A-OK, until our rental check "bounced" after our third month in operation! How in God's name could this happen? I questioned my colleague and she came back with some gobbledy-goop which I bought hook line and sinker. You'd think I'd learn to listen to my heart as well as my head; I hadn't – I'm fairly stupid on Mondays and Tuesdays – I get smarter through the week though! The Manager of this very toney professional building where we had our office came to us a few days later "cap in hand" requesting the rent money. To digress, my colleague and I had arranged to pay each month's rent on the basis of percentage earned. Because her income was 3 to 1 ratio of mine, she paid a higher percentage of the monthly rent. In theory that sounds fair and above board, but in practice it caused immense problems! I'd have to go each month and confront, as in challenge vociferously and even once or twice think seriously of going to Small Claims Court, to get her share of the rent! *Jake, Jake, this is a danger signal; get the hell out!* I couldn't because we'd made this payment arrangement a legal arrangement! Once again, stupid me, I was on the hook for the next five years of the lease, or get somebody else to take over my share. There was no "escape clause" in the lease because the city we worked in had a thriving economy, so once you were in you were stuck with the leasing conditions, which were draconian to say the least!

That's not all, I was soon to learn that NO ONE BUT NO ONE who'd dealt with this tsedreyter,[23] miscreant colleague walked away unscathed! I was no exception! I could not throughout the five years I worked with her find anyone to take over the rental lease! Although I advertised regularly, no one in the Industry was foolhardy enough to come and join forces (i.e., work directly) with my colleague! They were happy to send referrals, but not get involved in any "rumbles" with this Dybuk[24] – it appears everybody knew her better than Jake! But I forgot to finish my story with the business manager demanding his monthly rent. I had to use my Visa for that particular month's rent, although being promised by my colleague that she'd pay me back – it never happened! After that, approximately six months of our rental payment arrangement went along smoothly. I got the feeling that this modus vivendi was finally going to work out and in fact be quite successful! Then the rent check "bounced" and ONCE AGAIN was returned NSF! Without boring you with details, I'm not ashamed to say I went to this Cretin

---

23 eccentric
24 soul condemned to wander because of its sins

eleven times to get her share of the rent, which never happened! The business manager by this time was breathing down our necks, after three weeks of overdue rental payment – wouldn't you! I had to pull out the trusty Visa card ONCE AGAIN to pay this month's overdue rent! And ONCE AGAIN didn't get repaid!

A few months later I made the mistake of going out for a business lunch with my colleague. Then I found out where the money was really going!? The woman had an impulse control disorder and was in lay terminology a SHOPAHOLIC! After lunch, which cost me in excess of $100 – a lot more money in the mid 1990s than now, while strolling along a major street of this Midwestern city she stopped dead in her tracks! "I just have to have that," she stated emphatically, as she spied a jacket in a clothing store. She walked in, tried on an "all weather" coat, and then had the tailor make a few adjustments. She had just purchased a $1300 "impulse" – this I might add in the space of 15 minutes! That's nothing, three months later, after bitching about the two-year-old "piece of shit" she was driving, her comment not mine, she went car shopping with her "Platinum" American Express Card! Once again, after conveniently forgetting to pay her share of the rent of our very toney office for the THIRD TIME. This time she entered a high-end Asian dealership and asked to see two or three sports cars she'd observed from the showroom while driving by in her piece of shit!? She was shown and then taken for a scenic drive in one of these high-end sports cars, driving at speeds in excess of 100 miles an hour (160 km./hr.) to get a feel for the power, guts, performance, you name it, whatever turns you on!? When they returned to the dealership, she asked the salesperson when they could have the car ready for her!? He smiled and stated, "On Thursday," which was two days hence. Her response, "I need to have it by the end of today or you've lost a sale," caused nary a pause before his response sealed the deal, "No problem we'll have it ready by 4 p.m." THIS scenario just about sums up the level, or better stated, degree of impulse spending my colleague was capable of committing! Does the word pathological ring any clinical bells!? It did for me.

Unbelievable but true and to reiterate, she used her PLATINUM AMERICAN EXPRESS CARD TO PURCHASE THE CAR . One of seven credit cards she possessed! I know, I counted them! You haven't heard anything yet – and you thought the Tombstone Vignette was interesting. READ ON, READER, – READ ON.

This woman, in order to stay awake, because, in her defense she worked consistently 10- to 14-hour days, drank coffee to EXCESS! *Jake, how much to excess?* Oh about an industrial urn of coffee per day – the equivalent of 20–24 cups of coffee PER DAY!!? Her pallor was pasty white, she had irritable bowel syndrome and regular migraine headaches and YES she was absolutely addicted to coffee!! This self-indulgent cretin colleague also became very nasty when she thought her coffee supply was getting low!? How so you ask, she occasionally accused yours truly of "stealing her coffee cache," her words not mine! This woman's sympathetic and parasympathetic nervous system must have taken a pounding, because the resultant labile mood exacerbated her personality problems like nobody's business! As in very, very moody, irascible behavior. Woe-betide us if we ran out of coffee, which we never did, but we came close a couple of times! The fear and catastrophic response of potentially losing her daily "high" from the coffee would have been overwhelming, with a high risk of stroke/heart attack, without a doubt! Thank God and Jesus Christ I never faced that one with this Tsedreyter Cretin! I'd be the enabling fall guy in a client lawsuit after she jammed out during business hours, no doubt about it!

One weekend after completing back-to-back reports, after my colleague was up probably 24 hours AND using her coffee addiction to keep her awake, she decided she needed a "breather" – a few days in the mountains skiing was just what the doctor ordered! Subsequently, the story has it, as I wasn't there – I'm one of the few people who can't stand downhill skiing – my colleague, while driving to the mountains in her brand-new Asian sports car, fell asleep at the wheel at approximately 6 p.m.! Darkness had fallen and she went off the road and traveled, get this, approximately fifty yards (45 m.) into a snowy field by the side of the highway!

That's traveling at some accelerated speed and then some! She woke up around midnight, didn't know where she was or what had happened and tried to get out of the car, which was buried in the snow.

After approximately half an hour of struggling to open the door jammed against the snow, she made enough room to squeeze out of the vehicle. At this point, in pitch blackness, mind you, she retraced her steps by walking along the tread line back to the highway. She then "thumbed" a ride to a nearby ski resort and hired a tow truck at a 24-hour truck stand, UNBELIEVABLE but true! She told the tow truck driver some "cock and bull" story about her brakes giving out in order to elicit sympathy and got the sympathy vote big-time! I heard his decision was duly influenced when she leaned over and gave him an eyeful of cleavage with those C-cup bosoms. Subsequently she got a much reduced rate, yeah right, one starts to wonder doesn't one? That's the story I heard anyway – third and fifth hand.

Approximately one month later, she invited a mutual colleague to go skiing with her. The problem was my business associate's gigantic ego interfered with her reality testing concerning her ability to ski. She had always stated she was a "Black diamond" skier – meaning she could handle the most challenging hills. This was complete B.S., which nearly cost her her life! Unfortunately, our mutual colleague had taken her comments at face value, believing my business associate's ability to ski at an expert level! They took the gondola up to the top of this incredibly high and very steep mountain and our mutual colleague skied halfway down the hill, occasionally looking over her shoulder for our heroine – who never arrived! Our mutual colleague eventually got tired of waiting, skied to the bottom of this gigantic hill, and took the gondola back to the top. As she approached the top of the hill she saw the ski patrol taking a fallen skier, lying in the ski toboggan and covered with a blanket, down the hill. Our mutual colleague, thinking nothing of it, got out of the gondola and skied down the hill, back and forth in a diagonal manner, to increase the potential of finding our heroine. Two thirds of the way down, still no heroine and it was starting to get dark and our mutual colleague was getting worried! She decided to complete her ski run to the bottom and contact the ski patrol. She didn't have to! When she got to the bottom of the hill, beside the Ski Chalet there was a big "white board" with a message stating our heroine's name and the HOSPITAL where she could be reached!? Oh no, just great, you can imagine the response from our mutual colleague! She RAN not walked, into the Ski Chalet, explained who she was and got on the telephone pronto. Our heroine, according to a ward nurse, had sustained a moderate concussion and broken left clavicle, but would be okay and wanted visitors! It goes without saying that this was a costly weekend both emotionally and financially for our mutual colleague!

One other major issue before I forget! Our concussed, Tsedreyter heroine lady had MISPLACED HER PURSE and couldn't pay one cent of that very extravagant impulse for a break from work! Our mutual colleague, now our mutual benefactor, became our mutual cum enemy in very short order! She eventually got paid back but only after a lawyer was retained. I know because I saw the Letter of Warning and then the Letter of Intent, and it was a doozy! I began to worry big time about my own mental health, as I'd signed a five-year lease with our heroine, which was a binding contract. *Get out of it, Jake, get out!* Shush, I haven't finished yet. On to the next Vignette!! Reader, take a break from work, it gets better (or worse)!

VIGNETTE 35

Two years later – YES, I lasted that long – we met with my business associate's very expensive and very competent Chartered Accountant! He "blew my socks off" when he stated in a very forthright manner that my colleague's "depleted resources were a direct consequence of her excessive and impulsive spending habits"! No kidding, Ace! Shortly thereafter I tried sitting down with my colleague with the International, Grade A, Gold Standard professional reputation, for a heart-to-heart! Wrong – she sloughed me off like secondhand news, told me it was "all in my head" and that I was "conspiring against her," along with her very expensive and very competent Chartered Accountant – dun da dun dun! I had more than two years left in my contract as a co-signer on the lease. *But Jake, didn't you ask around and try to get somebody to take your place?* Of course I did, I told you that already. No one but NO ONE in the immediate geographic region wanted to take over my portion of the lease and deal with this cretin's behavior! I tried and tried and tried – by phoning friends, colleagues, friends again, even enemies. Nope, I was "on the hook" and could either pay out my portion of the remaining two years or sit back and take it – the contract was that binding. This woman had obviously done her homework and had covered her tracks and then some! Yes, I stayed and at great expense to my mental health and marital stability I might add! STUPID, STUPID ME. *(I think so too, Jake!)*

I started to ruminate about my current situation, my future and the drawbacks of working with this Cretin makhasheyfe,[25] including the stability of my marriage, which was, from my point of view, seriously affected by my colleague's narcissistic behavior! Are you thinking what I'm writing – *impulsive, narcissistic, grandiose, a sense of entitlement, lack of remorse – where's the checklist, Jake (you know the one I'm talking about)?* I was told I was an enabler and if I stayed in the current business arrangement, I deserved everything she dished out! People questioned my personal code of conduct and the ethics of staying in a business arrangement, or any arrangement with this Paskudnik.[26] Even her ex-spouse in so many words stated, "I told you so!" These "externals" felt it was only a matter of time until she'd start to hit on me financially to support her very impulsive and very destructive spending habits!

Then it happened and I was there! Remember the very expensive and very competent Chartered Accountant mentioned above – *yeah, sure we do, Jake!* One day, the very expensive and very competent Chartered Accountant was contacted by guess who? The Federal Government Income Tax Collection Agents! *Jake, why, pray tell?* Because he'd taken over as the Executor of our heroine's finances because she was hopelessly in debt? *That's "old news," Jake, we already know about that!* Okay,

---

25   witch
26   revolting, evil person

okay. He was told by them in no uncertain words that a check for $10,000 was expected, which unbeknownst to him, had been promised by my colleague to be paid three days hence, "as a show of good faith"!? He had phoned me to inquire if I knew anything about this arrangement and, by the way, he was TAPING the conversation! Oh great, what did I get myself into? *Jake, Jake, pay the two remaining years on the lease and get the hell outta there – are you a "mark" or what!* Okay, okay, why did I stay? Stupidity, pride, a sense of integrity to end what I started, the legal binding contract, I don't know – but I answered the Chartered Accountant's questions very thoroughly, as I had nothing to hide! He then stated, "I think it best we have a tête-à-tête with your colleague sooner rather than later!" I agreed and after a number of unanswered phone calls, written messages, and circuitous corridor encounters (she feigning time constraints), a meeting was eventually arranged, at which time my Paskudnik colleague attempted to blame everyone else, except her own ineptness, for her financial woes! JUST GREAT, basically here is what happened.

The meeting was ostensibly a diatribe between the Chartered Accountant, a highly intellectual and very experienced professional, challenging the veracity of another highly intelligent professional, with an international reputation AND very slick. *How slick was she, Jake?* The full extent of the woman's pathology, let's just say "Personality Disorder NOS," came out during that fateful meeting! Does that answer your question, Ace? More specifically, the frightening impact of her devious, manipulative ploys to discredit and redirect any responsibility for her current financial nightmare was projected onto other people! This was a sinister individual, no doubt about it! No qualms in denigrating, maligning, misrepresenting and bald-faced lying in an attempt to avoid responsibility for her actions! Her brilliant mind had never, ever been better! I'd seen her work magic in the Courtroom as an expert witness winning many complex cases, but her eloquence, or better stated grandiloquence this day topped them all! What finally broke her credibility was a combination of two issues. I'm going to start a new Vignette as the length of time required to describe these two issues requires further, separate stories.

VIGNETTE 36

THE CHARTERED ACCOUNTANT RECOGNIZED HE'D HIT A "STONE WALL" regarding the Cretin, Paskudnik's denial and rationalization of any responsibility for her financial dilemma. OUR financial dilemma, to be more accurate, as I was tied in legally by co-signing the Lease! He began by asking my colleague what made her return to the European country of her origin 10 years previously. I was dumbfounded but sat quietly, absorbing the interplay between these two verbal titans, syllable by syllable, phrase by phrase. After verbal swordplay of approximately ten minutes my colleague finally confessed that a home she co-owned, in another geographical location of this country, had been seized to pay "back taxes" at that time. She blamed her husband's financial incompetence, which might've been true, but by now both the Chartered Accountant and I realized the depth of the deceit we were dealing with! Again the question was asked by the Chartered Accountant why she and her husband *at that specific time* decided to leave this country?! She postured, "umm'd and ahhed" and then said nothing! The final answer, which was the true answer, was unceremoniously shoved in front of her! A letter from the Federal Government Income Tax Department, almost yellow with age, stating eight years of back taxes was owed and their home was being expropriated in order to retrieve taxable income, how much was not stated. Obviously, there was still a great deal more tax that was owed AND the Federal Government always gets its man or woman in this case! You guessed it – my colleague blamed her husband's ineptness and sat there wondering what her next move was! It was her "proof" against our "proof" in the diatribe that unfolded. Reader, forget that corporate merger, read on!

The Chartered Accountant then proceeded, in a carefully staged modulated voice, to describe, again with copies of letters from the Income Tax people, "requests" to pay the *remaining* back taxes, but by this time my colleague and her husband were in another country and immune to deportation. He then produced "warning" letters from the Income Tax people to respond to the request to pay the *remaining* back taxes. Lastly, a final warning letter was produced stating the back taxes *still owed* were collecting compounded interest, meaning interest on interest was accruing at an exponential rate and how was this going to be paid?!

Once again, my colleague sat there nonchalantly blaming her ex-spouse and his incompetence in managing their finances. Further letters from the Income Tax Department warned that returning to this country would initiate prosecution (i.e., jail time) by the Government if the back taxes owed weren't paid forthwith! By the couple's lack of response, it appeared they had no intention of ever returning! Oh yeah?

At this point the Chartered Accountant reminded me of Perry Mason, the lawyer from the 1950s television series – deliberate, methodical, and calculating – *get on with the story, Jake*, Okay, okay. The Chartered Accountant produced information, from whom I don't know, describing in law enforcement "speak" my colleague and her former husband's RETURN to this country, which was much to the delight of the Income Tax Collection Agents I'm sure! So, this dubious pair returned to our country from approximately three years overseas, where it appears they couldn't sustain the lifestyle to which they were accustomed! They'd come back to face the music, because they had no borrowing capacity due to their horrendous credit rating! Once again my Cretin, Paskudnik Colleague sat there impassively and began to YAWN! That did it, I was seething with hatred! Jake, calm down! Don't worry – eventually there is a good ending! There, I did it! I let the "cat out of the bag"! RATS, two in fact! The Chartered Accountant, who had forensic training, told me later that he'd seen this type of "frozen" behavior, that is, denial/rationalization, minimization throughout his long career. Corporate, white-collar you guessed it and I didn't say it! Anyway, not in this book I didn't.

The Chartered Accountant then proceeded to read an itemized transcript of the proceedings that occurred that fateful day when the Income Tax Collection Agents interrogated this dubious pair who had accumulated over $778,000 in back taxes, during a period of by now 10 years! To make a long story short, a decision was made to divide the taxable amount into equal shares, $389,000 owed by each party. From sources otherwise unstated, it appeared that the former spouse was well on the road to paying off his share. However, my Cretin, Paskudnik Colleague had not touched her debt owed and it was growing exponentially, every minute of every hour of every day! The laugh and it was a big one, was stated in one of the "bullets" describing my colleague's misunderstanding that the meeting with the Collection Agents was being held as a return home, "Welcome Wagon," in essence, a coffee klatch! The report further detailed her casual reaction to this unbelievable amount of money owed as an "obvious error" on the Government's part AND a complete misunderstanding of the motive for my colleague and her husband's departure to their homeland!? In addition, it described her exaggerated lack of comprehension that leaving this great country and moving to her country of origin would not have a repatriation consequence, AS IN JAIL TIME if she didn't pay her back taxes! They had cautioned my colleague a number of times about this attempted deceit, as it was highly unlikely from their point of view with her level of intelligence, educational accomplishments, and international reputation, that she didn't understand the consequences of Income Tax evasion. Unbelievable, but true and I sat there TOTALLY STUNNED. What to do? *Get out, get THE HELL OUT, Jake!* – Cool your jets, Ace, wait and see. On to the next and final Vignette!

VIGNETTE 37

LET'S GET BACK TO MY CRETIN COLLEAGUE'S $10,000 FANCIFUL, IN GOOD faith, back tax installment that she arranged without the knowledge of her legal Executor, the Perry Mason–like Chartered Accountant. He was fuming, his voice on the phone was controlled rage as he thought I was in cahoots with her! He knew she had absolutely no serious money or credit at, or anywhere near the vicinity of $10,000 to honor her "good faith" phone call to the Income Tax Collection Agents. What to do? Another meeting was held and I won't bore you with her carrying-on B.S. behavior – this time even more outlandish than described above! Anyway, the Chartered Accountant showed up ready to do battle as he brought a "Statement of Accounts" regarding her Portfolio. They were alone in her office and I was left to my own devices outside. After approximately 20 minutes the door opened and they both approached me solemnly. The gist of their request was that I take an envelope with thirty-five $100 bills to the Income Tax Collection Agents, in the hope that this portion of the $10,000 would be enough to appease them!?

Where this pair got the money is anyone's guess, but they did get some of the $10,000 guaranteed to be paid as a "good will" gesture – G...damn what a set-up! You guessed it – please, read on!! Reader, the story gets even better!

Here was the rationale given by the Chartered Accountant to me as a professional courtesy not as a directive, or I would've walked out then and there! My Cretin, Paskudnik Colleague had zero credibility with the Income Tax people, I was an unknown, a "go-between" but with some professional credibility. We had run out of time, as today was the deadline date and the Chartered Accountant had a pressing other appointment which he "could not miss" – GIVE ME A BREAK! Regardless, I believed him and from the expression on his face knew if this money was not taken post haste to the Feds they would be shutting down our operation even more post haste and how would Mr. Chartered Accountant collect his fee! Sorry for the "dig" but that's the way I felt! There was no choice – he looked at me imploringly and stated, "Will you do it?" My answer, "I don't have a choice, do I?" made me feel a little better, as in locus of control. From his facial expression he interpreted my response as "cocky" but let it go. Throughout the whole goings-on my Cretin, Paskudnik Colleague had returned to her office and was nowhere to be seen! *Jake, I don't believe it!? She did what again? She left you to face the music ALONE!? Are you surprised? Of course not, I hope stupidity doesn't run in your family!* Believe me, this happened! I put the thirty-five $100 bills into a legal sized envelope and left the office with 40 minutes to spare before closing time at the Federal Government building.

While zooming downtown, I had a chance to review the remaining year and a half I owed on my five-year lease arrangement with the Cretin, Paskudnik Colleague. Nothing came to mind as far as realistic quick-fix ideas, so I was stuck with this "gig" unless miracles happened, which when you need them they never do! I arrived with 15 minutes to spare, took the elevator up to the eighth floor and looked for the room number which was provided me regarding Income Tax Collection. There it was and there standing in front of the door was a 6'5" (1 m. 98 cm.) 240-pound (115 kg.), 30ish-year-old, Mr. Giant, Security Guard Person with a flak jacket. Can you believe it – a FLAK JACKET! There must be some pretty tough fraudsters out there! He loomed over me when I asked him to alert the Collection Agent with his walkie-talkie; he did so and a pregnant pause followed. Funny how physical size becomes exaggerated when you're waiting and you're scared! Mr. Giant Security Guard Person held the walkie-talkie to his ear, nodded and stated "follow me," got his keys out, opened the industrial-sized door, and we entered a crypt-like room, filled with too many desks. Serious people sat at those desks, Reader! Mr. Giant Security Guard Person made sure I walked beside and slightly ahead of him as we headed towards a desk labeled 28, with three stacks of files laying on it, very, very tall stacks!

Another huge man, I guestimated 6'1" (1m. 84 cm.) and approximately 250 pounds (120 kg.), was sitting behind the desk and when my name was mentioned as in business title, second name, followed by my Colleague's name, he mistakenly thought I was her – forgetting that similar sounding names can be used by both sexes. "Well… we finally meet," he stated, "I see you've brought the $10,000," and held out his hand to receive the envelope. It was a great big, thick, wide hand – one that could be used as a weapon real easily, or so I imagined – let me assure you his manner and size commanded respect! My response was a bit shaky, "Sorry but you've got the wrong person, my name is Jake Hagerman not…and…is a female name and colleague of mine." His startled response, as he looked down at me (I felt approximately half his size) was quickly followed by, "How well do you know…?" which SAID IT ALL. "Personally, not well at all [I lied but kept a straight face] but was asked if I could 'pinch hit' because her Chartered Accountant, who is the legal Executor of her finances, couldn't miss an alternate meeting."

His retort, "Mr. Hagerman, can I be frank?" sent a chill down my back. I nodded and he responded, "Ms.... has a very large file with the Federal Income Tax Department – are you comfortable dealing with her on a professional basis?" What was I supposed to say, "No, I think she's a 'slimeball' but I still work with her because I have integrity" – I don't think so! My response, "This woman has an international reputation in her field and for the most part is highly regarded" was all I could muster. *But Jake, why were you being dishonest but gallant at the same time, this doesn't make sense, she doesn't deserve it!?*

I agree my comment was a "stretch," a great big dishonest stretch – what can I say? *Jake, shush for a moment, can you still look at yourself in the mirror is the big question!* Okay, okay, at the time I thought it was a good answer; he was impugning a professional colleague, albeit one of dubious character with a lack of integrity a mile (1.6 km.) wide! His retort was chilling and succinct, "I would be very careful if I were you in future dealings with this individual," and with that he took the envelope, ripped it open and licked his thumb before counting the thirty-five $100 bills. "Mr. Hagerman, we're short by $6500."! I wasn't going to lie! "This is the money I was given less than one hour ago by Ms....'s Chartered Accountant, please give him a call to clarify the issue." This is all I could think of and wasn't going to fabricate some lame-brain story. The Collection Agent's subsequent comment was meant to comfort not maim, "I can see you have integrity, Mr. Hagerman, but keep your head up, please keep your head up and avoid any future involvement with this person! I'll give the C.A. a call on Monday." And with that he replaced the money in the torn envelope, wrote me a receipt, and called Security to escort me off the premises. Prior to leaving while waiting by his desk, he shook my hand, gave me a very slight smile, sat down, and returned to his audits. Mr. Giant Security Guard Person strode in and led me out, walking slightly behind me and to my right. As he escorted me to the very heavy looking, industrial-sized door he turned and stated, "I've seen grown men cry, even sob – destroyed and sent away by that guy, you've got the touch, buddy!" I presumed the Collection Agent had pre-warned the Security Guard about my Colleague's situation and to expect anything and everything, including I presumed, a ploy of resistance both active and passive. It didn't happen, so Mr. Collection Agent let me go unscathed. It was scary stuff nevertheless and the moral of the story: PAY YOUR DAMN TAXES.

When I got back to the office, my Cretin, Paskudnik Colleague had left for the day! Presumably to go skiing with her new boyfriend who'd bought her a double-sized elastic band to put around her wrist, to snap when she was driving TO KEEP HER AWAKE! Yes, she was still drinking an industrial sized-urn of coffee per day and still alive to talk about it. Of course she was – SHE had the constitution of a draft horse, Tombstone get over here – just kidding! I contacted the Chartered Accountant and gave him a "heads-up" about the remaining $6500. But he was gone as well – Fridays are Fridays are Fridays, you know the feeling, and "passing the buck" has a degree of comfort, doesn't it. One week later, my Cretin, Paskudnik Colleague received a letter that was "burning through the air" from guess who, the Income Tax Department. An ultimatum was being given, at which time you-know-who decided to pull the plug and declare bankruptcy! The Chartered Accountant was not surprised and in a ubiquitous, fateful, persistent way my colleague had won the battle by not going to jail and the Accountant's peremptory comment, "A severe emotional problem disallows her from ever changing those crazy spending habits she dug herself in too deep," was a brilliant brain synopsis – OF THE OBVIOUS but what the hell else was new? CAN YOU BELIEVE IT! Anyway, it was over!!

Folks – there is a God and Jesus Christ – approximately two weeks later while I was relieving myself in the men's room, a colleague at the urinal beside me began complaining about the lack of office space that he was experiencing in this "godforsaken building" and "Did I know anyone who was going to be moving out?" I just about collapsed, but then my exposed penis might have caused him to collapse, so I didn't collapse – just a joke, take it any way you want! I quickly got a copy of our lease, which was coming to its completion in 15 months, and asked if he'd be willing to take it over, or at least my half as soon as possible? He was new and didn't know about my colleague and her, to put it politely, "foibles." His next statement, "I like to work alone and would feel more comfortable taking over the entire lease as soon as possible, if that's alright?" IF THAT'S ALRIGHT just about said it all! Hallelujah! Please believe me, this part of the story happened exactly as I stated and with that request, my ticket to sanity was signed, sealed, and delivered! No amount of marketing had been successful and this option had just landed on my lap serendipitously, while I was answering the call to nature! Reader, I moved out the very next day, forget the goodbyes or whatever!! The new Colleague savior guy would have to deal with the Cretin, Paskudnik and her half of the lease! I just got my stuff together and MOVED THE HELL OUT as fast as my legs could carry me; no help was needed – my adrenaline did the trick! And with that I end the book. Phew, I'm tired of reliving past trauma and excising demons.

But Jake, THAT'S IT!?!! What happened to the Cretin, Paskudnik Colleague; don't end the book without telling us about the Cretin, Paskudnik Colleague! Okay, okay, almost exactly seven years later to the month, a colleague from the city where our business had been located sent me an e-mail suggesting I look at the local newspaper's business section she had included as an attachment. THERE IT WAS – BOLD AS LIFE!! My Cretin, Paskudnik Colleague had been laicizated, "defrocked" from her professional organization, sued for the expenses incurred during the legal battle which she failed to win and also sued by various clients who had been, I guestimated, collateral damage! I include her favorite expression "collateral damage," which she often used to rationalize her dirty dealings with angry, disconsolate victims – me included! My former colleague was currently incommunicado, nowhere to be found!

I had to end the story on a good note – justice had finally been served!! What eventually happened to this replicant of a human being was KARMA. Karma plain and simple! No one who intentionally harms and manipulates the way she did was going to get away from Karma eventually biting them in the ass. THAT'S IT and hopefully Karma doesn't bite YOU in the ass! Did you enjoy Section One of the book? I know I enjoyed dictating it! So Reader, what d'ya think? Now it's on to more serious practical stuff in Section Two of the book, please read on.

SECTION TWO

SHARKS, SLIMEBALLS, AND MALCONTENTS:
AN ORGANIZATIONAL SURVIVAL GUIDE

PREAMBLE

WELCOME TO SECTION TWO OF MY BOOK ENTITLED, "SHARKS, SLIMEBALLS, and Malcontents: An Organizational Survival Guide," a silly title actually but there it is. Hopefully, the contents of Section Two make practical sense and help you survive in the organizational "jungle" during your career. Quite frankly, without a composite skill-set to manage safely, you increase the probability of being scapegoated in today's work milieu! To be forewarned, this section requires an entirely different strategy from Section One, that is, thinking "outside of the box", applying the knowledge provided in Section Two with your current worksite problems in the most efficacious way possible. One last point, this portion of the book requires studious concentration and appears somewhat tedious at first glance but remember, its major theme is utilizing survival strategies at your place of employment to make it a safer place to work. Good luck, and now on to the more serious portion of the book.

As I think back, the concept of this section of the book was inspired after participating in a lecture-tutorial series during graduate school in the early nineteen eighties. It must have had an important influence on my life because I've remembered the general theme for thirty-five years and subsequently studied in the area, the information I gleaned which I now dictate in 2014.

The professor of the lecture-tutorial series would come to our weekly tutorial meeting with a discussion theme for the two-hour period written on individual pieces of paper, which he circulated to each of my student peers to explore and debate, as he sat back and enjoyed the combat! The "cut and thrust" would be intellectuals testing their knowledge and stomping on ill-conceived arguments with a vengeance. A particular pecking order of power, diplomacy, and malignancy soon found its way into the atmosphere of those Monday morning tutorials and woe betide if you were a non-contributor! It simply was not allowed and your passivity was quickly challenged by the aforementioned professor, who had a predilection for rapier wit and viperous quips that kept everyone honest, regarding who was boss. And also before I forget, he did not suffer fools gladly!

The first discussion entailed the following statement, typewritten in capital letters (personal computers had not yet been invented): "ARE YOU A JERK, ASSHOLE OR SLIMEBALL?" I beg your pardon, professors in those days did not begin tutorials with such vulgarity? Suddenly, after a few chuckles and quick repartee about the nonsensical nature of the question, the professor defined each of these words in the context of personality subtypes found in a typical work milieu. Specifically, a JERK was a socially inept obstreperous boob, an ASSHOLE – an irresponsible "lowlife" not necessarily stupid but at odds with everyone else, and a SLIMEBALL – a shrewd, clever manipulator who could be covert in his/her aggressive ploys and always with an "agenda" that meant the end justifies the means and usually at your expense.

The professor went on to describe these behaviors regarding the negative impact they had on input, throughput, and output functions of an organization, the employees, the constituent client base, and product development. Subsequently, the respective modus operandi of those individuals manifesting these character traits was examined and role-played in the tutorials. *How so, Jake?* The professor requested that we try to remember a persona in our past who best "fit the bill" for each of these personality subtypes, then conjure up and act out their behavior via role-playing. Believe me, the story line of the role-plays put things into perspective as we copied and play-acted personality traits of people we'd known, dated, or worked under. It was fun and everyone as I remember got into the spirit of "ham boning" a particular personality from the past. Once again at the end of the role-playing, we debated, dissected, hashed, and re-hashed the various characters that had been played out, attempting to make sense of this dialogue of free association.

The following Monday's tutorial discussion topic was entitled, DIGNITY OF RISK, as coined by Wolfensberger (1970). This concept pertained to the intrinsic feeling of power and increased self-esteem when an individual attempts something at which he might succeed or fail and had the courage/guts to try. We liked this topic and the professor asked us to list five areas both socially and professionally when we had demonstrated dignity of risk; why we identified the attempt as a risky venture; and the advantages and disadvantages of success or failure of initiating the particular activity at the time. The age range of the participants (my peers) was late twenties to early fifties, which also helped to put things into perspective regarding life experiences, successes/failures, achievements beyond the wildest imagination, and boring mediocrity.

The third discussion topic was entitled, THE POWER OF FAILURE, which captivated everyone's attention – we went at that one with gusto! How can there be power in failing at something? Once again the professor introduced the word "power" defined from his perspective, borrowing from physics, as the formula "force times distance squared." Or in common parlance, talk the talk and walk the walk squared. Specifically, as I remember: when we say we should do and when we don't, we won't succeed because we never tried, which increases fear of initiative, or words to that effect. Boy, did our "jerk, asshole, slimeball" characteristics come out in spades during the heated debate that followed in the tutorial. To be honest, all of us manifested in little bits and pieces these three characteristics, some more than others, but nevertheless! *Jake, get on with your point, I'm getting bored!* Okay, okay.

In a nutshell the professor, with each Monday morning tutorial session, cleverly orchestrated the interpersonal dynamics of most organizational infrastructures I've known or been acquainted with during the past forty-odd years! The dos and don'ts, the whys and wherefores, came out in these carefully crafted tutorial sessions, which combined a philosophical belief system and a theoretical basis. All of this effort was meant to form an applied practice with meaning and substance, developed, revised, and refined, and then implemented at the worksite. During each tutorial this process encouraged debate, dissection, and rumination of a novel topic. What transpired throughout the two-hour diatribe was a clarification of our personal belief system regarding organizations, the dynamics within, and how to think and analyze in an objective, "third party" fashion. In conjunction, we wrote term papers on various topics and at the end of the course were required to pass an examination that lasted four hours and evaluated the breadth and depth of our knowledge in the subject area. But most importantly, the tutorial taught us humility, compassion, insight, and ganef[27] (i.e., a thief's mentality without actually robbing anyone).

In writing this section of the book I hope I can "carry on the torch" my old professor lit and passed on to many of us years ago and provide you with some cogent information regarding organizational survival. Now on with Section Two!

---

27   thief

CHAPTER NINE

ORGANIZATION DELINQUENTS: MISCREANTS WHO CREATE SYSTEMIC TYRANNY

PREAMBLE

LET ME START WITH THE FOLLOWING STATEMENT, HAVING WORKED IN THE field of Mental Health and Social Services commencing in the early 1970s, including twenty-one years in mid and senior management positions. There are people in the workforce who for the lack of a better descriptor I label *organization manipulators*. These individuals exploit others in the workforce using cunning, guile, and ruthless conduct to perpetuate unresolved needs. There have been many books and peer-reviewed articles describing their behavior during the past thirty years, and I guess here goes another one. Hopefully this portion of the book provides practical, no-nonsense ways to identify dysfunctional working environments, the denizens of which are often inhabited by organization manipulators with predatory intentions. I have also provided various coping strategies to improve your quality of work life! Now, let's "cut to the chase" and please try and follow my directions throughout the book and also before I forget, I'm a "folksy" writer; get familiar with my writing style. It will make learning the information easier and more fun to absorb! But on with Section Two and also prepare yourself, the preamble goes on for a few more pages setting the stage for an interesting examination of the organizational manipulator.

While reviewing a book by Dutton (1998) I noticed a section that describes the *development* of organization manipulators with some important background information to keep in mind. I felt THIS was a necessary and important precursor before reading more academic information, so here goes.

A child's attachment with abusive parents, his primary caregivers, is a source of pain and misery! Not a great leap in logic but here's the problem – the RAGE that is experienced by the child can be seriously repressed and its expression distorted because of such delinquent parenting, until a similar intimate attachment is formed later in life. Specifically and according to Dutton, the child's underlying personality will remain dormant until an intimate attachment later in life "triggers" the emotional template developed in the original attachment experience. The upshot being, abusive people physically abused in their family of origin are at risk for ambivalent attachment. As well, faulty internal schemata, particularly self-concepts and expectations of attachment to other people, are fraught with rage and fear. These ingredients are the basic groundwork for abusive behavior to manifest itself in interpersonal relationships.

The following is a very important point to remember as you read through Chapter Nine's contents. Abusive childhood experiences extrapolate learned behavior patterns, as they influence avoidant-ambivalent bonding styles that generate tendencies which are excessively demanding and angry in adult attachments.

I'm not going to use diagnostic labels (e.g., psychopath, antisocial personality disorder, covert aggressive personality, malignant narcissist, sociopath) to describe the professional miscreants we occasionally meet during our careers, but rather, describe *behavior* that YOU the employee will undoubtedly encounter at some point in your career, that will cause undue stress, conflict, second-guessing your sanity, anger, anxiety, depression, guilt, shame, revenge. All the conflicted feelings that one exudes when juxtaposed with this type of malignant personality working in close proximity! Later on (i.e.,

Chapter Fourteen) I will give you some coping strategies/techniques regarding "set-ups," "cons," and other nefarious activities that can be inflicted on you by these contemptible, human replicants. But before I go on, let me provide a little bit of my own experience dealing with these personalities.

I have worked beside many, many organization manipulators during the past forty-odd years. Three individuals come to mind whose outlandish behavior was so extreme within their respective organizations that the regional newspapers became involved regarding the crises that ensued, and two of the three manipulators were investigated on regional television. Unfortunately and to minimize the problem, these three personalities with extreme behaviors were rationalized by management as *outliers* within the respective organizations' conservative working culture. Specifically, the erroneous conclusion from management's perspective was that the culprits' personality flaws (i.e., grandiosity, entitlement, lack of empathy) were too outlandish and quickly rationalized as a rarity. This mistake had the unfortunate consequence of diminishing the administration's perception of what was appropriate versus inappropriate social conduct amongst other employees, and the problem not only festered but grew in size (i.e., ripple down effect).

The lack of immediate action to resolve the problem caused friction amongst the employees, which progressed to open conflict and toxic human relations throughout the respective organizations. Eventually this caused the demise of the three amigos mentioned above, which was not so quick I might add. Why, you ask? It appeared the manipulators' pattern of behavior within the respective organizations was "familiar, regular and like it was rehearsed" (as quoted by one of the staff). An enhancement of irregularities that any number of staff manifested while performing their jobs!? I wonder. In English, the presenting behavior of the three amigos was not unique but exaggerated personality traits frequently observed in other colleagues. Management in essence had become desensitized to inappropriate conduct until its presentation became "an issue" as complaints came rolling in from *outside* the organization. Specifically, the local papers got involved, television next, and finally the regional government stepped in, took a look, and then stepped back stating it was the responsibility of the Executive Board of the respective organizations "to resolve the situation."

So what you say, it's a tough world, Jake, these organization miscreants are usually identified, caught and done away with (hopefully) by the powers to be! Don't be so quick on the draw is my answer! Some are and some aren't – the major problem is the CARNAGE they cause and leave behind unresolved when they're terminated. The staff left exhausted and recoiling from the destruction, often lack the requisite coping strategies to survive the emotional games during the manipulator's employment. But I digress.

Here are some things you need to know as foundation information regarding the modus operandi of the manipulator's intent to "own" you. Specifically, your self-esteem, creativity, and will to work constructively within that new organization you've recently joined, or the current one with which you've been employed for many years.

COMPETENCE AND LOYALTY

TO START WITH, THESE NASTY INDIVIDUALS CONSISTENTLY UNDERMINE your career by challenging your *competence* and *loyalty* (Babiak & Hare, 2006). Your competence is what keeps you employed, and organization manipulators see your strengths as beneficial to their purposes, however meaningful or furtive. Secondly, your loyalty to the organization is measured in terms of productivity, quality output, regular attendance, adherence to policies and procedures, and your positive work effort. If you begin to present as a threat or imply disloyalty to the organization manipulator, you will often be denigrated by him/her to colleagues, superiors, external sources, etc.

The nature of this ploy is to disparage your competence and loyalty regarding adherence to the organization's work protocol. Historically, your reputation has been made by the impressions you make with your colleagues, a lot of hard work has gone into honestly obtaining this reputation, which, in relatively short order, can be demeaned and substantially reduced by a clever manipulator. This "skullduggery" is often done behind your back before you know about it and have time to challenge its effect. By that time your credibility has been reduced, so when you try to address the situation to remedy the problem, it's too late. Consequently, your role can become the token scapegoat of your department, division, unit, which can have catastrophic results on your mental health and your reputation. A nasty position to find yourself in, and one which I've observed over many years, often for no other reason than YOU, through the "luck of the draw," were dealt an unfortunate fate, by working in close proximity with one of these divisive individuals. But how did it happen in the first place; what did you do to cause them to initiate a range war against you? Book (2009) suggests these people have an uncanny ability to observe and interpret vulnerability and with unusual accuracy, starting initially in many cases by assessing the GAIT of their intended target!

Please believe me, the standard employee is cannon fodder to be easily assessed and exploited by an experienced manipulator within a work environment. As I proceed with this Chapter take note, the nature of the manipulator's interpersonal conduct presents a marked risk for inexperienced employees being targeted and victimized. Let's get back to regaining your authenticity as a competent and loyal employee, shall we, what to do?

Some of the preventative measures to make sure your competence and loyalty are kept in check when disparaged by an organization manipulator include the following practices (Babiak et al., 2006). Unfortunately, making complaints describing a personality maladjustment of a colleague to a company H.R. representative or Senior Manager is not one of them and *loses* you credibility. You're simply not qualified to make a diagnosis unless you're a licensed psychologist, psychiatrist, or psychiatric social worker. Please, leave the diagnostics alone unless you're formally qualified to make such a clinical evaluation.

A better approach is describing the individual's *behavior*; its frequency, the pattern of circumstance, time of day, themes, anything that is relevant to the work at hand that challenges/

reduces the organization's mission/mandate, rather than presenting a subjective feeling or impression about a colleague that may not be perceived by other people, which could in effect, reduce your credibility to your listener; as mentioned above, a common occurrence originating from the organization manipulator is creating chaos amongst the staff members, for example, playing one staff member against the other by claiming something derogatory was stated by one towards the other. The success of this ploy depends on one or both parties avoiding confronting the person they think is talking negatively about them. This "divide and conquer" technique takes its toll as the staff tension increases, effectively shutting down communication and providing "cover" for the organization manipulator. This ploy allows the manipulator to control and isolate employees from each other and simultaneously conceal his/her abusive behavior.

The best defense against the divide and conquer ploy is developing a solid reputation and positive interactions with subordinates, peers, and senior staff by demonstrating talent and consistency, which increases credibility. Favorable comments about the organization, its operation, and a positive atmosphere during discussions with senior colleagues will be remembered. Questions asked by this level of management should be responded to with crisp, fact-based answers. Sincerity usually communicates competence, forthrightness, and loyalty, and will not be forgotten.

Know the Company's Policy-Procedure Manual and Code of Conduct expectations "like the back of your hand"! Go to the orientation sessions when you're first employed and ask questions of the Human Resources personnel so that you KNOW YOUR RIGHTS as an employee. This point cannot be stressed enough! When in doubt call the H.R. department representative and request a formal meeting to discuss your concerns.

PICK YOUR BATTLES CAREFULLY! No one is interested in a "whiner" (i.e., complainer) AND PLEASE rephrase your complaints with a positive twist. Use the old "bookends" technique learned in assertiveness training. Specifically, start with a positive statement regarding your concern, then slip in your critique and wait for the response and tactfully debate the response if you feel your point is being misunderstood. End the discussion on a positive note, thanking the individual for their time, etc. Long-term whiners hurt their professional reputation and credibility within the organization. People want to work alongside positive influences not "downers." Complainers are easy set-ups for the organization manipulator, who wants to place them in the scapegoat role – the old "top dog, bottom dog" role, to enhance his/her reputation as a "go to" employee.

Frankly, if you're already perceived by others as a chronic complainer, there is little dissonance produced when you find yourself being scapegoated. Basically, your lack of credibility and negative attitude as a malcontent downer mean you are not high on the organizational totem pole. The irony is your colleagues might even support and thank the organization manipulator for identifying your behavior as deleterious to the working conditions of the organization and the manipulator having the "guts" to address the problem. Nice hunh (eh).

Phew, what's next regarding organization delinquents, those miscreants who create systemic tyranny? How do you maintain your emotional stability in these situations?

HOW TO MAINTAIN EMOTIONAL BUOYANCY AND SURVIVE IN A POLITICAL ECOSYSTEM

ONE WORD AMONGST MANY DESCRIBES AN ORGANIZATION MANIPULATOR – NARCISSISM – cold-blooded, self-serving behavior, as they tend to have limited, if any capacity for demonstrating true empathy! To reinforce the need for self-aggrandizement, the organization manipulator uses control paradigms that include cunning, exploitive, manipulative behavior to achieve goals and all at the expense of your mental health! Employees are carefully chosen and predated upon, often very adroitly and with some degree of panache! The organization manipulator practices their skill-set of deceit daily, weekly, monthly, yearly with identified targets, usually "run of the mill" employees who, at first glance, appear normal. Specifically, the manipulator's predatory pattern of thinking and behavior has over decades become habituated, even refined, almost error-free in many cases. As a consequence, this method of conduct is often difficult to clearly identify and immensely destructive to the organization's infrastructure and its employees' collective mental health, and with time, many a reputation is ruined. What to do? Please read on.

I refer to Kuczmarski & Kuczmarski's (1995) norms for personal values, as a "jump off" point for discussion. One aspect of personal values I emphasize specifically is encouraging *intuitive thinking* to increase accuracy of appraisal by *feeling* if something is true! Intuitive thinking encourages the individual tapping into his/her emotions (the head/heart dichotomy) and in doing so better leverages his/her values in decision making. It also increases the ability of identifying inappropriate behavior by organization manipulators. Specifically, intuition combines both feelings and emotional input and is an underutilized skill. If learned and utilized properly it assists in "decision making, communication, leadership, motivating others and building trust" (p. 154).

Most organizational settings gather decision-making information in three ways: authority, logic, and science, frankly, a pedantic approach that is often assessed, screened for inherent weaknesses, and exploited by the organization manipulator. A parallel process of evaluation by the employee is influenced by *intuition*, specifically, feelings and sense experiences on decision making/options provided in making a decision. This approach increases analysis by an employee who becomes comfortable with the listening/feeling perspective intuition provides. An intuitive employee's examination of the organizational dynamics is often more objective and insightful, allowing a fresh perspective to be garnered. Intuitive thinking, feeling, and sensing are in contrast to the emphasis on "knowing" through authority, logic, and scientific thinking. In this regard, we need to encourage inner emotionally charged intuitive energy and insight, which brings a new perspective on examining organizational issues. This also provides further armamentarium against the organization manipulator's ploys which include deceit, cunning, guile, and exploitation. Haven't I said that one before? In essence, please listen to that inner voice while you plan your next move with these "cagey" individuals!

HOW TO ACCOMPLISH GOALS IN SPITE OF AN ORGANIZATION MANIPULATOR'S PRESENCE

IN PRESTON'S (1988) BOOK, *LEADERSHIP STRATEGIES FOR HEALTH CARE Managers*, the author suggests ten strategies for management to employ in an organization. I also think they're of merit for a "line" employee to keep in mind throughout his/her employment within an organization and as another "grab bag" of techniques to be utilized when experiencing distress in a dysfunctional working milieu.

In a workaday employment environment no one is perfect and demands can be placed on you that might be outside of your immediate job description. When individuals ask questions or when a problem issue arises, be able to assess as much as you can about the problem and those challenges and demands being faced that influenced the colleague's desire to seek YOU out specifically. Remember the old saying, "nice guys finish last" and in the context of *not* becoming a "mark," as in completing a colleague's dirty work. Try to understand the purpose of WHY you are being sought out.

Don't take anything for granted and ask questions to clarify any issue presenting inconsistencies. Examine your daily accomplishments and subjectively "guestimate" your colleague's as well – gauge any disparity and be cautious of over-solicitous behavior. This will keep you from becoming complacent and allow you to maintain a competitive spirit, especially when confronted with a manipulator's request for information about a certain project, ongoing job function, or any other arbitrary request. Please remember the broad perspective surrounding the initial request (bigger picture) – this will keep you on your toes.

Try to maintain an optimistic attitude at your worksite, despite carrying the weight of negative information about a manipulator's behavior, or your observations of others being harassed by this individual. Challenge catastrophic thinking paradigms by "thought stopping" and counting by threes backwards from 100 to interfere with emotional escalation; practice diaphragmatic breathing to regulate heart rate – counting up 1–4 while inhaling, pausing for a count of two and then counting down 4–1 while exhaling. Lastly, optimism is contagious; your positive approach to your job, albeit working in a living nightmare when predated upon, allows others to benefit from your emotional strengths.

Keep your objectives and those of the organization in mind at all times. Objectives allow you to remain on track while working for, with, around an organization manipulator whose demands, surreptitious behavior, and charm are all the while undermining your confidence and positive approach to your work and quality of work life. To reiterate, keep those goals, both short and long-term, in mind at all times.

Know your strengths and weaknesses! This cannot be stated enough: KNOW YOUR STRENGTHS AND WEAKNESSES. This will help to improve your skill-set by challenging those areas needing to be improved, thereby reducing (hopefully) your vulnerability when an organization manipulator wants to exploit you. I say again more softly this time, know your strengths and weaknesses, remember the person who appears "normal" stated above – yeah right.

Learn and know your job inside, outside, upside down, right side up – this knowledge competency reduces boundary encroachment and manipulation by an organization manipulator who is immensely skilled at discerning vulnerability and exploiting unmercifully a mediocre to poor performer.

Deal with any conflict openly and directly AS SOON AS POSSIBLE. Unresolved conflict allows divisive behavior to be utilized by the organization manipulator, who, while operating from the sidelines, loves to set up antagonistic he said/she said "range wars" between colleagues. I have observed this strategy countless times in my career and the loser is most often your reputation, which remains in the organization long after you've departed. Why use direct confrontation with a colleague to resolve the conflict? The answer: because it sends a message that you and the opposing party had the "guts" to challenge the problem appropriately (i.e., directly)! Your actions and style of conflict resolution, or lack thereof, will be carefully appraised by an organization manipulator, which is translated quickly that you will not "truck" with underhanded, devious behavior! Please, a silly point to bring up but an important one nonetheless: If you haven't approached a problem or conflict head on with an opposing, over- zealous colleague, try giving it a shot; it will work wonders for your self-esteem! Some unsolicited advice, remember to use tact, as in the bookends "plus minus plus" assertiveness technique to reduce any potential aggression. Moving on: If you want results – pass around the credit; the team becomes the benefactor of your generosity – greed and self-aggrandizement are not acceptable. Work quietly, effectively, and efficiently within the organizational milieu and the success of your work performance should be traced back to you, not always, but most often. Now on to Chapter Ten, "Adult Children of Alcoholics" and their impact on the organization.

CHAPTER TEN

ADULT CHILDREN OF ALCOHOLICS (ACOAS) IN THE ORGANIZATION: HOW TO IDENTIFY AND WHAT TO DO

PREAMBLE

I BEGIN CHAPTER TEN WITH THE FOLLOWING STATEMENT, WHICH SHOULD be common knowledge to those individuals who are clinically trained and qualified. Persons raised in a dysfunctional family often *repeat* the same patterns of behavior learned in their families, in the organizations in which they work. Further, during the past thirty years since Wotititz's book *Adult Children of Alcoholic Parents* (1983) was published, we have observed that many of the behaviors considered "normal" for individuals in organizations are actually a repertoire of behaviors of an active addict or a non-recovering co-dependent. In conjunction, many organizational processes labeled acceptable in the worksite are a repetition of the same addictive behavior "cloaked" as corporate structure and function.

ACOA BEHAVIOR

WOTITITZ (1990) STATED THAT THE FOLLOWING PATTERNS OF BEHAVIOR and personality traits expressed by a consensus of Adult Children of Alcoholics (ACOAs) describe the characteristic manner of responding in their environment and the problems derived from their dysfunctional upbringing. Specifically, ACOAs:

A. guess at what normal is;
B. have difficulty following a project through from beginning to end;
C. lie when it would be just as easy to tell the truth;
D. judge themselves without mercy;
E. exhibit more difficulty having fun;
F. take themselves very seriously;
G. have difficulty with intimate relationships;
H. over-react to changes over which they have no control;
I. feel they are different from other people;
J. are either super responsible or super irresponsible;
K. show extreme loyalty, even in the face of evidence that the loyalty is undeserved; and
L. display impulsivity – they have a tendency to quickly "lock" themselves into a course of action without giving serious consideration to alternative behaviors or possible consequences. This impulsivity leads to confusion, self-loathing, and loss of control over their environment. In conjunction, they spend an excessive amount of energy cleaning up the mess.

In an article entitled, "Control, Attachment Style, and Relationship Satisfaction Among Adult Children of Alcoholics," Beesley and Stoltenberg (2002) describe the ACOA's tendency to develop an exaggerated need to control situations and/or people in order to mediate the chaos and unpredictability of the alcoholic families in which they grow up, and that they generalize this behavior to adult relationships.

No one knows exactly how many active addicts there are in Canada or the United States. To date, there are no accurate statistics for alcohol, drug, food, sex, work, or relationship addicts. In this Chapter, the manner with which the Adult Child of Alcoholics (ACOA) repeats dysfunctional behaviors learned from their upbringing, while employed in organizations, is addressed and a working solution to the problem is subsequently provided.

An ACOA is an individual who was raised in a family in which one or more parent was an alcoholic, or in a family that repeats alcoholic or addictive patterns. As a consequence, adult children may not be addicts themselves as adults, but have a predilection to become an addict under the right circumstances (Schaef & Fassel, 1988). Statistics vary on the number of ACOAs in the United States. Goldberg (1986) suggests approximately 15% of the U.S. population (i.e., 40 million), but this estimate is viewed by many as a conservative evaluation. The writer could not find any statistics regarding the prevalence of ACOAs in Canada, but a conservative number is probably two million.

ACOAs face enumerable problems at the worksite. A number of factors consistently presented by ACOAs have a negative impact on the organization's political ecosystem. The following categories are examined from Goldberg's (1986) research regarding the myriad of difficulties exhibited in the workplace by ACOAs, which are still cogent in 2014, more specifically:

A. *Perfectionism/self-criticism*. Most ACOAs feel a job duty must be done perfectly and often denigrate themselves when even the smallest mistakes are made. Praise is frequently disregarded because of the self-critical nature of ACOAs – they find compliments difficult to believe or accept. One consistent byproduct of the self-critical nature of ACOAs is problems with overtime. They want the product/work widget to be completed "perfectly" and the content of a product is often revised and revised and then revised once again.

B. *Workaholism*. For many ACOAs, overwork is the addiction of choice at the worksite. They often manifest an inability to make personal boundaries, have a feeling of inferiority and insecurity, and generally are unable to say no to their colleagues' demands. This passivity consequently reinforces and escalates a behavioral problem that contaminates the work environment. A general statement can be made that most ACOAs are better at work than their personal relationships. This weakness is highlighted by the fact that many ACOAs have anticipatory and performance anxiety regarding interpersonal contact at work.

The writer has frequently heard mid and senior management staff compliment an ACOA's dedication and productivity, "Jill has excelled at this job since the beginning, I don't know where she gets her energy – but it's too bad she's not a people person." Unfortunately, due to the chronic anxiety ACOAs exhibit, they have a tendency to be hypervigilant and chronically seek approval at the expense of their emotional and physical health – it can be very exhausting attempting to meet unattainable goals.

C. *Rigidity in thinking.* ACOAs are generally rigid in their thinking patterns, more specifically, they interpret problems from a black-white/right-wrong perspective. This rigidity, in conjunction with the perfectionism previously mentioned, reinforces a belief that there is only one correct way of examining a project or problem. The downside of approaching problem-solving in a linear manner is the reduction in flexibility and options to resolve the situation. This rigidity in thinking processes/stratagem has obvious repercussions causing ongoing problems at the worksite. Specifically, the ACOA will frequently provide an affirmative response regarding the way a problem should be resolved, but then go in another direction – doing things their own way.

Thus, commitments from ACOAs at the worksite regarding methods of evaluation to find a viable solution can often be misleading and create interpersonal conflict. The person on the receiving end of these misunderstandings frequently doesn't know what he/she did wrong! In these situations they often acquiesce to the ACOA's behavior, which has an undermining effect on morale in the workplace environment.

D. *Crisis handling.* ACOAs are usually very adept at resolving crises and maintaining poise when the environment around them is fraught with unpredictability. Their family upbringing has conditioned them to maintain a comfortable emotional state, under the most extreme conditions. The obvious carryover of this strength during a worksite crisis, from the perspective of their colleagues, is a perception of a positive attribution (e.g., admiration). In a competitive industry where "quid pro quo" is the norm, acknowledgment of this strength can be unintentionally misused as reinforcement – praising the ACOA's calm, cool and collected behavior "under fire." The major problem as conveyed to the writer by many ACOAs is their comfort level in being calm throughout these stressful situations. They frequently state they thrive in crisis situations, which allows them to feel in control because they are so practiced at being in control from an early age. Specifically, ACOAs are raised in homes where inconsistent parenting practices by their addicted parent(s) are the norm; where lack of structure in the household is the norm; where their parent's impulsive and often violent overreactions to otherwise normal, day-to-day intangibles contravene the ACOA's ability to feel emotion at any depth. In essence, the ACOA's upbringing has conditioned him/her to feel comfortable with intense feelings and conversely to misinterpret and mistrust softer, more sensitive "welfare emotions," which contributes to interpersonal barriers at the worksite.

E. *Teamwork*. Generally ACOAs are *not* team players; this deficit is attributed to an inconsistency in being taught the basic rules of cooperation in the family unit during their upbringing. More specifically, the family has often been described as a painful/fearful period in the ACOA's life. As a consequence, many ACOAs are socially inept, have difficulty adjusting to interpersonal workplace demands, and prefer to be left alone. Conversely, please read the following section on factors contributing to a normal worksite atmosphere.

WHAT FACTORS CONTRIBUTE TO A NORMAL WORKSITE ATMOSPHERE

MANY FACTORS CONTRIBUTE TO A "NORMAL" WORKSITE ATMOSPHERE; however, the following organizational elements described by Martin (2012) represent a good starting point. *Four* interrelated, healthy functioning components of an organization's group dynamics enable a strong organization to be developed. These components include *morale, unity, cohesion,* and *mood*. This allows its employees to perform at an optimal level, being fully motivated and engaged, and where there is satisfaction and the intrinsic feeling that "I'm involved in something special."

1. The first ingredient, *Morale*, is the willingness of an individual, a team, an organization to win and to succeed. Morale has also been described as the mental toughness and determination to "soldier on" despite hardships, obstacles, and failures. When organizations have elevated morale amongst its employees, individuals can maintain focus on a positive outcome. Hope is also enriched in these positive environments and a feeling that we will accomplish the goal and be successful.

2. The second ingredient for a successful work environment is *Unity*. Unity is the willingness to subordinate individual goals to those of the team, group, or organization. To function optimally as a coherent unit, the organization's employees must subordinate their personal goals and aspirations to those of the entire group. Specifically, the group's potential to achieve a positive outcome can be drawn from the individuals' motivation and satisfaction from their respective roles in a team/organization.

3. The third ingredient, *Cohesion*, is the ability to function as a whole, as a well-oiled machine. Well-led Units within an organization are highly cohesive, having a strong unity of purpose. Poorly led units frequently suffer poor cohesion and have low unity. The negative effect of reduced cohesion and unity is often the disintegration of the unit, as a cycle of poor morale and lower cohesion ensue.

4. The fourth ingredient for a successful work environment is *Mood*. Keep in mind, when employees complain within an organization it doesn't necessarily equate with bad morale. However, the opposite is quite true! When the organization's employees stop talking, that is, when there is confidence that open disclosure is a threat to job security/safety, an internal problem exists. The lack of comfort in disclosure is a mitigating factor that has a negative effect on performance. In these situations, management should have been aware of or informed a long time previously that a

problem exists. Three examples of conditions *reducing* a positive mood amongst the organization's employees include:

   a. ACOAs' behavior, eroding the organization's effectiveness/efficiency within its infrastructure;
   b. Poor leadership; when the constituent body of employees feels the Executive doesn't have the welfare of its membership at heart;
   c. Insufficient workload; when the employees have too few things to do or to keep busy, this is a pre-condition for the malcontents of the organization to work their vitriol. Conversely and to reduce employee misconduct, experienced managers keep their employees busy (i.e., developing projects with strategic meaning), which usually increases morale, unity, and cohesion and also prevents a deterioration in mood that often accompanies idleness and boredom.

ACOAS' DISRUPTIVE BEHAVIOR AT THE WORKSITE

SO NOW YOU'VE READ THE "IDEAL" INGREDIENTS OF A STRONG ORGANIZAtion, built on a foundation of high morale, unity, cohesion, and positive mood. Conflict begins to occur when the organization employs an ACOA, whose characteristic pattern of dysfunctional behavior begins to undermine the Unit's/Organization's "balance" and trouble is not just around the corner – it has arrived!

Goldberg (1986) identifies three major reasons why ACOAs are poor team members: (a) they have difficulty listening and communicating; (b) they have difficulty giving and receiving criticism; (c) they have a strong need for control. In general, ACOAs were raised in a conflicted family environment and consequently could not rely on their parents. A standard complaint the writer has heard from ACOAs is, "I was always let down as a kid (by my parents) and don't trust very easily," which is one major indicator why ACOAs are so doubtful of other employees' motives and are themselves controlling. In conjunction, ACOAs have trouble with authority or perceived authority figures. Typically managers and supervisors are viewed as surrogate parents and ACOAs often seek from them a consistency they never received from their caregivers while growing up. Unfortunately, it can lead to a "two steps forward, one step backward" paradigm, if professional intervention to correct the problem is not sought out. Specifically, the upheaval in the ACOA's childhood home affects their interpretation of a supervisor's intent. While growing up, ACOAs never knew how a parent was going to act, so now, when they're requested to see a boss, they often panic!

The mistrust felt from ACOAs can be very burdensome and over an extended period, draining of time, energy, and patience. This is observed when the boss inevitably does not fulfill the ACOA's emotional demands and is met with veiled contempt, hostility, and rejection (i.e., projection) from the ACOA's unresolved family history. In these situations, some bosses react by taking on quasi therapy roles with ACOAs such as mentoring and protection, to give the ACOA a fighting chance, reminders of past failures made good due to the boss's intervention. Frequently, these efforts from the boss can provide sustenance for a while and even allow subtle changes to occur, but as a matter of course (from my consulting experience), the ACOA's "drama" overtakes the positive changes that have occurred and the employer is left wondering, "and after all I did for Joe he hasn't changed – what happened?!" ACOAs' behavior towards their supervisor/boss is typically dualistic. They can admire the boss, acquiesce to his/her power, attempting to meet each request – or they can resist and be an oppositional, defiant subordinate. The ACOA's problem is not necessarily task specific or being able to do his/her job properly, but rather, the lack of a human relationship skill-set, setting in motion a frustrating paradigm of conflict at the worksite.

INTERVENTIONS WITH ACOAS IN THE WORK ENVIRONMENT

WHAT TO DO? QUICK ASSESSMENT AND INTERVENTION IS OF THE HIGHEST priority before the organization begins to lose staff, unwilling/

unable to deal with the ACOA's day-to-day conduct! Here are some suggestions that may be considered to resolve the ACOA worksite problem: Please keep in mind, children who grew up in an alcoholic home typically develop similar personality traits and characteristics as their alcoholic caregiver(s). It is therefore necessary to put in place a well-defined intervention program that has been empirically tested and has efficacy (e.g., S.H.A.P.E.). The S.H.A.P.E. program incorporates a cognitive behavioral and solution-focused therapeutic approach and has proven successful with ACOAs (Adamson & Ahmed, 2011). The organization's support for such a treatment initiative is necessary to allow the following interventions to be successful, without appearing draconian. I have incorporated Woititz's (1990) suggestions with some additional observations which are as follows:

1. For reasons stated (see #6 below), have an intervention team, as opposed to an individual, seek information from the ACOA's supervisor and collateral sources, which confirms the ACOA behavior is a problem and requires intervention. Of note: Usually, by the time the intervention process has been identified, the ACOA has created substantial interpersonal problems within the organization and quick, decisive action is necessary and required.

2. During the intervention phase, describing the ACOA's behavior should be verbalized nonjudgmentally. It is most crucial at this phase of the intervention process to recognize the ACOA is operating from a conditioned, response paradigm regarding stress, the interpersonal worksite demands, and the ACOA's inability to use effective coping strategies. Specifically, using ineffective coping strategies with the interpersonal job demands creates problems and makes the ACOA's behavior appear parasitic in its presentation amongst colleagues. The colleagues expect the give and take of teamwork and conversely are faced with the ACOA's rigid, self-absorbed, "loner" attitude/deportment/passive and active aggression, which undermines the effectiveness of team performance.

3. The intervention team formally meets to discuss the identified staff member's behavior. If the behavior reflects the criteria of

identified ACOA characteristics, this requires an immediate action plan. Subsequently, a decision is made to address the problem with the ACOA and seek his/her feedback regarding the identified issues at hand. At this point, each member of the intervention team should comprehend and communicate clearly the consequences of the ACOA *not* beginning a recovery program.

4. The consequences must be stated in a tone that conveys clear, immediate, and important action! That is, a statement of intent by the organization's management informing the ACOA that continued employment, without entering a recovery program, will result in termination from the job! A tough but honest approach to challenge the ACOA's defense system (i.e., denial, rationalization, projection) has to be taken! Most importantly, the message conveyed highlights the intervention team's commitment to follow-up on the stated consequences forthwith. As well, it is often determined that colleagues frequently propped up the ACOA by rationalizing the problem; denying a major problem exists; and minimizing, that is covering up for the ACOA with enabling behavior. Obviously, this process only aggravated the situation and perpetuated the ACOA's dysfunctional behavior and its harmful effect on positive team functioning within the organization.

5. After the intervention with the ACOA there is continuing work. All the employees of the worksite who had contact with the ACOA can be, at some level, functioning as co-dependents, especially if the ACOA's behavior was not challenged and allowed to continue over a chronic period of time (e.g., 6 months+). The colleagues should be encouraged to attend a support group within the organization, supervised by a member of the intervention team, or their designate, who is trained in S.H.A.P.E and ACOA behavior and its residual effects on those around them.

6. Lastly, there is no one way an organization recovers from ACOA or co-dependent behavior. I strongly recommend that relying on the efforts of a single company representative (e.g., EAP counsellor, H.R. designate, Consulting Psychologist) is *not*

Chapter Ten | 193

realistic (i.e., this can be very exhausting work for one person) but rather, the organization trains an intervention team to work with ACOAs with the following issues addressed:

    a. Prepare information, education and support for the intervention and treatment of ACOA behavior;

    b. Operate as a "think tank" to address the implications of ACOA behavior and the entire system's (e.g., division, department, unit) recovery, which has been negatively affected within the organizational environment; and

    c. identify the structures and processes that facilitated the ACOA to operate longer than six months (i.e., normal probation period) within the organization and rectify any weaknesses in the system.

Now it's on to Chapter Eleven, evaluating the political ecosystem of an organization, more specifically: your "location" within the organization; "emotional safety"; and "navigation" to help guide you through the day-to-day stressors and obstacles interfering with your quality of work life. Don't worry, after several reviews, it should be easy to put into practice.

CHAPTER ELEVEN

EVALUATING THE WORKPLACE POLITICAL ECOSYSTEM:
LOCATION, SAFETY, AND NAVIGATION

PREAMBLE

PREVIOUSLY, IN CHAPTER TEN, MARTIN (2012) IDENTIFIED *FOUR* ORGANIzational elements that contribute to a "normal" worksite atmosphere. Let's reiterate these four components: morale, unity, cohesion, and mood. But what about the organization's flexibility quotient for change and what distinguishes a healthy from a dysfunctional organization? Please, read on.

DETERMINING CHANGE THRESHOLD WITHIN THE ORGANIZATION

IN CHAPTER NINE WE DISCUSSED TEN STRATEGIES TO EMPLOY THAT INFLUence a successful work experience, followed in Chapter Ten by highlighting four organizational elements that contribute to a normal worksite atmosphere. But what about three important ingredients a person should assess when entering a new job – *location, safety, and navigation*. Let me digress before we go on.

Over forty years ago Mott (1972) identified three characteristics that distinguish healthy from unhealthy organizations, which are related to the effectiveness of the organization: adaptability, flexibility, and productivity. *Adaptability* refers to the ability of an organization to change and resist becoming rigid in its functioning and operating procedures vis-à-vis its task environment (i.e., the part of the organization related to goal attainment efforts). *Flexibility* differs from adaptation in regards to response time. Adaptability is concerned with long-term adjustment, whereas flexibility is concerned with adjusting to internal and external demands. The *productivity* characteristic is concerned with the amount of products or services provided by the organization.

Healthy organizations are self-renewing and self-examining in an effort to maintain adaptability, flexibility, and productivity. Key internal dimensions in these organizations achieve integration and congruity *amongst* the dimensions. In conjunction, they have consistency and congruity with their task environments. The key internal dimensions in which planned change may be made include employees, structure, technology, and task (Leavitt, 1965).

This is a lot of information to "chew on" but it's important to know the theoretical foundation of what makes a healthy organization and how it maintains itself. Continuing on, bear with me please.

Organizational "health" provides *internal adjustment* activities aimed at having the people, structure, technology, and task of the organization work in harmony. From the writer's perspective a chronic problem with two or more of these dimensions can cause internal health problems for the organization. A second aspect of organizational health refers to the organization's adjustment to the demands of the task environment. In conjunction, good *external adjustment* is essential for organizational health and vitality and is best achieved through the reciprocal exchange of knowledge, products, and other resources between the organization and the agents in its task environment (Alderfer, 1976).

The maintenance of organizational health requires an active process of planned change and adjustment to avoid crises. There must be constant efforts to achieve integration and wholeness within the four internal dimensions of the organization (i.e., people, structure, technology, and task) as well as adjustment to the task function of the work environment. This ongoing process of adjustment to internal and external demands requires both resources and commitment from the organization's management, as well as a long-range perspective. Specifically, short-run cost-effectiveness should not be achieved at the expense of long-term health and growth.

So now, what about location, safety, and navigation in an organization? That was part of Chapter Eleven's title – enough digression, here we go.

LOCATION

SO NOW YOU'VE JOINED AN ORGANIZATION AND ARE "ITCHING" TO PROVE your worth, but before you do, please remember there is NO PERFECT organizational infrastructure. Let's pause and take a backwards approach to the location issue. I would suggest and for peace of mind you review the following *ten disqualifiers* of an organization and then "locate" yourself, or where you think you fall within your current imperfect work environment, we'll go from there.

But Jake, what d'ya mean "locate yourself" especially after reviewing the negative things about an organization. Shush, just do what I ask and read carefully the following ten factors suggested by Kuczmarski & Kuczmarski (1995), which I've expanded upon and endorse wholeheartedly:

Ten factors that *decrease* employee satisfaction include:

A. *Values Gap* – There is often a disparity between the values of management and the values of employees within the same organization. Specifically, management preaches one set of values to employees but practices a different set themselves. After a while you can spot the inconsistency a mile away, which becomes an invaluable tool for assessing an imbalanced and dysfunctional organization infrastructure.

B. *Theory vs. Practice* – Many of the norms and values that are developed and nurtured within organizations are not positive.

Rather, they are negative forces that act to create tension between management and the employee. Look for a negative valence that festers, diminishing positive interactions (i.e., power struggles) between management and employees.

C. *Insufficient Feedback, Rewards, and Recognition* – To understand the impact they are making, employees depend on feedback and view it as an incentive. Conversely, management in a dysfunctional organization rarely does a good job of letting employees know specifically how they are performing; nor do they acknowledge the contributions of their employees. There are often few nonfinancial rewards in these companies. Specifically, descriptive praise and nonmonetary recognition are rarely used by management – when this happens a lethargy often prevails – need I say more.

D. *Lack of Trust* – Many employees are frustrated because management doesn't trust them. Employees perceive that they are not given enough responsibility and "ordered" to do monotonous tasks of which they quickly tire, the feedback loop is closed, and frustration threshold is low. Not a lot of incentive to stay is there.

E. *Low Job Satisfaction and Self-Esteem* – Employee job satisfaction is low in many undesirable organizations because individual self-esteem and perception of self-worth are low, and management refuses or does not care to resolve the problem at hand.

F. *Minimal Teaching and Mentoring* – If the leaders are willing to help teach new members how to do their jobs well, there is less confusion among employees about the organizational norms and values. Conversely, very little teaching occurs within dysfunctional organizations and mentoring is almost nonexistent. Yet if provided, it has the power to transmit knowledge about norms and values to employees and increase feedback and job satisfaction. If you're faced with this minimal teaching/mentoring problem, think about looking for "greener pastures." Specifically, if there is no change over a six-month duration, you could be at risk of becoming part of the problem.

G. *Personal Values Are Disconnected to Those of the Organization* – If norms and values are established within the workplace, they have the potential to empower employees. If organizations can influence their employees to tie their personal goals to those of the workplace, then they will nurture long-term relationships together. Unfortunately this rarely occurs, or does not occur in dysfunctional organizations.

H. *Minimal Professional Impact and Growth* – Employees seek to make an impact and are happier when they feel they do so. Employees want professional growth; conversely, a lack of job opportunities and/or mobility reduces morale, which can affect job satisfaction, which occurs frequently in dysfunctional organizations.

I. *Lack of Commitment to Values* – Many organizations make efforts to create norms and values but fall short in demonstrating commitment to the values. Employees are able to detect a divergence between their organization's stated norms and the values and mechanisms to reinforce them. Many organizations express a commitment to professional growth and development, but do little to instill trust in their employees, provide training, or reimburse development courses. Obviously this is bad news; you should be wary of this inconsistency and proceed cautiously, as professional development is required to improve your cadre of skills and competencies.

J. *Values-less Leadership* – The leadership within the organization does not convey the values that the organization espouses. This is a big one; be sure you have a comfort level "from the gut" about the leadership under which you work. Think about this one and listen to your heart as well as your head and paycheck.

Before you rate your imperfect organization regarding these ten destabilizing characteristics, please review the following tenets (Cherniss, 1980), which should help to clarify your evaluation:

A. the valence of power an organization exhibits regarding bureaucratic mentality affects job stress and burnout, which are correlated with level of staff autonomy and control;

B. greater centralization and formalization within an organization are associated with greater alienation, stress, and burnout;

C. creativity and innovation are stifled not by the formal role and power structures, but by subtle norms that define the institutional atmosphere. The extent to which innovation, creativity, and risk-taking are rewarded is an important aspect of an organization's normative structure and contributes to your mental health as an employee. Please, keep this in mind as you read on.

NOW come three issues to help appraise the first element, "location," regarding evaluation of the organization's political ecosystem. *Finally, Jake, I thought we'd never get there!*

The *three* critical components of organizational design used to "locate" yourself within an organization's political ecosystem are the normative structure, the power structure, and the role structure (Cherniss, 1980). These three components determine to a great extent the amount of role conflict and ambiguity experienced by a staff member. *Dysfunction* in these components can cause job insecurity and fear, which interferes with the initiation of "dignity of risk" – attempting new and innovative projects. Remember this while "locating" yourself within the imperfect organization's template of work demands, expectations, and short- and long-term goals. Are you comfortable and feeling fine about this process thus far – hope so, let's move on.

Conversely, these three components can also determine the extent to which a staff member's job is interesting, challenging, and stimulating! They also influence the amount of autonomy, participation, and control available to a staff member on the job site. All of these factors ultimately influence the extent to which staff members experience psychological success in their work, which in turn affects the burnout rate in a work setting. Or, as I always say to disgruntled staff coping in an organizational environment, "work milieus can appear to be a tropical paradise then turn quickly into cyclones; please learn to manage the transition." The moral of the story: be prepared to combat any unlikelihoods that spring up out of nowhere, or in other words, Murphy's Law prevails! Let's move on to emotional safety.

SAFETY

Okay, here you are in a brand new job and work environment. What do I do to assess the emotional safety of the present worksite? Hopefully you've got a fair understanding of where you're "located" from the information provided above. The following ten questions developed by Kets de Vries & Miller (1987) can start the ball rolling regarding your assessment of the emotional "safety quotient" of the imperfect organization you've recently joined. As no organization is perfect, I've taken the liberty of expanding the answers to the questions below, taken from my experiences over the years:

1. *Generally, what is the working environment like?*
   Are your colleagues friendly, detached, fearful, goal directed?

2. *What does the organization stand for? What are its goals?*
   Is the Mission/Mandate of the organization and the method to obtain the organization's goals readily available for the employees? Do the goals seem realistic?

   Do they seem far-fetched given the nature of the organization's staffing population; service provision; general level of competence; budget? Have you reviewed the Annual General Report from the past two–three years? Does it mesh with the organization's grand scheme(s)?

3. *What is the "Vision" of the CEO who runs the organization?*
   Is the vision of the organization something you feel is "right for you" in regards to your professional qualifications and ability to fulfill the job duties and mandate of your unit within the infrastructure of the organization?

4. *What aspects of the organizational functioning are important to the leaders? What stimulates them, gets them excited, angry, pleased?*

Once again, carefully read the President's Annual General Report over the past two–three years and talk to people within and external to the organization. This will give you a cross-referenced data base from which to assess your emotional safety within the organization and ability to realistically meet the demands placed on your unit and you personally.

5. *How are crisis and critical incidents dealt with?*
   A very important point – over your probation period determine the ways and means with which the organization resolves crisis and critical incidents. Do the resolutions appear fair, unfair, draconian, over- or under-resolved?

6. *What kind of people do well in the organization?*
   Another important point – can you identify those factors that facilitate promotion? Are promotions given as a result of fair and transparent evaluation procedures, including both objective and subjective assessments of the incumbent's skill-set?

7. *What are the measures of performance and the criteria for rewards and punishments?*
   How does the organization objectively and subjectively measure performance and what are the criteria for rewards and punishments? Do you feel comfortable with the ways/means the measures of performance assessed are utilized? How arbitrary are the measures; how precisely are they evaluated by the criteria? What is the margin of error?

8. *What are the criteria for selection, promotion, and termination?*
   See #7's response.

9. *What kind of organizational "war stories" and rituals exist? What are the taboos?*
   Very important to know – learn to recognize, slide and "side-step" potential hazards to your emotional safety before you become victimized by your naïveté as a new employee. Do not underestimate the organization's rituals, taboos, and war stories. All three will "flesh out" the nature and code of conduct emanating from the organization's infrastructure.

10. *What is the nature of the organization's structure? (this is discussed in a later Chapter)*

Is it traditional "top-down" hierarchical; matrix system of management – functional based, cross-functional based, etc. How does the vertical dimension of the power structure interact with the unit's horizontal functional and cross-functional service provision? All of this is important information to glean while assessing your emotional comfort zone: specifically, the safety quotient of the organization and your mental health as an employee.

So now you've gone over these ten characteristics to help determine the safety quotient of the organization and its ability to provide a quality of work life for you during the course of your employment. If you read Chapter Eleven a few times you should be able to pick out major organizational themes at your current place of employment and prioritize the critical information you require to allow the most expedient decision-making. The analysis of your worksite, its strengths and needs, takes time, but then "Rome wasn't built in a day."

Now I want you to review again the *location* and *safety* sections. This will allow greater ease of "navigating" within your organization's political ecosystem because your next job in this process is examining the five factors below. These factors increase your understanding of what causes stress, but before starting, let's recap a few things about you, the organization, and its impact on your mental health.

To reiterate: *Locate* yourself by reviewing the ten factors mentioned above that *decrease* employee satisfaction within an organization – go ahead, DO IT. Next, review the ten questions just listed describing a "healthy" organization to help you determine a *safety quotient* regarding the organization's capacity to meet your quality of work life. Go ahead, DO IT. This exercise should get you primed for the next and last element of evaluating an organization's political ecosystem, NAVIGATION.

NAVIGATION

A GOOD WAY TO SYNTHESIZE THIS SECTION IS DEVELOPING AN UNDERstanding of stress management, its principles, and how it can help you navigate in your current job within the broader context of an organizational milieu. If *location* and *emotional safety* have been assessed effectively, then becoming aware or increasingly aware of stress management as an indicator of your internal dialogue is also required. It will help counteract the many stressors that increase the pressure(s) at your current job and increase your ability to navigate through "uncharted waters." Politics aside, it will allow a greater comfort in assimilating and maintaining a mind-set that is flexible, astute, and forward thinking. That being stated, please review the following definition of stress management and the five principles of preventive stress management as developed by Quick, Quick, Nelson & Hurrell, (1997):

"Preventative stress management is an organizational philosophy and set of principles that employs specific methods for promoting individual and organizational health while *preventing* individual and organizational distress" (Quick et al., p.149)

Principle 1: *Individual and Organizational Health Are Interdependent (person-organization fit)*

An obvious point – organizational stressors have the potential to create substantial ill health among employees, and distressed employees can create considerable organizational dysfunction. In conjunction, organizations cannot achieve a high level of productivity, adaptability, and flexibility without an emotionally healthy worker. As well, individuals may have a great deal of difficulty maintaining their psychological and physical health in unproductive, rigid, and unchanging organizations. The worker's skill-set must be able to meet the organizational goals and requirements. Organizational health and vitality contribute to individual health; they are interchangeable and axiomatic for optimal emotional health within an organization. But what happens if this is missing in my organization, you ponder – you've got some thinkin' t'do is the obvious answer, and guess where I'm going with that one!

Principle 2: *Leaders have a Responsibility for Individual and Organizational Health*

A leader's responsibilities include diagnosing organizational stress, selecting organizational and individual methods of preventive stress management, and implementing programs designed to address the particular needs of the organization. Employees also have responsibility for their health as individuals and for the health of the organization. An individual has a responsibility to contribute to the organization and participate in efforts to combat organizational distress and, to be perfectly blunt, anything less is immature and hazardous.

Principle 3: *Individual and Organizational Distress Are Not Inevitable*

Although the stress and demands in the worksite are not inevitable and should not be viewed as such in a competently run organization, distress resulting from stress and demands is also *not* inevitable. Keep this in mind while you navigate your way through your organization's political ecosystem.

Principle 4: *Each Individual and Organization Reacts Uniquely to Stress*

The title says it all; people perceive stress and react in unique ways. The feasibility, acceptability, and effectiveness of preventive stress management interventions vary among organizations and individuals. The uniqueness of employees and organizations requires that interventions be chosen and implemented in light of the particular characteristics and needs of the individual and the organization being served. Flexibility is the key word here, and anything less at your worksite should be viewed as substandard. Basically, is your organization functioning as a flexible, fair, and robust working environment that meets your emotional make-up? If not, think about moving on; an abrogation of responsibility when analyzing this area of worker-organizational interface is a recipe for disaster. Think about it carefully; pride aside, your talents and skill-set may be better appreciated somewhere else!

Principle 5: *Organizations Are Systemic*

Organizations are systemic, "open systems" that have a life cycle of growth, maturation, and death as well as varying degrees of health and vitality (Miller & Friesen, 1984). They often face different developmental issues of growth and deterioration like human beings. The nature of the stressors faced by an organization, as well as the nature of the demands generated within it, may change over the course of its life cycle. Most importantly, the strategies and techniques that are effective in managing stress at one stage of an organization's existence may be ineffective at a later stage.

Lastly and to reiterate, YOU the employee should study, study, and study again the five principles of stress management mentioned above to facilitate proper *navigation* through your journey at the new job. This, in conjunction with a thorough assessment of the *location* and *safety* aspects of your job, will further your ability to evaluate the organization's political ecosystem. This assignment should be completed throughout your probation period and periodically during your employment!

Now on to the next aspect of appraising the work environment: Organizational Dynamics – Positioning, Meta-Communication, and Guile (Ganef).

CHAPTER TWELVE

ORGANIZATIONAL DYNAMICS: POSITIONING; META-COMMUNICATION; GUILE (GANEF)

PREAMBLE

IN CHAPTER ELEVEN WE DISCUSSED EVALUATING AN ORGANIZATION regarding three personal domains: *location, emotional safety,* and *navigation*. This assessment helps to build a bridge of knowledge to the next, more in-depth analysis concerning *organization dynamics,* which increases your chances of identifying the ploys of a manipulator. Specifically, understanding organizational dynamics will enhance your ability to obtain positioning and assimilate the knowledge of meta-communication and guile, which, when linked with location, emotional safety, and navigation, effectively build a strong foundation from which to work. But prior to discussing the three postulates of organizational dynamics there are four broad characteristics that must be reviewed (Burnham, 1995). *Here we go again, Jake.* Okay, okay, just bear with me.

The four characteristics to keep in mind and evaluated using "broad strokes" at your place of employment and throughout a probationary period include: morale (there's that word again); the organization's ability to change its working structure; the organization's administration ability; and lastly, the organization's effectiveness in strategic planning.

Positioning, meta-communication, and guile come into play later on, after you've evaluated the strengths and needs of the organization's ability in the four characteristics just mentioned. When evaluated they should provide a "roadmap" of the organization's ability to furnish a quality of work life for you within its infrastructure. Therefore, during your probationary period, keep in mind the organization's ability to articulate, provide and facilitate these four characteristics occurring.

Upon entering the worksite and throughout the first few months ask yourself: Does anything in the organization's work protocol appear irregular upon first review? Specifically, is the organization unable, unaware, or indecisive as manifested by the lack of consistency, or inconsistency in successfully implementing one or more of these four characteristics? Notwithstanding, problems will present themselves over time, so be patient when assessing the organization's ability to attend to these four characteristics. Let me describe them in detail.

MORALE

First, the *morale* of the organization generally reflects how well the organization is functioning as a place of work on a day-to-day basis, essentially, the "mental health" of the organization. Burnham (1995) states morale refers to three issues:

A. How well the employees like working in the organization; do they like their employee colleagues; do they feel valued; would they rather be off work than at work?
B. How well do the employees like the kind of work they're doing? Is the work challenging; is it boring; can they use individual judgment in getting the work accomplished?
C. Do the employees like working for the management team and does management listen to the employees' ideas?

The next characteristic involves your assessment of the organization's ability to competently effect change within its infrastructure.

CHANGING THE ORGANIZATIONAL STRUCTURE

SECOND, *CHANGING THE ORGANIZATIONAL STRUCTURE* CAN BE TRAUMATIC, whether the change is in the form of deletions, additions, or modifications. To lessen the impact of change and for the organization's wellness, the organization management should be using an "open" style of change process. Specifically, the affected employees working in the areas to be changed are involved in the decision-making process. The process of how organizational change manifests itself, and how widely that process might be shared within a company, is another focus point. Gathering information from the organization's various working levels increases transparency and allows a "tracing" to be identified about the effects of the change to various parts of the organization's infrastructure. The results via feedback to the management allow them to make adjustments regarding the division to be changed and how the rest of the organization will be changed, thereby necessitating "tweaks" or adjustments in other divisions to accommodate the modifications. You should ask yourself, how well does the organization function in this area, allowing management to use small samples of information to avoid the high costs of reducing the employees' esprit de corps (i.e., the ambiance in the working environment). It also serves the objectives of management and helps plan future steps, involving all levels of employees and done in a systematic manner. Basically, the question you ask yourself is, do I feel involved in the organizational change process? If not, there could be an inherent problem in flexible management and you might be an "unhappy camper" down the road; think about it.

CHANGING ORGANIZATION ADMINISTRATION

THE THIRD ORGANIZATIONAL CHARACTERISTIC TO BE APPRAISED INVOLVES the *company's ability to change organization administration*. Please don't take this one for granted, as the detail and precision an organization utilizes in changing its management cadre is vitally important to the organization's morale amongst other things.

When the organization decides to change management, there should be "ownership" regarding the change, a rationale of what precipitated the change with objective data to support the decision. This is completed with the organization's rationale for taking the corrective action – suggestions and recommendations take the place of solid conclusions and remedies, specifically a flexible approach at this juncture. In the end a clear picture of what precipitated change, why it was needed at that specific time, and the expected benefits from the new management structure should be articulated. Anything less regarding feedback to the constituent employees will leave people wondering what transpired, why it happened, and could this happen to me without my knowledge (as one possible negative outcome).

The fourth characteristic to evaluate is the organization's effectiveness in strategic planning.

STRATEGIC PLANNING AND EVALUATION

STRATEGIC PLANNING AND EVALUATION ARE OFTEN DIVIDED RESPONSIBILI-ties, which need to be combined for maximum effectiveness to be achieved. There are two types of evaluation: formative (ongoing) evaluation, which supplies corrective information to the efforts in programs or other change-producing activities throughout the project's development; and summative (end) evaluation, which provides a sum total of the program or change effects, an assessment at the end of an activity about the results of that activity – basically an accountability statement. Strategic planning is a set of activities meant to help an organization change to meet some designated outcome or goal. The achievement of the goal cannot be realized without some midcourse corrections. Strategic plans are visions of where an organization wants to go, and some changes may be made in order for the objectives to be achieved. Specifically, an organization may be forced to reduce/remove some of the old processes in order to increase efficiency/effectiveness.

To accomplish these new objectives, short-term goals are set as markers to guide the proper movement toward a longer term goal. In conjunction, as Burnham (1995) states, strategic plans are visions of the future of the organization's plan of action and are commonly shared among the members of the organization. Evaluation and strategic planning go hand in hand in making an organization a better place to work. The evaluation function is a monitoring device for innovation or other changes to an organization. Most importantly, the involvement of the stakeholders, management, and clients is important to achieve the best possible results from an evaluation activity.

Okay, so now we've covered four interrelated characteristics of an organization's style of doing business, but how do these foundation structures impact on positioning, meta-communication, and guile?

POSITIONING

YOU'VE COMPLETED THE PROBATION AND DECIDED TO STAY ON, BECAUSE employment at this imperfect organization feels okay. Ah, but how about positioning you ask? Placing yourself in the most advantageous position (politics aside) to allow upward mobility (if that's what you want) or at least emotional comfort and reduced fear of potential exploitation by an organization manipulator. Guess what, a perfect, prescriptive answer doesn't exist to my knowledge, but I'll try to provide what I think is a fair compromise. If you follow these strategies you may find your behavior and reputation enhanced, thereby increasing the potential for organizational reward (e.g., promotion, positive reputation, reduced potential for exploitation).

Strategies Enhancing Positioning
The University of Michigan's Medical Center's Management Expectations (Marszalek-Gaucher & Coffey, 1990) can be used as a reference guide because it identifies behaviors that influence a foundation of trust, collegiality, and respect to develop. This allows optimal *positioning* to unfold for new employees in a new job. That

being stated, a number of factors should be used to increase your positioning potential, which include:

- Developing and supporting a work environment where every employee's capability is improved. Yes, you work within and for your team, so become a team player if you weren't already. Ego be damned, help out your colleagues, when the time arises it will work wonders for your reputation.

- Secondly, influence a work environment where you, the individual, become an integral part of the unit, department, or division's improvement process. Encourage interdepartmental problem solving; solicit and utilize input from your colleagues and work cooperatively with other departments within the organization. This unselfish, collegial attitude will be identified, your credibility increased, and the potential of being violated by an organization manipulator reduced.

- Thirdly, promote an environment of open communication and shared appreciation of your colleagues' contributions. Utilize effective listening skills by not interrupting a colleague, which lets them know that you're attempting to understand their position. This behavior begins the affiliation process and should not be underestimated as an entrée to establishing rapport and respect.

- Fourthly, create an atmosphere that promotes and encourages innovation and creativity and does not catastrophize mistakes or foster blaming.

- The fifth and final point, foster an environment that values diversity and sustains multiculturalism. This is an obvious statement in 2014, but deserves to be repeated. Learn about the diversity of your organization's employee cultures in order to better understand their customs and viewpoints. Promote respect and build the differences of the group as a strength, not a weakness.

The next area to become familiar is meta-communication, the coded and often masked meaning behind a statement. This is a very important skill to acquire and refine; please attempt to learn and appreciate its power.

META-COMMUNICATION

ORGANIZATIONAL "SCRIPTS," THE META-COMMUNICATION OF THE ORGANIzation, are written over time by long-term employees and are usually codified by understanding *the message behind the message* between co-workers, management, union officials, etc. To help you learn the meta-communication of the organization, you should keep in mind *four* principal features that have been identified by Kets de Vries et al. (1987) and are here expanded upon.

a) Thematic Unity

Organizational "goings on" should be interpreted in one interconnected, cohesive observation. Specifically, a commonality amongst the organization's global themes occurring throughout the first weeks/months that you work in this new environment should become increasingly apparent! Conceptually, a unity or theme of organizational protocol begins to present itself which allows the following extrapolation. Can I envisage myself working within the organization's operational boundaries? Do I like the organization's style of problem solving, doing business, risk taking, liberalism/conservatism? All of this information should be absorbed – certainly by the end of a probation period. If not, "get the hell out of Dodge" as the expression goes because you're probably in an enmeshed or disengaged infrastructure, which diminishes transparency of communication – obviously this is not good.

b) Pattern Matching

When involved in organizational diatribes between departments, units, and collegial relationships, people tend to seek out a "fit" between the current event and past events in an attempt to make things meaningful, ostensibly looking for patterns of repetition. Pattern matching or interpreting the present dynamic(s) in terms of past events causes us to relive it and react as we did at a previous time. Unfortunately, what was an appropriate reaction in the past is often no longer effective. Please beware of making this generalization, which can be a grave mistake! Rather, carefully assess the current problem to reduce the tendency of impulsive "knee-jerk" responses based and influenced by previous, habituated behavior; you will save yourself a lot of problems and heartache.

c) *Psychological Urgency*

You should, with practice, be able to understand the dynamics of the issue being addressed and the "text" of the most pressing problem(s) to be solved. Begin by prioritizing the problem and look at the flip side of the problem, which is usually the answer to the problem in broad strokes. Subsequently, compartmentalize the problem by breaking down its components and assessing, then prioritizing which aspect of the problem you can successfully address. Attempt to solve the problem after you've aligned its degree of difficulty from your perception of it on a weak to most difficult continuum. As you answer each aspect of the problem, you should be increasing your confidence to continue. From this beginning and the success you achieve in solving aspects of the problem, you will begin to understand the problem's overall psychological urgency vis-à-vis the greater impact on the organization. Often what we perceive as overwhelming and stressful upon first review changes after a few attempts to problem-solve. Specifically, anxiety dissipates and there is less fear of "dignity of risk" – actually risking a confrontation with the problem at hand. With practice this problem-solving approach should become a comfortable option for addressing most dilemmas faced by your role within the new organization. Try it out.

d) *Multiple Function*

Organizational theme(s) can have various meanings depending on how you interpret them and on different points of view (i.e., defensive processes; key dynamics; interpersonal relationships, their patterns and effect on the organization, etc.). These issues may also be played out simultaneously, concurrently, and at individual, management, and organizational levels of the political ecosystem. If you hadn't guessed, thematic evaluation is a tapestry of complexity, but then so is the conduct of an organization manipulator!

By now it should be obvious to YOU, the stakeholder of your mental health, that becoming familiar with these rules of interpretation is vital! Learning the basic organizational themes and patterns of the dynamics of these themes played out at your worksite will allow you to interpret them quickly. With practice over time, the significance of issues that initially seem meaningless or chaotic can be interpreted at their proper level of importance. Have confidence, you will become adept at learning the organization's themes of communication, and your ability to interpret them will become "second nature" with practice, practice, and more practice!

GUILE (GANEF)

AN OLDER TEXT BY MALONE & PETERSEN (1974) VERY ADROITLY DESCRIBES how to deal with organizational politics as a manager, which in my estimation can also be utilized by all employees. Without belaboring the issue of guile or in Yiddish "ganef," a thief's mentality without actually stealing, there are *four* key areas you can adopt to increase your effectiveness in handling politics and promote your reputation/success within an organization. Some of this information may overlap previous sections, but it doesn't hurt to be redundant for your benefit (does it?).

A. *Build a positive political image*: Simply put, consistent good work and the appropriate use of your ability usually "wins the day"! How so? By increasing the frequency of contact and interest in others; knowing people by name and giving them credit or recognition to acknowledge their work and personal achievement; showing tact, sensitivity, and respect for other people and your contacts with them.

B. *Deal with political realities*: Organizational politics are realities we have to deal with! Be wary of cliques and if you join one, don't be surprised if anything you disclose *is not* perceived as confidential and discussed in open forum! Expect fairly consistent action and support among the members within a clique. If one member is opposed to an idea or program, the others are apt to be against it as well. Please be careful and be aware of this one looming its big rotund head.

C. *Prevent political breeding grounds*: Avoid using the same source as your informal channel of communication, this is a big "no-no" as that person comes to depend on the power of their informal "expert" role as your confidant, which in turn can work against you with a "falling out" and in times of distress and political action. Ostensibly, the information you seek or have disclosed to that person in the past may be misrepresented to save someone's job, career, whatever, and leave you "hung out to dry."

D. *Sidestep political schemes and power plays*: Challenge the temptation of listening to gossip and keep in mind the alternative of refusing to listen. Explore issues and differences between people openly and impartially. Avoid the tendency to "carry tales" or listen to unverified rumors. Stay focused on work objectives and avoid entanglement with conflicting factions and schemers. Colleagues respect "apoliticals" – it's that simple

Following these rules will help you stay "on top of the game," and games are usually orchestrated by an organization manipulator, if you hadn't already guessed it; if not, you haven't been reading the damn book!?

Now on to Chapter Thirteen, "The Matrix System of Management – Strengths and Needs" or stated more accurately, "Survival in the Matrix System – How to Manage Successfully," but you be the judge. The next Chapter is somewhat more academic and complex than Chapter Twelve, but nevertheless very important to understand! Unfortunately organization manipulators abound in the Matrix infrastructure; hence the information imparted is from both a theoretical and practical perspective and identifies coping strategies to utilize for survival.

Organization manipulators analyze, request, require, demand, and damage your quality of work life as mentioned above. Unfortunately, the matrix management system has been a frequent territorial domain of this devious individual. Sorry, I didn't mean to stress you out (twice now), but this is a fact of work life! Have courage and please read on.

CHAPTER THIRTEEN

THE MATRIX SYSTEM OF MANAGEMENT: STRENGTHS AND NEEDS

PREAMBLE

THE DEFINITION OF MATRIX MANAGEMENT IS A STYLE OF MANAGEMENT where an individual has two reporting superiors (bosses) – one a functional expert, usually from administrative services, who manages everyone with the same functional specialty regardless of their project team assignments, and the other, operational, a project manager in charge of everyone assigned to the same project (Hatch, 2011). Since employees often possess a skill useful to more than one project team, they may be assigned to one or more projects and thus report to multiple project managers as well as a functional boss from administration.

Matrix systems in organizations were designed to be *fast and flexible* when compared to other structural types of organizational designs, where change involves restructuring the whole organization (Hatch, 2011). As a consequence, matrix structures developed within organizations adapt well to rapidly changing environments. It would appear that the highly educated professionals typical of matrix structures can handle the greater complexity of working in an environment requiring them to juggle the demands of multiple managers and ever-changing work requirements. Aha, you say, isn't this "tailor-made" for the average Mental Health/Social Services organization with its highly educated cadre of staff, eager for flexibility and ongoing change to stimulate the drudgery of daily case work? For the most part a big resounding YES – but only if the matrix system is effective!

To reiterate, matrix management superimposes the management of individualized projects, thereby establishing a *multiple command system*. It is a type of organizational management in which people with similar skills are pooled for work assignments, resulting in more than one manager. Managers in the various functional areas supervise the "talent pool" for the project teams and determine the availability of skills for various projects. Team members may return to their functional specialities or transfer to new project teams when a project is completed.

A political agenda may arise if the project leader, the team of committed subordinates, and the demands of the project do not mesh well, or the project's functional manager is *not* qualified in the profession he/she is overseeing at the worksite and does not comprehend the professional context from which another discipline works, or their point of view. This can cause and has caused numerous problems in Health Care/Social Services projects, which have been the bastion of matrix management structures. For instance, the following is an example I present to illustrate my point.

A peer review (i.e., feedback) is requested by a functional manager regarding a subordinate's work performance, who is qualified in another profession from the functional manager. Frequently and under these circumstances, the real purpose and true intent of the request for the "evaluation" is often disguised. The functional manager uses the information from the subordinate's peers, whether biased or not, to form the basis of an evaluation that is contrived to meet the political agenda of the functional manager. In conjunction, he/she might or might not have informed the subordinate, or for that matter the project manager, that a peer review of the subordinate has been requested. A silly rhetorical question – does this nefarious conduct enhance trust, fair play, and esprit de corps amongst the team? I think not! In my experience the opposite occurs – regardless of the project manager's protestations, the functional manager's behavior sabotages the working atmosphere of the project and instills fear of retribution if the request is not followed! Under these circumstances and especially if the subordinate is a perceived threat, outcast, or malcontent, it is not uncommon for the project manager *not* to be included in the information loop (believe it or not) especially in dysfunctional organizations, where clandestine meetings, duplicitous behavior, and innuendos abound, combined with "cut-throat" ambition, which is a lethal combination to say the least.

Please, beware of the following presenting behavior by a functional manager; think "obvious" as in disingenuous and the rest falls into place: specifically, a lubricious, "smothering" approach with a tendency to be indirectly domineering (e.g., veiled threats) during interpersonal encounters; the glad hand/stout colleague, you're a good guy/gal trust me routine (or else is often implied). This not so clever ruse is often employed by an individual trained in another profession and unversed in yours, attempting to be collegial but basically a troglodyte who wants to dominate you at your expense. *But wait just a minute, don't be so judgmental, Jake; they oversee my career, quality of work life, and keys to my promotion, yeah right give me a break!?* If you encounter this approach or intuitively feel it being attempted, ask yourself, "why the overkill already, I smell an organization manipulator"; need I say more! Let's move on to something more positive, shall we.

To be effective the matrix system requires collaboration, openness, and effective problem solving rather than traditional administrative approaches (e.g., blaming), which tend to occur in dysfunctional organizations, and the directive "command style" approach found in many functional, albeit imperfect organizations. An obvious point, the success of the matrix system is dependent on the sensitivity brought to bear in the quality of working relationships fostered between the employees, their ability to deal with conflict and work well within groups, AND the commensurate communication skills to carry this off. The intrinsic ability to work through problems, admit mistakes, and accept you were wrong (for once) and then get on WITH BUSINESS is a tough row for many to hoe! In the writer's experience, cross-functional (i.e., matrix systems) management requires leadership adept in critical thinking processing – anything less is a recipe for disaster.

Specifically, different philosophical camps often emerge in a matrix system during project development and implementation that often challenge even the most mild-mannered Mental Health/Social Service practitioners. What to do? First, let me digress and give you some background before we continue.

Many years ago Argyris (1973) contrasted matrix management with the traditional hierarchical organization, the latter dependent on the pyramidal administrative ladder. Specifically, as one goes up the ladder, power and control increase, availability of information increases, the scope of decisions made and the responsibilities involved increase. Conversely, implicit in the matrix system are generally opposite tendencies. If the matrix system is to work successfully and at its fullest potential, it requires managers who have effective two-way communication, acknowledge employee vulnerability, and have the ability to "think outside of the box." The sine qua non of the matrix system working effectively is "active" engagement, a demonstrated concern about working relationships and mutual respect developed with and between colleagues. Ideally, a project team utilizing the matrix system requires intense collaboration and interdependence to be successful (Sargent, 1983). "Great," you say, "we're trained practitioners in the helping profession, this is like falling off a log; what's the problem?"

It's simply this, in practice the "soft" supportive, quasi-therapeutic approach required for a successful matrix system frequently does *not* occur consistently enough in evolving projects because of the tight time lines and budgetary restraints. If management and the team lack sufficient training and fail to reinforce the ingredients required for the matrix system to work effectively, team members still tend to be competitive, trust issues arise, and "turf" protection abounds. A desire for visible power and traditional top-down organizational behavior patterns begin to emerge or re-emerge, which can be detrimental to the project. This I believe is the crux of the problem!

The level of power in matrices is often described as *strong*, *medium*, or *weak* depending on the level of power of the project manager. Most importantly, for a matrix management style to be effective, the functional and operational managers must have *equal weight* in controlling the individuals in their matrix. Generally, in real life application, the functional reporting relationship between the project manager and project workers is stronger, because the project manager controls the worker's compensation and evaluations. Unfortunately, this can create problems with a functional manager who micromanages, is not interested in an equal valence of power with the project manager, and wants greater control of all aspects of the project/job areas.

Specifically, problems tend to occur when the functional manager has a need for greater scrutiny and involvement in the day-to-day operation of the project, personally or through a designate. This intrusive behavior can undermine the vested authority of the project manager and increases the likelihood of a toxic work environment. Problems occur in a matrix system when a worker is involved in several projects simultaneously and their time on a specific project is disputed and/or diluted as a result of the conflict between the functional manager and the project manager. KEEP THIS IN MIND as employees in the Mental Health/Social Services Industry may become collateral damage in these disputes, which occasionally results in messy, litigious outcomes – not always, but sometimes. We'll talk about the three matrix levels (i.e., strong, medium, weak) later on. For now, let's précis the advantages/disadvantages of the matrix system.

The *advantages* of the matrix system especially for project management include flexibility – individuals can be chosen according to the needs of the project. The use of a project team facilitates viewing problems in a different way, as specialists have been brought together in a new environment. Project managers are directly responsible for completing the project within a specific deadline and budget, allowing greater transparency and tighter quality control and quality improvement.

The *disadvantages* of the matrix system for project management can include the following: A conflict of loyalty between project team practitioners/management designates and the project manager over the allocation of resources. This frequently occurs in the Mental Health/Social Services Industry when resources are supplied by government for specific purposes. The interpretation of how to spend the project money and issues of the service provision, quality control, and cost-effectiveness issues are often debated, with little or no sensitivity to underlining philosophical perspectives from the various professional constituents. The outcome can be an operational intransigence between conflicting philosophies/belief systems creating communication problems, the dreaded turf wars interfering with the project's ongoing maintenance and functional lines of authority – which compromise getting the project completed on time!

Projects can also be difficult to monitor if the turf wars between team members and management cause teams to seek, then request and receive too much independence. An extension of thought is required here. The matrix system requires flexibility, speed, and efficiency to operate at an optimal level. If the concern is not meeting the pre-arranged time lines, people go looking for flexible ways to problem-solve the dilemma, which often includes increasing costs if more professionals are requested by the project teams once the project is under way. But why would they deplete a fixed budget by hiring more staff in these circumstances? One answer, a "more is better" mind-set can evolve regarding expansion of staffing. This is usually a result of infighting amongst the team members and management when the conflict is not carefully examined and resolved. One often observes a knee-jerk reaction to resolve the dilemma(s) by hiring more people to get the job done within the time lines. If this happens the problem(s) can *increase* because of operating on a fixed budget, which can be depleted at an alarming rate, exponentially in some cases. With each additional staff person hired, the pressure to perform may increase the error rate. It sounds like old fashioned "circular logic," doesn't it?

The government work milieu is not free enterprise with private financing, but instead is played out within a strict economic boundary, cost wise. The infighting "fireworks" usually begin slowly and then proceed if unresolved, with more passion and vitriol as the project continues and the money is drained. Specifically, "Oops, the completion deadline is looming, what do we do now" syndrome comes into play! Personalities can "act out" unmercifully when dealing with highly educated bureaucrats promoted from the ranks who want to take over!

Consequently, the project managers and professional team workers can find their opinions disregarded in very short order. NOW we're dealing with ego, power, control, and the final authority from a functional manager who oversees everyone and likes to "crack the whip." Are you frightened just a little? You should be; if you've ever been ensnared in one of these power plays, it isn't fun. Many a professional reputation has been stained in these circumstances and it's tough making a comeback! I know, I've been there.

Taken from a different slant and from an optimist's point of view, the matrix system is a concept that initially has great appeal because it draws on the full potential of the human resource capabilities of the respective, imperfect organizations. In theory it frees up leadership for everyone concerned and does not rely on a few people who have positional power. HOWEVER, there are inherent problems with the matrix structure in a single, multidisciplinary, or cross-functional team when a number of these cross-functional teams are working simultaneously, requiring people to relate to one another vertically, horizontally, and diagonally, all at the same time.

In the Mental Health/Social Services Industry, the overriding concern about matrix management is how to make it work. Upon first glance, the matrix structure appears dynamic and innovative, but it requires both ability and willingness to serve more than one boss to derive any potential benefits and this may have more to do with culture and behavior than any intrinsic organizational design. Please, keep that in mind.

HISTORICAL CONTEXT

HISTORICALLY, THE MATRIX SYSTEM WAS IN VOGUE IN THE 1970s AND '80s in such organizations as Xerox, Digital Equipment Corporation, and Citibank, which employed a two-boss matrix management structure, as they sought to maximize productivity and harness resources. The matrix approach appeared to keep organizations "agile," but by the late 1980s it was clear that it wasn't such an easy task and corporate enthusiasm began to wane. Specifically, the structure was often too complex to be effective. What worked well in corporate free enterprise organizations did not translate easily in alternative, not-for-profit working environments.

Specifically, in the not-for-profit organizations, people working in matrix teams seemed unable to negotiate satisfactorily over resource issues and cost allocations; individual team members and their managers couldn't agree where responsibility should lie. As a result the early enthusiasts for the matrix system began to revert to simpler structures. By the 1990s matrix management had developed into several modifications (i.e., subsets), which included (Reh, 2013): "virtual teams," the focus being increasingly on customer service and speed of delivery; the *ad hoc* project team, where members often belonged to different functions but were loaned out to work for a period of time according to the project need; the *cross-functional* team, which was comprised of people with different functional skills working towards a common goal such as gathering information, making decisions, and generating support from stakeholders to achieve their objective; and lastly, the *self-directed* team, which was empowered to make decisions and take actions to resolve day-to-day issues. Self-directed teams may consist of people within one function or across functions but they are driven more by initiative than corporate directive.

In the 1990s it appeared the matrix system was still the most popular structure for product developers capitalizing on an organization's ability to draw on the competence of the whole workforce, but realistically could this be consistently achieved? What characterizes the matrix's strengths is how to get beyond hierarchy and how to get people in multi-disciplinary teams to work together effectively, allowing everyone coming together to brainstorm their ideas at the beginning of the project. In the Mental Health/Social Services Industry this did create problems based on philosophical differences of service provision, as mentioned above. For instance, the "medical model," with a top-down hierarchical management approach, and the rivalries between various professions (e.g., psychology vs. psychiatry, nursing vs. other professions) often created challenges in changing the "mind-set" that had been inculcated for decades (i.e., this is the way things should be done for this project, let's do it my way)!

This rigidity is not easy to change, and many a "range war" developed as a result. In this working environment the matrix system leaders were required to be influencers, facilitators, and persuaders. However, the issue of who wields the power was still an obstacle in decision-making, especially when there were conflicting interests at stake.

THE PROBLEM IN A "NUTSHELL"

GENERALLY SPEAKING EMPLOYERS WANT TO USE TEAMS THAT MANIFEST coordination, cooperation, and flexibility. This has been a hard nut to crack from the writer's experience working in the field of Mental Health/Social Services Industry. How so? Here goes. The Matrix Model of Management identifies that organizations and industries in the private sector have vertical chains of command but also have people working horizontally, across their functional specialization. In theory, employers harness the services of employees irrespective of their function, to work collaboratively on key projects. On such projects the matrix manager can pool the necessary resources in order to achieve what from the strategic objective is the overriding priority. However, as you've probably picked up, in most organizations functions are the number one way to do business within the organization, and getting work done cross-functionally (i.e., matrix system) is difficult at best.

In the not-for-profit government-funded organizations during the past three decades (at least) organizations have tried to solve this problem by changing the culture or by restructuring, but very little progress has been made. Functional *silos* still don't cooperate with one another (e.g., psychology is still viewed as the handmaiden of psychiatry), operational processes are reworked and reworked to death, and long cycle times to get projects achieved are the result. Keeping this in mind, how do you survive as a Mental Health/Social Service employee in the matrix system?

HOW TO SURVIVE IN THE MATRIX SYSTEM OF MANAGEMENT

BEFORE I GO ON, HAVE I LEFT ANYONE BEHIND? IF SO, HANG TIGHT AND BE patient; this matrix thing should come together with time and careful review. Let's continue, shall we? In the Mental Health/Social Services sector, the two basic reasons that cross-functional operations and projects aren't working well entail a greater refinement of the horizontal dimension in those organizations using the matrix system of management. Defining the horizontal dimension involves alignment around the customers' needs (i.e., patients, families) and how best to service provide these identified needs within the staffing and operational budget available. When there is a token restructuring within an organization, there is typically a rearrangement of reporting relationships – in effect, the vertical dimension of who reports to whom.

HERE'S THE PROBLEM, and it's a great big one! The restructuring is often *not* affecting alignment in the horizontal dimension – the dimension that interfaces with the patients and their families. Structure is concerned with reporting relationships, and alignment is about including everyone in the same direction to meet the strategic objectives and satisfy the patients and families. This can cause and has caused politics to rear its ugly head. Simply stated, in order to successfully achieve this alignment with the constituents, you have to address VERY CAREFULLY the horizontal dimension where the work gets done and include input/feedback from the constituents. How do we do this effectively? Carefully evaluating the type of matrix system subtype you work in will address most of the overriding issues. Please read on.

As mentioned above, there are *three basic forms* of matrix management (Reh, 2013). The *weak matrix* entails the project manager overseeing staff from different functions but still reporting to his/her functional manager. Such a structure enhances the possibility for communication across functional areas, but it's still hierarchical and for this reason retains most of the problems associated with a functional organization (beware of this one). The *strong matrix* entails the project manager being independent of functional management. It is the role of functional managers to support the project by providing technical expertise and assigning resources as and when required. In this structure there is potential for conflict between the project manager and the functional manager over resource assignment and cost allocation – as a result excellent communication, strong relationships, and a flexible working culture are required (i.e., please evaluate the strengths of leadership between the project and functional leader and then decide, do I stay or do I transfer?). Lastly, in the *balanced matrix* power and accountability are shared equally by the project manager and functional manager. Not surprisingly this style of matrix management is the most difficult system to maintain because power sharing is tricky and not always easy to maintain. The likelihood of working in a balanced matrix is low but if you do, please learn as much as you can about your respective managers and their respective philosophies both clinically and administratively.

Whichever subset your current matrix structure entails, there are a number of matrix management challenges in those working milieus that have relatively weak accountability and influence, and operate without appropriate authority. By the way and to reiterate, this has occurred frequently in the Mental Health/Social Services Industry, which receives most of its revenue from the government. What to do about the matrix system in this situation? The Summary should clarify what you need to know.

SUMMARY

ACCORDING TO HALL (2013), MATRIX MANAGERS NEED TO MAKE SURE that team members comprehend the matrix working paradigm and change their behaviors accordingly to meet the needs of the team and the demands of the project (i.e., *Context*).

A matrix system is intended to improve cooperation across professional disciplines, but it can easily lead to increased bureaucracy, more meetings, and slower decisions where too many people are involved (i.e., *Cooperation*).

The project leader needs to have competence in all aspects of management of the project, or risk becoming a handmaiden to the whims and fancies of the functional manager! Specifically, the matrix system is often dependent on "strangers" (i.e., program manager) who don't have direct control but indirectly have incredible influence on the team's morale (e.g., budgetary restraints). In this regard, there are many factors that can undermine trust (e.g., cross-cultural differences between professional disciplines; miscommunication through technology) and when trust is undermined managers often *increase* control. Centralization can make the matrix slow and expensive to run in these circumstances, with high levels of cost escalation. It is imperative that matrix managers build trust in distributed and diverse teams and empower people, even though they may rarely have time to meet face-to-face, as described in the functional manager's role (i.e., *Control*).

Lastly, *Community* – the formal structure becomes less important when getting things done in a matrix system, so both the functional and project managers need to focus on the "soft structure" of networks, communities, teams, and groups that need to be set up and maintained to get things done. If this is done competently in your imperfect organization, great. If not, think about other options, including moving on.

That's it, good luck in all future endeavors as you work cooperatively in your organization, and now it's on to the final Chapter which describes "Set-ups, Cons, and other Nefarious Activities."

CHAPTER FOURTEEN

SET-UPS, CONS, AND OTHER NEFARIOUS ACTIVITIES

PREAMBLE

AFTER READING ABOUT THE MATRIX SYSTEM OF MANAGEMENT IN CHAPTER Thirteen, can you see how "ripe" a work environment is for the organization manipulator to exploit opportunities, impugn colleagues to achieve devious ends, and seize the opportunity to become more entrenched in the organization's power structure? A Mental Health/ Social Service worker has to be very wary of this type of organizational management system; it has its strengths, no doubt, but also pitfalls for those inexperienced line staff unwary, or lacking experience working in a multi-tier, cross-functional system of management. Information, or more precisely, miscommunication can quickly become a manipulated resource as in indirect, "masked," and incomplete communiqués – all instigated at the whim of the project or functional manager, who may be an organization manipulator or influenced by a manipulator. Now, moving on, the following sections detail coping strategies (once again) to help you survive at your worksite. The writer has incorporated the information reviewed from several noted experts (e.g., Babiak; Clarke; Dutton; Simon) to provide the broadest base of knowledge when interpreting the manipulator's behavior. More in-depth reading by these authors can be located in the Reference section of the book.

SET-UPS

How to Handle a Manipulator Boss, Peer, Subordinate

At most worksites the organization is expected to take the side of your *boss* regarding disagreements over your performance. As mentioned above, the best defense is to ALWAYS perform to your potential and complete the tasks assigned to you, unless they are illegal, unethical, or violate safety or security procedures (Babiak et al., 2006). Be open about your performance and ask for regular feedback, if this is not forthcoming, you've got a problem.

Next, always complete and submit a written memo (yes, in writing) to a boss you've assessed as an organizational manipulator, which reflects your understanding of his/her directive. The memo entails discussing your understanding of what exactly it is you have been requested to do, the timetable, the assistance you expect from your co-workers, etc. (e.g., boss, peers). Ask to meet with your boss to review your requests and keep a personal copy of the documents. Come to these meetings with several solutions that you've developed and assess as reasonable options. The organizational manipulator should view this initiative as you being a results-oriented employee who is boundary specific, yet wants to achieve a mutually agreed-upon goal. The next suggestion may appear counter-intuitive but if you can, build a reasonable working relationship with your boss, hard as it may seem; address this chore without losing self-respect or self-confidence. He/she "holds the cards" and has the power and authority to make your quality of work life miserable. Regardless, this request is a work in progress and can be a hard one to achieve, to put it mildly. Conversely, appearing less than forthright and worse, argumentative, with these individuals is a recipe for disaster – you have to play this one cozy!

With a *co-worker* deemed untrustworthy and/or ruthless with a manipulative bent, build open and honest relationships with your boss and peers, follow policy/procedures, and if you're required to work closely with an unreliable colleague, don't fall into the trap of doing their work for them. To get these predators off your back you will often be tempted to capitulate. Colluding with them is a mistake; you will likely be "done in" politically when you're no longer useful and most often to mask their poor work performance. Aggressive confrontation with these co-worker/miscreants can often be dangerous as it will undoubtedly be manipulated, "spin doctored" in lay terminology, as you being the instigator of the problem, not them. They have learned and become VERY adept at charm, manipulation, and guile and if you think you can defeat them over time – good luck, they can and will rip your heart out! Specifically, your attempts at one-on-one confrontation are a policy of action with good intentions, but often twisted by the manipulator to meet their needs/desires, after carefully assessing your motive and nature of request. BE CAREFUL and listen to your intuitive side before taking action. We will discuss coping strategies below in much greater detail.

Organizational manipulators, if you hadn't already guessed it, rarely make good subordinates! Their tendency to lie, manipulate, con – using "the end justifies the means" rationale is the antithesis of an ideal colleague (no kidding). When you're around an organizational *subordinate* who is a manipulator, use the following techniques to "cushion" the impact of their negative behavior:

A. Be very careful about boundaries – they have a tendency to collect and use information against you, all with the pretence of developing a solid, working relationship.

B. Try to remain in control, as you will be emotionally challenged by their unsavory, clever ploys to manipulate you.

C. Be aware that the organization manipulator's description of a situation is often fabricated, with omissions of very important detail. Do not take at face value what they state actually happened, or the manner in which they state it happened.

D. Keep written notation of your interactions with subordinate organization manipulators; time has a habit of interfering with memory accuracy and a written account completed no later than 24 hours post conversation, meeting, etc., can be worth its weight in gold AND a job or career saver.

CONS AND OTHER NEFARIOUS ACTIVITIES

THE TACTICS AND STRATEGIES OF THE ORGANIZATION MANIPULATOR ARE subtle and developed in *stages*. In the early stages, they complete a micro then macro analysis of the organization, its policies and procedures, and the behavior of the employee constituents, ostensibly asking themselves "what operational style must I utilize to fulfill self-gratifying needs and how effectively will my behavior be detected by my colleagues and the management system in place." Most importantly, *from the beginning* they examine their colleagues' weaknesses in order to exploit them in the future when the time arises. Subsequently, the organization's rules and protocol being learned and absorbed by manipulators are subtly challenged, then violated. With time, colleagues become desensitized to this odd "testy" behavior and if the manipulators are confronted about their unsavory conduct, they will plead ignorance and, being new in the organization, will often request another assignment "to prove their worth.". Unfortunately, this usually includes one caveat – that the job requires little staff interaction, please keep this in mind! This allows greater opportunity for victimizing without being detected, as the manipulators' job function in this new role does not require close working relationships with their colleagues.

As progress occurs in time, the organization manipulators' detailed knowledge of the rules and regulations of the worksite increases their ability to talk their way out of compromising situations when complaints start "rolling in." They become VERY ADEPT at covering up their mistakes, transgressions, and overt errors. Keep this one in mind as well! They increase their expertise at challenging the protocol at *all levels* of the organization's infrastructure, but most importantly, identifying individuals (i.e., "marks") within the work environment and exploiting the colleague's weaknesses. Remember the identified presentation style of the functional manager to be wary of mentioned a few pages ago!? But I digress.

Do they worry about getting caught? Yes and no; often their narcissistic personality traits, which include grandiosity and self-entitlement, interfere with insight. Remember, they are lacking in empathy with little conscience about the consequence of their actions to others, which allows the "cold blooded" exploitation of their colleagues. The ability to learn and exploit any situation to meet their needs has been developed and refined to such a degree that the potential for error is much reduced relative to the normal employee. Therefore the risk of being caught, albeit low, is worth the risk of continuing to function in the same devious manner, which has become habituated. When they're eventually caught in their deceitful dealings and feel the organization will "win" against them, they often capitulate and move on, or attempt to eliminate the complaint, using whatever unsavory means they have at their disposal (e.g., emotional blackmail – quid pro quo "I helped you in the past, now you have to help me"; or else is either stated outright or implied). Regarding this last statement, organization manipulators have a habit of compiling dossiers on their victims that will be used against them when action is needed for basic survival at the worksite. Hollywood movies aside, this actually happens in real life, so don't be a victim!

As stated many times in the book, organization manipulators identify vulnerable people and use the power of knowledge of the system, its operational protocol, and identified weaknesses to target and exploit their colleagues. Clarke (2005) states *the key factors* manipulators look for include a victim's vulnerability, low self-esteem, desire to change, and a yearning for a better life. Consequently, a systemic approach entwining their victim's behavior is devised, which entails the following paradigm of exploitation: The organizational manipulator often begins by breaking the victim's confidence, making the individual fearful of challenging the manipulator's behavior towards them. To reinforce how serious the intention, confrontation and intimidation ploys are "acted out" against the victim numerous times. This maintains the "top dog–bottom dog" relationship, which over time crushes the incentive to initiate any retaliation (i.e., learned helplessness). This behavior establishes the consequence of challenging the manipulator's authority and once fear is established the manipulator "tweaks" the relationship any time he/she feels the victim is losing their "bottom dog" position – thus the fear and control is maintained and the victimization persists.

In conjunction, the organization manipulator usually pushes colleagues away from the "mark," isolating the individual, impugning their sense of worth and ability to achieve success without the "support" of the organization manipulator. Typically, this bullying and manipulative behavior eventually reduces the victim's self-esteem, allowing the manipulator to better meet his/her need for power and control. Remember, the lack of conscience of such manipulators allows them to feel little to no remorse/guilt regarding their transgressions with the victim/colleague.

SO, if you get that intuitive "gut" feeling about Mr. Nice Guy/Girl at the office after they habitually overstep their boundaries with you, they could be initiating an exploitive situation with serious negative consequences for your emotional health and reputation! Think about it; your career is the means with which you make a living and your mental health is a precious commodity and not to be tampered with.

IDENTIFIERS – PROBLEMATIC BEHAVIORS THAT INDICATE TROUBLE LIES AHEAD

A LIST OF PROBLEMATIC BEHAVIORS IDENTIFIED BY BABIAK ET AL. (2006) are often observed in *clusters* and initiated by the organization manipulator, they include:

A. *Inability to form a team* – the organization manipulator is unable to form a workable team. More specifically, they find fraternizing, "teaming up" with colleagues whom they view as adversaries very difficult. In conjunction, the organization manipulator withholds and distorts information to the detriment of the team and habitually disrupts the homeostasis, or balance of the team. They are highly competitive people who frequently attack, berate, and denigrate. In conjunction they can't take directives unless it suits their purpose, they dominate and bully – we've heard that one before, haven't we?

B. *Inability to share* – their personality style requires them to work parasitically. Specifically, they don't like to share the credit where it's due. Organization manipulators tend to "keep out of the loop": they will provide information when it suits their purpose and with an ulterior motive.

C. *Disparate treatment of staff* – disparate treatment of "marks" is often subtle and very often only known to the victim. Subsequently, the victim's passive behavior disallows forthright action to be taken by management, which could rectify the problem if management knew about the problem earlier.

D. *Inability to tell the truth* – organization manipulators are pathological liars and because they don't manifest guilt in doing so they habitually cross over from truth to lies, and no one knows the real story for a very long time. Questioning their integrity is inviting RETRIBUTION with a capital R.

E. *Inability to be modest* – the organization manipulator's continuum in this context ranges from immodesty to arrogance and the consistency of this behavior on a day-to-day basis is what is most often identified by their co-workers. In a sentence, there is no such thing as genuine modesty among organization manipulators.

F. *Inability to accept blame* – organization manipulators rarely take responsibility for their actions, in fact they tend to project the blame onto their colleagues, which identifies to a "T" active instrumental aggression.

G. *Inability to act predictably* – organization manipulators ARE INCONSISTENT and tend to disrupt, embarrass, behave irrationally and as "loose cannons" on a regular daily basis at their place of employment, but not usually in front of superiors.

H. *Inability to react calmly* – in conjunction with (g), organization manipulators are unable to act calmly and rationally when faced with a crisis or under pressure. In general, and when *out of corporate visibility*, organization manipulators frequently display

Chapter Fourteen | 235

over-reactive behavior or in more conventional terminology become "drama queens" when faced with these circumstances. The effect of this outlandish behavior is a reduction of team cohesion/morale, and because senior management is not there to witness the behavior, it may continue for a very long time;

I. *Inability to act without aggression* – organization manipulators are masters of manipulation, intimidation, and coercion. Direct, "in your face" bullying can be a major presenting feature. Those who intercede, be it supervisory level, management, or consultants, do so at the risk of being sued or at least threatened with litigation. Remember, organization manipulators are scheming, intelligent, and ruthless. They have evaluated the organization's strengths and needs and will challenge the source of their discomfort with a retinue of "ammunition" regarding organization failures, short-comings, etc., to defend their actions. The presenting aggression, both active and passive, has to be seen to be believed, it ain't nice, and has in my professional experience caused many a senior manager to "squirm" in his/her boots. It's a "game," and manipulators are Masters if not Grand Master chess players instigating this very ruthless and destructive game! Metaphors aside and for your future well-being, BE VERY CAREFUL!

So, how do we effectively challenge the organization manipulator's "nefarious" conduct? Please read on.

HOW TO EFFECTIVELY CHALLENGE NEFARIOUS BEHAVIOR BY THE ORGANIZATION MANIPULATOR

A NUMBER OF EXCELLENT COPING STRATEGIES (SIMON, 2010) HAVE BEEN identified to keep in mind when involved with an organization manipulator. The following protocol should provide you with coping strategies and a greater sense of personal empowerment:

A. *Accept no excuses* – Don't accept rationalizations for the Manipulator's inappropriate, aggressive conduct. Simply don't accept the rationale they provide, it is totally irrelevant. The "bottom line": don't accept or be influenced by any excuses they offer for their conduct.

B. *Judge actions not intentions* – Judge the behavior itself; remember, organization manipulators are brilliant impression-management operators. Behavior patterns from the organization manipulator provide the information you require about his/her character – observe and appraise THE BEHAVIOR.

C. *Set personal limits* – Know your personal boundaries and what you'll accept or not accept from a colleague before you take some counter-measure. As well, what is the level of confrontation you're prepared to make in order to defend yourself? Identify your personal boundaries or risk exploitation by a very shrewd and ruthless manipulator.

D. *Make direct requests* – Use "I" statements and avoid generalities. Make clear your boundaries with the manipulator, which influences reduced distortion regarding what you expect from them. If their response is not clear to your direct request, you may be set up in a "top dog–bottom dog" relationship – beware and look out!

E. *Accept only direct responses* – As an adjunct to (d), insist on clear, direct answers, respectfully assert yourself, and expect a forthright response. Answers that are exaggerated, understated, or "masked" suggest they are attempting to manipulate you.

F. *Stay focused in the present* – Watch out for diversionary and evasive behavior from the organization manipulator. Stay in the "here and now"; their willingness to change as a result of the point you're making of your confrontation will give you an indication of how flexible they are in modifying their behavior towards you. In essence, do they change their tactics as a result of your confrontation and do you really care at this point – hopefully not, but it's your choice.

G. *When confronting aggressive behavior by the manipulator, keep the responsibility on the aggressor* – Specifically, the focus of your statement should be on what the manipulator did to injure your self-esteem. Don't be sucked into their attempts to rationalize and shift blame. Ignore their rationalizations and continue your questioning using the "broken record" technique (i.e., repeating the point) most of us learned in assertiveness training. Keep the focus on the manipulator changing a specific behavior that has impugned your integrity; they usually try to "slip and slide" out of any responsibility for their actions. WATCH FOR THIS MANEUVER!

H. *When you confront, avoid sarcasm, hostility, and demeaning behavior* – Organization manipulators construe any kind of confrontation as a CHALLENGE, which precipitates an attack, and ATTACK they will! Generally, as stated before, they project blame, deny and rationalize to avoid responsibility for their inappropriate behavior. Consequently, you should assert in a steady "off the shoulder," nonaggressive manner and simply identify the manipulator's inappropriate behavior. Remember, confrontation with tact is necessary with this type of individual – please, learn to confront tactfully and avoid denigration; it only escalates the problem at hand.

I. *Avoid making threats* – NEVER THREATEN but take action to protect yourself and achieve your needs. This is not as easy as it sounds when involved in close-quarters "combat" with this type of ruthless personality; keep focused on a positive approach while defending your position and with practice (there's that p word again) it will become easier.

J. *Take action quickly* – Organization manipulators lack internal controls, as has been stated above. They aggressively seek out and attempt to "steamroll" to achieve their goals at your expense. Be ready to confront their tactics and then respond in an assertive, boundary-specific manner. Get away from the "bottom dog" position and seek a better balance of power.

K. *Speak for yourself* – If you have the courage, strength of character, and willpower, deal with the organization manipulator by yourself; don't find a "defender" as it identifies your passivity and potential for future exploitation. When you're alone with a manipulator, assert for what you want openly and directly. That being stated, this is easier said than done, but you have to start somewhere and with practice, setting boundaries should become easier.

L. *Make reasonable agreements* – Make agreements that are "transparent" and open to scrutiny by others, honor your contract, and expect this in return. Be wary of being cheated and remember the manipulators' proclivity to use guile in crafting lies to meet their needs at your expense! Try to propose as many "win-win" scenarios as you can. This tact dissipates the manipulators' tendency to compete at all costs to win and reduces the frequency of conflict. They most prefer a "win-lose" situation with you the identified "mark" ending up in the "bottom-down" position. They will also accept (with chagrin) a second best option, a "win-win" result, yes, you heard it right, a "win-win" second best option.

M. *Be prepared for consequences* – The organization manipulator WANTS TO WIN in their interactions with you and can be as vindictive as hell, so prepare yourself for antagonistic behavior and take appropriate action to protect yourself. Assess the continuum of responses the manipulator might make against you and if possible as stated above, confront the manipulator on a one-to-one basis to show strength. As an adjunct and when necessary, involve yourself with a strong support network to decrease the manipulator's power against you. I said Support NETWORK not Defender; there is a big distinction.

N. *Be honest with yourself* – Know your own needs, desires, abilities, strengths/weaknesses because the organization manipulator will assess and attempt to "press your buttons." THAT I CAN GUARANTEE! Deceiving yourself, or better stated, deluding yourself about your strengths and needs can quickly place you in a subservient "bottom-down" relationship with this devious and tenacious individual. KEEP AWARE of the "dance with the devil" paradigm that can play out with an organization manipulator. Forget ego; your mental health is not worth the risk! Let me expand on this "ego" thing for a moment. Dutton (2012) has characterized the personality traits of an organization manipulator very adroitly to include ruthlessness, charm, focus, mental toughness, fearlessness, mindfulness, and action (pp. 185–86). These formidable opponents choose to apply the different personality traits depending on the circumstance they encounter – as Dutton states, "fading in and out to match the soundtrack" (p. 186). Specifically, the manipulator chooses the right trait or set of traits to match the context of the situation in which they find themselves with a "mark" and initiate their predatory behavior to meet their need for power and control. At this stage, after reading the book, do you still think you can match their cunning and guile? Hmm, I hope not. Please, don't tempt fate and try to prove me wrong, not when this tyrant's "gig" is at full ram speed. Their behavior has been rehearsed, habituated, and "acted out" since childhood and certainly by late adolescence/early twenties is refined and pathological in nature. But there I go repeating myself again.

Hurrah, I've finished Chapter Fourteen and the book. I hope you've enjoyed reading about the misadventures of many of my colleagues in Section One. Having a sense of humor in this demanding field has kept me going during the past forty-odd years. Did you find Section Two's tapestry of worksite intrigue, the whys and wherefores of organization manipulators in twenty-first century employment settings, worthwhile? Regardless, my final suggestion to enrich your quality of work life is this – *stay mentally tough*, use the information provided above, and *watch your boundaries like a hawk! Lastly, when in need of a laugh re-read Section One – the endorphins always need lubrication.* Good luck in all future endeavors and hopefully we'll meet one day.

Sincerely with regard,
JAKE

REFERENCES

Adamson, D., & Ahmed, A.G. (2011). *Addiction and co-occurring disorders from a SMART recovery perspective: A manual for group therapists.* SMART Recovery Bookstore.

Alderfer, C. (1976). Change processes in organizations. In M.D. Dunnette (Ed.)., *Handbook of industrial and organizational psychology* (pp. 1591–1638). Chicago, IL: Rand McNally.

Argyris, C. (1973). Today's problems with tomorrow's organizations. In Jong S. Jun & William B. S Storm (Eds.), *Tomorrow's Organizations: Challenges and Strategies.* Glenview, IL: Pearson Scott Foresman.

Babiak, P., & Hare, R.D. (2006). *Snakes in suits: When psychopaths go to work.* New York, NY: HarperBusiness.

Beesley, D. & Stoltenberg, C.D. (2002). Control, attachment style, and relationship satisfaction among adult children of alcoholics. *Journal of Mental Health Counseling* 24(4): 281–298.

Book, A., & Costello, K., & Wheeler, S. (2009). Psychopathic traits and the perception of victim vulnerability. *Criminal Justice and Behavior* 36, no. 6:635–48.

Burnham, B.R. (1995). *Evaluating human resources, programs, and organizations.* Malabar, FL: Krieger Publishing Company.

Chernis, C. (1980). *Staff burnout: Job stress in the human services.* Beverly Hills, CA: Sage Publications.

Clarke, J. (2005). *Working with monsters: How to identify and protect yourself from the workplace psychopath.* Sydney, Australia: Random House.

Dutton, D.G. (1998). *Violence and control in intimate relationships: The abusive personality.* New York, NY: The Guilford Press.

Dutton, K. (2012). *The wisdom of psychopaths: What saints, spies, and serial killers can teach us about success.* Toronto, Canada: Doubleday.

Goldberg, R. (1986). Under the influence. *Savvy*, July, 1986, pp.51–60.

Hall, K. (2013). *Making the matrix work: How matrix managers engage people and cut through complexity.* Boston, MA: Nicholas Brealey Publishing.

Hatch, J. (2011). *Organizations: A very short introduction.* Oxford, UK: Oxford University Press.

Kets de Vries & Miller. (1987). *Inside the troubled organization: Unstable at the top.* New York, NY: New American Library.

Kuczmarski & Kuczmarski. (1995). *Values-based leadership: Rebuilding employee commitment, performance, & productivity.* Englewood Cliffs, NJ: Prentice Hall.

Leavitt, H. (1965). Applied organizational change in industry: Structural, technological and humanistic approaches. In J.G. March (Ed.), *Handbook of organizations* (p. 1145). Chicago, IL: Rand McNally.

Malone, R., & Peterson, D.J. (1974). *The effective manager's desk book: Improving results through people.* West Nyack, NY: Parker Publishing Company, Inc.

Marszalek-Gaucher, E. & Coffey, R.J. (1990). *Transforming healthcare organizations: How to achieve and sustain organizational excellence.* San Francisco, CA: Jossey-Bass.

Martin, R. (2012). *Brilliant manoeuvres: How to use military wisdom to win business battles.* Kent, UK: Global Professional Publishing.

Miller, D., & Friesen. P. (1984). A longitudinal study of the corporate life cycle. *Management Science*, 30, 1161–1183.

Mott, P.E. (1972). *The characteristics of effective organizations.* New York, NY: Harper & Row.

Preston, P. (1988). *Leadership strategies for health care managers.* San Antonio, TX: Preston, McTavish & Co.

Quick, J.C., Quick, J.D., Nelson, D.L. & Hurrell, J.J. (1997). Preventive stress management in organizations. Washington, DC: American Psychological Association.

Reh, F.J. (2013). Matrix management. about.com.guide.

Sargent, A.G. (1983). *The androgynous manager: Blending male & female management styles for today's organization.* New York, NY: American Management Association.

Schaef, A., & Fassel, D. (1988). *The addictive organization.* San Francisco, CA: Harper & Row Publishers.

Simon, G. (2010). *In sheep's clothing: Understanding and dealing with manipulative people* (2nd Ed.). Marion, MI: Parkhurst Brothers, Inc., Publishers.

Woititz, J.G. (1983). *Adult children of alcoholics.* Deerfield Beach, FL: Health Communications, Inc.

Woititz, J.G. (1990). *Adult children of alcoholics* (expanded edition). Health Communications, Inc. Deerfield Beach.

Wolfensberger, W. (1970*). Normalization: The principle of normalization in human services.* Toronto, Canada: National Institute of Mental Retardation.

CPSIA information can be obtained
at www.ICGtesting.com
Printed in the USA
LVHW080216030419
612725LV00002B/2/P